THE ART OF SICILIAN COOKING

ANNA MUFFOLETTO

Drawings by Ed Nuckolls

Gramercy Publishing Company

•

New York

This edition is published by Gramercy Publishing Co.,
distributed by Crown Publishers, Inc.,
by arrangement with Doubleday & Company, Inc.

h g f e d c b a

1982 EDITION

Library of Congress Cataloging in Publication Data

Muffoletto, Anna.
    The art of Sicilian cooking.

    Reprint. Originally published: Garden City, N.Y.:
Doubleday, 1971.
    Includes index.
    1. Cookery, Italian. 2. Sicily—Social life and
customs. I. Title.
TX723.M76 1982   641.5945'8   81-13512
ISBN 0-517-37074-3   AACR2

To my mother, Lucia Muffoletto, with love and appreciation for having taught me the fine art of Sicilian cooking, and for having given me inspiration and assistance in writing this book

CONTENTS

Introduction   *ix*

In Praise of Sicilian Festivals   *1*

Soups   *23*

Pasta—Over Two Hundred Varieties   *30*

Rice Specialties   *51*

The Sicilian Egg Basket   *58*

The Cheeses of Sicily (Chart)   *64*

Fish—From the Waters of the Mediterranean   *67*

Meat and Poultry—Thank Sicily for the Meatball!   *81*

Bread—The Staff of Life   *114*

Vegetables and Salads Reign Supreme   *127*

Sauces   *160*

The Spice and Herb Rack   *166*

Fruits of the Earth   *172*

Desserts, Desserts   *186*

The Wines of Sicily (Chart)   *207*

Index   *213*

Recipes followed by an asterisk (*) may be located by referring to the index.

INTRODUCTION

I'm an American, but Sicilian by ancestry. My paternal and maternal grandparents immigrated to the United States in 1888, became stalwart Americans, but remained Sicilian by tradition. They bore their children here and raised them as full-fledged Americans, but the Sicilian tradition was strong and remained an integral part of family life.

My grandparents and relatives left Sicily for the challenge and opportunity offered in America. They transplanted their roots to Buffalo, New York, and retained all the customs, culinary specialties, and folklore of their abandoned homeland.

My first trip to Sicily was in May 1960, seventy-two years after my grandparents had left. It was a wonderful trip and a true revelation. My first stop was Cefalù, the birthplace of my grandparents. How strange it felt to visit their home and visualize their lives there, to stare at our few remaining relatives and seek resemblances. Pasqualina Muffoletto, my Sicilian cousin, aged eighty and a *monica di casa* (a nun who lives in her own house and takes care of the sick and needy of the village), smilingly mused, "You come seeking relatives, and instead you find antiques!"

In Cefalù, I walked along the narrow, geometrically patterned streets, remains of pre-Hellenic, Byzantine, and Arabic constructions, toured the famous and magnificent twin-towered Norman cathedral started by Roger II in 1131, inhaled the sweet aromas of olive, eucalyptus, and orange trees of the nearby terrain, bathed my eyes in the beautiful faded pastels of the houses, and felt the softness of the sunset over the tranquil sea. I understood my heritage.

During this first of many trips, I made a complete tour of the island—starting at Cefalù, circling westward to Palermo, Segesta, Trapani, Erice, Marsala, Selinunte, Sciacca, Agrigento, Syracuse, Catania, Mt. Etna, Taormina, Messina, and back to Cefalù. Each city and province was more beautiful than the last, and each day brought a new experience. Frankly, before my first trip I was aware only of the tradition of Sicily and totally unaware of its incredible beauty and rich history, made evident by ancient temples and theaters, warm tropical climate, clear green waters, lovely rose-tinted beaches, volcanic mountains, and friendly and exotic-looking people.

I was familiar with Sicilian food, certainly, but I did not associate it with the past, nor had I experienced all of the authentic island flavors, spices, and aromas. To taste Sicilian food is to taste the ages, to sense nature, to feel the people, and to know and love the land.

Sicilian cooking—and what is Sicilian cooking?
Isn't it Italian cooking? How is it different?

Influenced by Greek and Arabic cuisines principally,
and French, Italian, and Spanish cuisines as well,
Sicilian cooking is a composite of exotic, varied, and
exceptional dishes.

It is *deliziosa!*

The burnished gold of the crusts, the fragrance of sugar and cinnamon they exuded, were but preludes to the delights released from the interior when the knife broke the crust; first came the spice-laden haze, then chicken livers, hard-boiled eggs, sliced ham, chicken, and truffles in masses of piping-hot, glistening macaroni, to which the meat juice gave an exquisite hue of suede.

From *The Leopard* by
Giuseppe Tomasi di Lampedusa

These few mouth-watering lines describe vividly the cuisine of Sicily: strong and subtle, earthy and sophisticated, exotic and exquisite.

Sicilian cooking is Italian cooking, but it has distinct differences. It is not coarse or heavy, as so many people describe Southern Italian cooking. Its differences lie in its heritage, its people, and its past. As I briefly unfold the history, you will discover the people of Sicily and the pleasures of Sicilian cooking, which has developed from some of the most dramatic events in the annals of time.

Sicily is known to have been inhabited as far back as the Stone Age, and a journey through Sicily is really a journey through time.

The island of Sicily, ideally located between Africa and Europe, in ancient times was called Trinacris (triangle) because of its shape. Varied and colorful, having the strength of mountains, the breadth of sea, and the fertility of plains, Sicily is unique in climate and natural beauty.

Still standing, like lovely mute ghosts, are magnificent theaters, rare art treasures, impressive temples and monuments as constant reminders of the glories of the past. Through the centuries Sicily was conquered, inhabited, and dominated by the Phoenicians, the Greeks, the Romans, the Vandals, the Goths, the Byzantines, the Arabs, the Normans, and even the Spanish. The hardships and suppression the Sicilians endured under the sway of many ruthless exploiters is still evident in the faces of the people and in their quiet resignation to their sorry plight. But yet, as if to make up for this rampant exploitation, the Sicilians inherited an extraordinary cultural legacy.

Although Sicily is a small island, it has nine major cities and provinces. Each has its own story, its own connection with medieval and modern times. Each has produced famous writers and artists, such as Pirandello, Bellini, Lampedusa, and Verga, and each has made significant contributions to the cuisine. It's no wonder Sicily won the praise of both Pindar and Virgil in their poetry.

This island of exotic odors, pungent flavors, interminable processions, brilliant sun, violent landscape, and ubiquitous cactus trees has produced a cuisine reflecting the influences of the European occident in the eastern provinces, and the Middle East in the western provinces—a blending of the tastes of France, Egypt, Spain, Greece, Italy, and Albania.

Sicilian cooking is similar to Neapolitan cooking—sumptuous and spicy—not subtle like that in Tuscany or delicate like that of Lombardy in Northern Italy. Basically, the cuisine is composed of foods cultivated in the arid soil of the terrain, nurtured in the warm sun constantly smiling overhead, and abounding in the clear waters of the Mediterranean Sea surrounding the island.

The foods, beverages, spices, and herbs forming the backbone of the cuisine are:

pasta	olives	cactus fruit
rice	onions	oranges
pizza	cauliflower	lemons
meatballs	zucchini	ice cream
sausage	fennel	ices
fish	orégano	cassata
cheese	mint	cannoli
artichokes	sesame seeds	biscotti
burdocks	melon	espresso
eggplant	grapes	muscatel
tomatoes	nectarines	Sicilian gold
capers	figs	anisette

MEDITERRANEA

PALERMO

MARSALA

AGRIGENTO

SICILY

SEA

MESSINA

TAORMINA

CATANIA

SIRACUSA

RAGUSA

IN PRAISE
OF SICILIAN
FESTIVALS

The shrill, mystical sounds of bagpipes; the penetrating, pathetic wailing of novenas; the strong, stark colors of costumes; the religious, superstitious decorations on carts and fishing boats; the somber, impressive processions; and the gay, colorful carnivals—all depict the drama and importance of Sicilian festivals.

The word *festa* in Italian (*festinu* in the Sicilian dialect) means feast, holiday, holy day, birthday, festivity, and merrymaking. Festas occur in every month of the year and are based primarily on the saints' days of the Christian calendar, and in remembrance of deceased relatives, in appreciation of bountiful harvests, in exultation of the blessed sacrament of marriage, and in triumph in the miracle of birth.

Festivals are a form of devotion, and Sicilians pay tribute regularly to their favorite saints with vivid pageantry and undaunted faith. Then, after their devotion is paid, they rejoice in the streets with parades, music, bright lights, amusements, and special holiday refreshments.

Without exception, every hamlet and family has its own special fête days; however, only the universally commemorated Sicilian holidays are described in this chapter.

December 13

LA FESTA DI SANTA LUCIA
THE FEAST OF ST. LUCY

Santa Lucia, patroness of Syracuse and all who suffer from eye diseases, is worshiped throughout Sicily, the rest of Italy, and even Sweden on December 13. Lucy, a beautiful young Christian maiden with sparkling eyes, was born in Syracuse, Sicily, in A.D. 283. Her rejection of a heathen nobleman resulted in the gouging of her eyes and eventual death by torture.

In Syracuse, the festival begins with the joining of dignitaries, clergy, religious societies, and laymen clad in green tunics with magenta sashes (the saint's colors), carrying lighted torches, marching in procession to the *duomo* (cathedral), where the Christian martyr is represented holding her eyes in a vessel.

This holiday is also called the Festival of Lights, and St. Lucy is often referred to as the Saint of Light. According to legend, St. Lucy went blind on December 13, the shortest day of the year according to the ancient Julian calendar.

Legend relates that during a great famine Syracusians went to the *duomo* to invoke the assistance of Santa Lucia. While they were praying, a ship carrying grain came into the harbor and saved the city. *Cuccia* (grain kernels) are traditionally eaten on December 13 to commemorate the miracle of food.

Cuccia
CHICK-PEAS AND WHEAT KERNELS

On St. Lucy's day, *cuccia* is eaten the whole day long as a breakfast cereal, thick soup, dessert, and even as a snack.

½ pound dried chick-peas	2½ to 3 quarts warm water
1 pound wheat kernels	1 tablespoon salt

Wash chick-peas and wheat kernels with cold water; drain; cover with cold water; soak for 4 hours or overnight. Drain; place in a large kettle; cover with warm water; add salt; bring to a boil. Stir, lower heat, cover, and simmer slowly for 1 to 1½ hours or until chick-peas and kernels are tender but firm. Correct seasoning if necessary. Serve hot, at room temperature, or cold as:

Breakfast cereal—Heat *cuccia;* add butter to taste. Serve with milk and sugar.

Thick soup or side vegetable—Heat *cuccia* with ¼ cup olive oil, ½ cup chopped parsley or fennel leaves; sprinkle with freshly ground pepper to taste. Serve hot or at room temperature.

Dessert—Serve cold with cream, sugar, and cinnamon.

SERVES: 6 to 8

NOTE: Canned chick-peas may be used instead of dried; mix in with wheat kernels after they have been cooked. Heat and correct seasoning if necessary.

LA VIGILIA DI NATALE
CHRISTMAS EVE

The religious preparations for Christmas actually begin nine days before with a novena and a twenty-four-hour fast, from sunset of December 23 to sunset of December 24.

The tradition of displaying a miniature *presepio,* or manger, in every Italian home originated seven hundred and fifty years ago with St. Francis of Assisi. Made of clay or wood, these small charming figures depict the Holy Family, angels, shepherds, and pastoral scenes. In many families, the *presepi* are generations old and cherished heirlooms.

During Christmas week, shepherds come down from the hills with *ciarmeddi* (bagpipes) to play tender pastoral hymns before the mangers displayed in shops and homes. They are rewarded with gifts of money and food. *Ninnareddi* (carolers) are welcomed warmly also as they visit homes singing Christmas carols.

Christmas Eve in Sicily, as in other parts of the world, is strictly a family affair. After a twenty-four-hour fast, a Christmas Eve supper, *il cenone,* is served for all to enjoy. *Il cenone* is an elaborate meal, but a meatless one on Christmas Eve. As many as ten to twenty fish dishes are prepared, with eel being a popular favorite, accompanied by seasonal vegetables such as artichokes and burdocks, fancy plaited breads, baskets of prickly pears (*fichi d'India*), fresh figs, blood oranges, apples, Zibibbo grapes, spumoni (a rich triflavored ice cream), Christmas cookies, roasted chestnuts, hazelnuts, almonds, and walnuts. Small steaming cups of strong coffee and liqueurs provide the perfect ending to the special feast.

A typical Christmas Eve *cenone* is given here for your holiday enjoyment:

Il Cenone

CHRISTMAS EVE SUPPER

LINGUINI WITH ANCHOVY SAUCE*
COLD EEL IN CARPIONE
SARDINE BUTTERFLIES*
COLD SEAFOOD SALAD*
HOLIDAY FRITTERS*
EGGPLANT QUAILS*

CORBEILLE OF FRESH FRUIT AND ROASTED NUTS
SPUMONI
CHRISTMAS COOKIES
CAFFÈ ESPRESSO
SAMBUCCA LIQUEUR

Chilled white Segesta wine is an excellent choice with this meal.

December 25

NATALE
CHRISTMAS

Christmas Day is a family holiday shared with friends and antic-ipated the whole year long. Ardent suitors send flowers to their loved ones, warm wishes are exchanged freely on the streets, and peace and love are in the air as well as in the hearts of all Sicilians. Gifts are exchanged not on Christmas but on January 6, the Epiphany.

Christmas, apart from being an important religious holiday, is paramount in its epicurean offerings. Christmas breakfast starts off with brimming cups of warm, eggy-wine *zabaglione,* and thick wedges of delicately textured *panettone,* speckled with raisins and citron.

My Sicilian family, the Muffoletto clan, always gathered at Grandma Greco's house for an annual Christmas banquet. The menu included seven courses of Sicilian specialties, all made from scratch, with each branch of the family contributing a dish. Mother baked long braided loaves of Sicilian bread and a huge assortment of Christmas cookies; cousins Sara and Clara offered noodles and ravioli floating in a thick meat sauce—a specialty of Aunt Florence —the menfolk always tended to roasting and carving the many plump capons selected for the occasion.

There being thirty in attendance, long tables covered with Grandma's finest hand-embroidered linens were joined together, running through the living and dining rooms and even the kitchen. Shortly before the banquet began, doilied platters of hot and cold antipasto (prosciutto and fresh figs, stuffed mushrooms, roasted peppers, eggplant salad), baskets of crusty bread, and many bottles of Uncle Marty's homemade wine were spread along the tables. Then, a small voice was chosen to say grace and *la festa* began to the cheers of *"Buon Natale! Buon appetito!"*

Pranzo di Natale
CHRISTMAS DINNER

HOT AND COLD ANTIPASTO
CAPPELLETTI IN TASCA
SPINACH AND MEAT RAVIOLI*
BAKED GOLDEN CAPON WITH SAUSAGE STUFFING*
MINTED PEAS
SWEET AND SOUR ZUCCHINI*
GOLDEN BRAIDED LOAVES*
MIXED TOSSED SALAD
BRANDIED PEACHES AND CHERRIES
STRUFFOLI*
CHRISTMAS COOKIES
TORRONE
CAFFÈ ESPRESSO
SICILIAN GOLD LIQUEUR

Verdicchio and Valpolicella wines may both be served if Eloro Bianco (white) and Eloro Rosso (red) are unavailable.

December 31

NOTTE DI CAPO D'ANNO
NEW YEAR'S EVE

On New Year's Eve in Sicily, private parties are planned with friends and relatives to welcome in the new year. At the stroke of twelve, one of the guests, armed with a broom, sweeps out the old year and opens the doors and windows to let in the new year. Dried herring, cut in pieces, is savored by everyone; it supposedly brings luck and good fortune in the new year if eaten at midnight.

A traditional midnight supper, rustic and tasty, is served for all gathered.

Cena di Notte di Capo d'Anno
NEW YEAR'S EVE SUPPER

PIZZA MUFFOLETTO*
SWEET SAUSAGE AND PEPPER FRY
SESAME-SEED ROLLS*
OLIVE RELISH*
MANDARIN ORANGES
TOKAY AND MUSCATEL GRAPES
CANNOLI*
CAFFÈ ESPRESSO

Capo Rosso or a good-quality chianti is appropriate with any rustic meal. Red wine should be opened half an hour before serving to bring out the bouquet, and served at room temperature.

January 1

CAPO D'ANNO
NEW YEAR'S

On New Year's Day, the air is filled with excitement and gaiety prevails. Even though much of Sicily is depressed economically, Sicilians are always optimistic about the future and welcome each new year with aspirations of prosperity and good times.

Children receive *strenna,* or money gifts, from their parents, while friends and relatives send flowers and mistletoe to one another. Mistletoe in ancient times warded off illness, and hung over doorways of homes, barns, and stables protecting families and animals. Today, every Sicilian household hangs a twig of mistletoe over the doorway also, but now it's solely for luck.

Lentils are ritually eaten on the first day of every new year. They're considered to induce health and wealth, which is a little ironic since lentils are the poor man's staple.

New Year's dinner is one of my favorites; it's certainly a spicy way to ring in the new year.

Pranzo di Capo d'Anno
NEW YEAR'S DINNER

ANTIPASTO ANCHOVY-PEPPERS*
GOOD-LUCK LENTIL SOUP*
SWEET AND SOUR RABBIT*
CRISP-FRIED ARTICHOKE HEARTS*
ARANCINI*
SWEET FENNEL AND LETTUCE SALAD*
RICOTTA PIE
CAFFÈ ESPRESSO
ANISETTA

Faro wine is outstanding with white-meat roasts. Bardolino is a fine substitute.

February 5

LA FESTA DI SANT'AGATA
THE FEAST OF ST. AGATHA

St. Agatha, patroness of Catania, was put to death by a Roman prefect in 251 because she refused to yield to him. The beautiful virgin's breasts were severed during her torture, making her the patron saint of nursing mothers and women suffering from diseases of the breast.

Thousands journey to Catania each year for three full days of religious pageants and public festivities. Crowded streets, gaily decorated with colored paper flags, flowers, streamers, and people shouting *"Evviva Sant'Agata!"* ("Long Live St. Agatha!") make the festival one of the most colorful in Sicily. At night, small electric lights, in a variety of designs, transform the city into a virtual fairyland.

During the festival, *calia* carts line the streets, selling thirst producing goodies. *Calia* is something to chew on, and these carts may hold as many as twenty different "chewables" in neatly arranged piles: salted pumpkin seeds, sunflower seeds, roasted chick-peas, and roasted *fave* (broad white beans), *semenze* (calabash seeds), *nocciolini Americani* or in dialect *nuccidi Americani* (peanuts), *carrube* (St.-John's-bread), roasted chestnuts, *lupini* (yellow beans with slippery skins), *torrone* (nougat), and strings of cookies. *Olivetti di Sant'Agata,* pistachio or almond cookies, are eaten traditionally on this day.

February 15

SAGRA DEI MANDORLI IN FIORE
ALMOND BLOSSOM FESTIVAL

Although this festival is only four decades old, it certainly should be given mention for its beauty and charm. Agrigento, or Agrigentum, a typical Mediterranean town exceptional for its archeological heritage, climate, and scenery, sponsors the festival in mid-February, when the almond trees are in full bloom.

Along Agrigento's Valley of the Temples stand incredibly beautiful limestone temples rivaling those in Greece. The valley blends rows of blossoming almond trees against a verdant spring green. The flowers, fragrant and fragile, turn into almonds and significantly bolster the economy of the Agrigento province.

Confetti, the renowned Italian sugar-coated almonds, are inscribed in the tradition of many celebrations. At weddings, white almonds perfumed with orange blossoms, denoting fertility, are passed by the bride to her guests. At baptisms, pink or blue almonds, depending on whether it is a boy or girl, are enclosed in net sacks tied with a satin ribbon and given as favors in memory of the occasion. Red confetti appears at graduation parties and green confetti at engagements. And if a silver or golden wedding anniversary is celebrated, confetti appears again tinged with silver or gold.

LA FESTA DI SAN GIUSEPPE
THE FEAST OF ST. JOSEPH

In the Bible, St. Joseph is described as a humble carpenter from Nazareth, "a just man," and a pious and kind protector. To the Italians, he is the patron saint of carpenters, cartmakers, unwed mothers, and orphans—one of the most beloved of all saints.

Devotion to the saint is reflected in the feasting, merrymaking and sharing with the needy on March 19, the anniversary of St. Joseph. Festivities vary throughout Italy, but nowhere is the day so characteristically and picturesquely commemorated as in Sicily. Weeks in advance, every village selects an orphan boy, a poor young girl, and an old carpenter to portray the Holy Family. On March 19, the Holy Three, simply and typically dressed, mount mules and parade through the village, where they are cheered and given gifts of money and food.

La Tavola di San Giuseppe is a meatless feast table, prepared and given to those in need: orphans, widows, cripples, and beggars. Usually, nineteen people are invited to the banquet in keeping with the fact that the holiday is celebrated on the nineteenth, but often many more are included. Everyone in the village contributes what he can to the banquet: money, food, flowers, candles. In small villages, the banquet is given outdoors; but in large cities and various locales, feast tables are prepared indoors.

Customarily, many people make the rounds, visiting several feast tables the day before or the morning of the feast to admire the culinary artistry and table decorations. The long feast tables, extending through several rooms, are laden with an array of traditional foods; thick lentil soup, hearty minestrone, *pasta con le sarde* (spaghetti with sardines and fennel), fried fresh sardines, double layers of stuffed sardines, chunks of fresh chilled fennel, large black oil-cured olives, fried artichoke hearts, stuffed baked artichokes, stuffed escarole rolls, fried cauliflower rosettes, spinach and asparagus *frosce* (omelets), braided bread wreaths, large navel oranges, pomegranates, *sfinge di San Giuseppi* (crullers), *struffoli* (honey-dipped cakes), and *crispelle* (honey-dipped rice fritters shaped like sausages).

St. Joseph's day begins with morning mass, followed by the parade of the Holy Family and then on to the *banquetto*. The victuals are blessed by the local priest and the meal begins to the cheers of *"Viva San Giuseppe!"* Traditionally, an appetizer of orange slices, stalks of fresh fennel, and black olives is served; then tureens of soup, bowls of pasta, platters of fish, omelets, and vegetables, and fruits and sweets are passed family style in a continuous round until everyone is sated. Intermittently during the meal, *"Viva San Giuseppi!"* is shouted in tribute and admiration for the good saint.

Upon leaving, each guest receives a sack containing a small loaf of holiday bread, an orange, and some sweets to take home in remembrance of *la festa di San Giuseppe*.

Sfinge
SICILIAN CRULLERS

CHEESE FILLING:
1 pound ricotta cheese
¼ cup confectioners' sugar
2 tablespoons minced candied orange peel
2 tablespoons minced candied citron
½ teaspoon cinnamon

CRULLERS:
1 cup water
1 tablespoon shortening
⅛ teaspoon salt
1 cup sifted flour
4 large eggs (at room temperature)
1 teaspoon vanilla
1 quart frying oil
Confectioners' sugar

Combine cheese filling ingredients and refrigerate.

Place water, shortening, and salt in a saucepan; cook over high heat until shortening melts. Turn off heat. With wooden spoon, stir in flour all at once and cook over medium heat, stirring constantly, until mixture leaves sides of pan and forms a ball (about 1 minute). Remove from range and cool.

Add eggs to mixture, one at a time, beating hard for approximately 1 minute after each addition. Stir in vanilla.

Heat oil in frying kettle to 370° F. (hot enough to brown 1-inch bread cube in 1 minute). Slip batter from tablespoon into hot oil and fry until crullers are golden—about 3 minutes. Fry only 4 or 5 crullers at a time so they will have room to expand and move.

(Crullers turn themselves as they cook.) Remove with slotted spoon and drain onto absorbent paper.

Before serving, split crullers in half and fill with cheese filling, dusting tops with confectioners' sugar.

YIELD: Approximately 1½ dozen

End of March to Beginning of April

PASQUA

EASTER

Holy Week, the week before Easter, involves outstanding daily commemorations. Easter Sunday is eagerly welcomed, for it denotes the end of the gloom and fasting of Lent. The glory of a resurrected Christ pervades the spirit of the Sicilians, making the holiday both reverent and joyous.

Easter is celebrated brilliantly throughout Sicily. In Piana d'Albanese, or Piana dei Greci, an Albanian town in the hills near Palermo, where Greek rites and religion are still practiced and the Albanian language is spoken, Easter is especially colorful. A Greek high mass is performed by a priest in beautiful ornate robes designed with small red crosses. The young ladies of the town attend services wearing heirloom costumes adorned with embroidered vests and capes, unique wide silver belts, gold chains, earrings, and rings. It is remarkable how this small colony of Albanians has been able to preserve its language, customs, rites, and religion even though its ancestors came to Sicily in the fifteenth century.

Food plays a symbolic and important role in the Easter festivities. The egg is the Christian emblem of the Resurrection, and Sicilians make charming miniature pastry baskets nesting colored eggs called *Buba cu l'Uova** for their Easter breakfast. A delicately flavored Easter broth, brodetto Pasquale, usually starts the holiday *pranzo* (dinner). Baby lamb, agnellino Pasquale, signifying the Lamb of God—the Christian sacrificial symbol—is a popular favorite. Roasted artichokes and spring salad are typical accompaniments. Yeast breads, shaped like crowns and studded with colored eggs, represent the crown of thorns Jesus wore on the cross; they're used as center-pieces as well as being part of the meal. The traditional finale to the Easter feast is *Cassata,** a rich cake consisting of several layers of sponge flavored with wine or brandy and alternating with grated chocolate, candied fruit, and whipped heavy cream.

Buba cu l'Uova
EASTER EGG BASKETS

5 cups sifted flour	1 dozen eggs, raw and colored
1 cup sugar	1 1-pound box confectioners'
5 teaspoons baking powder	sugar
½ teaspoon salt	¼ cup shortening
1 cup shortening	Water or milk
4 eggs	1 teaspoon almond extract
1 teaspoon vanilla	Multicolored cake-decorating
½ cup milk	sprinkles

Preheat oven to 375° F. Grease twelve-sectioned muffin pan.

In a large bowl, sift together flour, sugar, baking powder, and salt. Cut in shortening with pastry blender or 2 knives until mixture resembles coarse cornmeal. Make well in center; drop in eggs, vanilla, and milk; mix until dough is smooth and cleans sides of bowl. Gather up with fingers; form into ball.

Turn dough onto lightly floured board; roll out on large sheet, ½ inch thick. Cut dough in 12 rounds to fit muffin cups (about 3 inches in diameter). Cut 24 3-inch strips from dough (for basket handles). Line cups with rounds, pressing gently with fingers to fit cups. Place 1 raw colored egg in center of each cup. Place 2 strips, criss-cross fashion, over each egg, pressing strip ends over rounds to seal edges. Bake until lightly browned—15 to 20 minutes. Cool 5 to 10 minutes before removing from muffin pan.

Combine confectioners' sugar with ¼ cup shortening and enough water or milk to make a smooth paste. Frost baskets, and decorate sides and handles with colored sprinkles. Using same frosting, pipe names of family and friends on baskets with pastry tube and decorator's writing tip.

YIELD: 1 dozen

FESTA DEL CARRETTO
FESTIVAL OF THE SICILIAN CART

One of the highest expressions of folk art is the Sicilian cart, *il carretto*. One of the most impressive celebrations is the Festival of Carts, or the Feast of St. Alfio, in Trecastagni near Mt. Etna.

The festival begins on the night of May 9 with a mad race around the environs of Mt. Etna; then, at daybreak of May 10, a colorful procession of Sicilian carts unfurls along the road traversing the woods of Mt. Etna, leading to the sanctuary at Trecastagni. The drivers and passengers of the carts, in brilliant costumes of linen and silk, parade in front of the sanctuary with highly decorated marionettes, telling ancient tales to the gathered crowd. Eating and dancing render this one of the favorite festivals for both the young and the old of Mt. Etna.

The actual craft of making Sicilian carts began in the late eighteenth century after the first roads were paved in Sicily. Drawn by plumed mules, donkeys, or horses, the tall, two-wheeled lightweight wooden vehicles, painted the most vivid of oranges, yellows, and greens, are used for carrying everything: hay, harvests of grapes and vegetables, animals, and even the family. Religious or political themes are painted on the side and back panels, and elephants, serpents, or horns are carved on the shafts or wheels to ward off accidents and the *malocchio*—the evil eye.

Bagheria, twenty-five miles from Palermo, is the center of this dying craft. Since *carretti* cannot compete with motorized vehicles and because they are prohibitive in price, fewer and fewer are being made each year. The skilled artistry required to make the carts is no longer encouraged—a real loss.

Nonetheless, small-scale picturesque carts are being manufactured by the thousands for the tourist market. The charming souvenir replicas are sold in every pastry and souvenir shop. They're sometimes filled with an exquisite assortment of marzipan or delicious cookies. The combination of the *carretti* and a little *dolce* (sweet) is a wonderful way to remember Sicily.

Marzipan

Marzipan, small almond paste confections, are shaped and colored to resemble ripened fruit. Martorana Cathedral in Palermo, where both Greek and Catholic rites are practiced, is famous for its marzipan. The Martorana technique dates back to the eighth century, reproducing the vibrant colors and shapes of fresh Sicilian fruit realistically. Understandably, then, Sicilians also call marzipan *frutti alla Martorana.*

2 pounds almond paste (purchase from gourmet shop)
2½ pounds confectioners' sugar
3 egg whites
2 ounces glucose (purchase at drugstore or gourmet shop)
Few drops almond or rum extract
Vegetable (food) coloring

Mix almond paste with confectioners' sugar and egg whites until mixture is smooth. Pour in glucose and almond extract and beat until smooth. Place mixture into china or ceramic bowl; cover with damp cloth (to prevent crust from forming) and refrigerate for 30 minutes.

Portion marzipan into small bowls; tint with vegetable coloring and shape as directed, or shape first and then paint with vegetable coloring. Dust hands with confectioners' sugar before shaping. Use approximately 1 to 3 teaspoons paste for each fruit as required.

India figs (prickly pears): Tint paste pale green; shape into figs; paint one side pink. Paint dots with brown vegetable coloring.

Bananas: Tint paste yellow. Form into tiny banana shapes, making one flat side and two parallel ridges on top coming together at each end of fruit. Paint in lines along ridges and tips at stem with brown coloring.

Strawberries: Tint paste deep red. Form small balls and elongate one end to resemble strawberries. Make pinholes all over with toothpick and paint pinholes green.

Oranges: Tint paste orange. Form into round balls and indent deeply on one end. Make marks all over with toothpick.

Lemons: Tint paste yellow. Form into round balls and elongate to resemble lemons. Make marks all over with toothpick. Paint stem ends green.

Peaches: Paint paste pale yellow. Form into small balls with ridges in centers. Paint one side pink to resemble ripened peach skin.

Pears: Tint paste pale green. Form into small pear shapes. Use cloves for stems (cut off clove heads for base stems and use spikes for top stem end). Paint one side pink to resemble ripened pear skin.

June

LA MATTANZA
THE TUNA KILL

Tunny fishing has stood for centuries and perhaps since prehistoric times as a principal productive occupation for Sicilians along the Trapanese coast. In Lavanzo, sketches depicting tunny fishing date as far back as the Paleolithic period.

The method of tunny fishing, so deeply rooted in the local economic life, is based on tradition and religiously continued year after year. It is a complicated and arduous operation that takes over a period of three months. During the first days of April, seven large nets are lowered into the deep Mediterranean waters in a line of passages and left until the beginning of June. Then fishermen, with long harpoons, force large schools of tuna through six obligatory passages, closing off each passage or net so that the fish are unable to turn back. Finally, they reach the seventh net, the so-called "chamber of death." An Arabic-sounding dirge, *La Cialoma di li Tunnari* (Song of the Tuna Fishermen), often heard in the Mediterranean, is sung at the time of the "kill" in grave and dramatic tones.

At the ultimate moment of the kill, the fishing crew gathers around the chamber of death and waits for the order to kill from the *rais,* or captain. During the kill, the crew starts wailing *La Cialoma* while rhythmically pulling up the net. Masses of tuna are forced to the surface, where they are speared with harpoons and hooks and thrown into a barge nearby. The kill is both physically and emotionally exhausting. The large fish fight violently, jerking away, diving back into the water, hitting and throwing themselves against the net, one on top of the other, causing a mountain of white foam to form which soon turns bloody red.

The desperation of the fish, the excitement of the fishermen, and the shrieking commands of the captain make the operation of tunny fishing a highly dramatic and impressive spectacle similar to an encounter between the primitive forces of nature or a pagan religious rite.

When the last tuna is being pulled from the net and as the last note of *La Cialoma* fades, the barge heads in the direction of the neighboring tuna canneries for immediate production.

In the canneries, not one bit of the fish is wasted. The white or meatiest part of the tuna is preserved in olive oil; the rest in salt. The bones of the fish are crushed and fed to animals, and the fermented refuse is used as fertilizer.

The Trapanese province is famous for its fish dishes, and many are Arabic in name and origin. It appears that during the Crusades, Trapani, "the city of four winds," was the stopping point for all ships sailing to the Orient.

Cùscusu

Cùscusu (an Arabic term meaning ground food) is made in the province of Trapani exclusively and is patterned after couscous, an Arabic meat and cereal stew. *Cùscusu,* however, is made with a combination of tunny and white fish and a mixture of fine and coarse semolina (an Italian grain cereal similar to farina). Its difficult preparation involves rubbing the semolina grains between the palms of the hands with a little oil and steam until the grains swell. This process is extremely laborious and requires a great deal of skill.

I have used bulgur (cracked wheat) in this recipe, since it is an excellent facsimile of semolina in both texture and size and requires very little preparation.

Cùscusu can be easily prepared in a specially made couscous cooker called a *couscoussière* (available in gourmet shops), but a colander or steamer snugly fitted into a kettle and lined with cheesecloth (so grains will not seep out) may be improvised.

NOTE: Tunny is a tuna variety found in warm waters of the Mediterranean. Tuna sold in the United States may be used or any of several fresh marine fishes related to the mackerel.

CEREAL:

½ pound bulgur (cracked wheat)
½ teaspoon saffron
½ teaspoon cinnamon
½ teaspoon ground cloves
½ teaspoon nutmeg
2 tablespoons olive oil
Salt and black pepper

STEW:

1 medium onion, minced
2 cloves garlic, minced
2 tablespoons olive oil
3 ounces (½ small can) tomato paste
1 cup dry white wine
1 cup clam juice
1 cup water
2 bay leaves
5 sprigs parsley
½ teaspoon salt
1 pound whitefish bones
1 pound fresh tuna or swordfish steaks
1 pound turbot or haddock, cut in 3-inch pieces
1 pound scallops

Cover cracked wheat with water; stir in saffron, cinnamon, cloves, and nutmeg, and soak for 30 minutes. Drain over steam kettle. Line colander with layer of cheesecloth and fill with cracked wheat. Bring liquid in steamer to a boil; cover colander, and steam for 30 minutes. During steaming, baste wheat with olive oil and season with salt and pepper to taste.

In a saucepan or bottom of *couscoussière,* sauté onions and garlic in hot oil; stir in tomato paste, white wine, clam juice, water, bay leaves, parsley, and salt. Add fish bones; cover and simmer slowly for 25 minutes. Strain sauce and return to saucepan. Add tunny fish, turbot, and scallops. Place wheat in steamer over fish and simmer until fish is opaque and fork-tender—5 to 8 minutes.

Heap wheat around a large, deep bowl or soup tureen, leaving a well in center. Fill the well with fish stew and serve immediately.

SERVES: 6

NOTE: Whiting, cod, and flounder are other varieties of fish that may be used.

June 24

LA FESTA DI SAN GIOVANNI BATTISTA
THE FEAST OF ST. JOHN THE BAPTIST

The feast of St. John the Baptist, patron saint of love and marriage, is an important holiday for young hearts desiring romance. Everywhere in Sicily, bonfires illuminate the streets. Stewed snails and suckling pigs are eaten on this day, and young girls play the game of trying to find out who their prospective husbands will be. They cast molten lead into a basin of cold water, and if it takes the form of a boat, fish, or paddle, he'll be a fisherman; a saw or plane, a carpenter; and so on.

Young ladies begin early in life to prepare for marriage by making a dowry of fine table linens, bedspreads, sheets and pillowcases, personal garments, and underclothing. Many of the linens are artistically edged with hand-made lace and whole bedspreads are crocheted in intricate patterns and designs. The complete hope chest may take as long as ten years to make, and it is truly a beautiful endowment for the bride and her future family. A week or two before the wedding, the dowry is exhibited to friends and relatives for admiration and boasting in the community.

The marriage ceremony and reception may be simple or elaborate, depending on the prestige and affluence of the couple and their families. The wedding banquet is elegant, and not everyone can afford it. Nevertheless, a large assortment of cookies, made by the bride's family, wedding cake, and confetti favors are a must at every wedding.

Sposalizio
WEDDING MENU

EST! EST! EST! CHAMPAGNE TOAST
CONSOMMÉ
GNOCCHI AL FORNO
ROAST SQUAB IN POLENTA NESTS
STUFFED MUSHROOM CAPS
ARUGULA SALAD
SPUMONI
WEDDING CAKE
PYRAMID OF COOKIES
CAFFÈ ESPRESSO
CONFETTI FAVORS

Chilled white Faro wine or Soave is served with the entrée and Muscatel with the wedding cake.

August 1 to 15

FERRAGOSTO
FEAST OF THE MADONNA

Ferragosto means vacation time for all Italians, and the Catholic Church has scheduled the Feast of the Madonna to coincide with this holiday. Messina, one of the most beautiful cities, on the very tip of the northeastern coast of Sicily, sponsors the most outstanding festival of the Madonna of the Assumption.

Religious floats with labored elaborations praising the Madonna, parade through the main streets of Messina daily. In the center of the town, the handsome *duomo* houses a most spectacular astronomical clock in the campanile. Each day at noon, gilded figures enact the legend of the Madonna of the Letter.

The lion roars, the cock crows, the angel passes,
the Madonna blesses, Christ appears,
the dove flies, the church arises,
death moves its scythe, the days turn.

Another impressive sight to see is two immense figures, *I Giganti,*
Mata and Grifone, the mythical founders of Messina, sitting majesti-
cally on horseback, carved in wood and papier-mâché, dragged to
the beat of drums by men wearing white shirts and trousers accented by red caps and sashes who amuse the gathered crowds.

The festa lasts for two full weeks, during which folksongs, dances,
water sports, colorful illuminations, and special foods are the main
attractions. Stands are set up to sell grilled sausages and peppers,
pizza, clams, *polpi* (octopus), fritters, ice cream, ices, seeds, nuts,
and candy.

Mid-October

SAGRA DELLA VENDEMMIA
FEAST OF GRAPE-GATHERING

The fruits of the earth—olives, grapes, and wheat—gave birth to
oil, wine, and bread, and linked the people of Sicily with the earth
and the vine. The vine best characterizes the sweat and toil of the
peasants while also providing necklacelike stretches of beautiful
Sicilian landscape.

In mid-October, La Sagra della Vendemmia, an annual con-
secration of grape-gathering, is enhanced with a cortege of beautiful maidens and a lovely queen.

Wine carts and floats carrying winepresses and bushels of grapes
parade in splendor through the main streets of Catania, Palermo,
and Messina. Shops and restaurants line tables and chairs in front
of their establishments for people to sit, drink, and be merry during
the parades and festivities. Wine is sold from large barrels centered
on the long tables and usually people bring their own olives, bread,
salami, and cheese to compliment the wine. The gay feasting and
flowing of wine continues as long as there is oil in the lamp and
bread on the table.

IL GIORNO DEI MORTI
ALL SOULS' DAY

One would immediately think All Souls' Day or the Day of the Dead would be a totally somber holy day. On the contrary, after visiting the graves of departed relatives and paying their respects, Sicilians celebrate in true *festa* style. They feel their departed would want to be remembered happily and joyously. The children particularly enjoy this holy day, for if they have been "good" they're rewarded with beautiful candy dolls (*pupi di zucchero*) given to them by the souls of their kind, deceased relatives.

The custom of doll giving is particularly popular around the Palermo area, where folk art is more visibly expressed. The large and small sugar-cast statuettes, glaringly attractive with gold and silver tinsel, portray fair ladies, historical figures, and plumed knights. They appear in pastry shops about two weeks before the holy day and are coveted by all boys and girls.

Fave dei morti (beans of the dead), although not authentically Sicilian, are also characteristic of All Souls' Day. Shaped like beans, *fave dei morti* are actually small almond cakes tinted white, pink, and chocolate.

Fave dei Morti
PISTACHIO COOKIES

⅔ cup sugar	2 cups sifted flour
½ cup butter or margarine	1 teaspoon vanilla
2 eggs	1 cup ground pistachio nuts

Preheat oven to 400° F. Grease two baking sheets well.

Cream sugar, butter, and eggs together. Stir in flour gradually and beat until smooth. Add vanilla and pistachio nuts; blend.

Break off small pieces of dough (about 1 teaspoon each) and form into kidney-shaped beans. Place 1 inch apart on greased baking sheets and bake until cookies are lightly browned—about 10 minutes.

YIELD: Approximately 9 dozen

SOUPS

"Tutto fa brodo!" is an Italian expression meaning "It's all the same!" Perhaps this is true of chopped liver, but not of *minestra* or *brodo* (soup). Each Sicilian soup recipe is unique and nutritious and has the flavor of the provinces.

Among the poor, soup is eaten with large pieces of bread to soak up the broth. It may be the whole meal; but often it is the only meal of the day. Possibly this is why Sicilian soups are substantial, strong, and economical. Combinations of home-grown vegetables or meat bones boiled with carrots, celery, tomatoes, and onions are the principle ingredients of basic soups.

Usually *brodo* is served for *cena* (supper) in place of pasta. Since supper is eaten late and not too far from bedtime, lighter meals are better before sleeping. Often soup dishes are listed with pasta dishes in restaurants, but both are never eaten at the same meal. *Il primo* or first course offers pasta or soup. The second course, *il secondo,* consists of meat, poultry or fish, vegetables, and salad, and the meal ends with fruit or cheese and/or dessert.

Minestrone di Lenticche
GOOD-LUCK LENTIL SOUP

1 pound lentils
Water
⅓ cup olive oil
1 large onion, chopped
6 stalks celery, chopped
3 sprigs fresh mint (or 1 tablespoon dried)

1½ teaspoons salt
½ teaspoon black pepper
1½ cups cooked rice or noodles (optional)
1 cup grated Parmesan cheese

Wash lentils with cold water and discard bits of rock. Place in a large kettle and cover with 1½ quarts warm water. Bring to a boil; drain and set aside.

In a large kettle, heat oil and brown onion and celery for 3 minutes. Add lentils and sauté for 5 minutes.

Cover with warm water (about 2 quarts) and stir in mint, salt, and pepper. Bring to a boil; cover and simmer until lentils are tender but not mushy—45 minutes to 1 hour. Mix in cooked rice, and correct seasoning if necessary. Serve hot or at room temperature with grated cheese.

SERVES: 6 to 8

Fritteda

SWEET AND SOUR MINESTRONE

Actually, *fritteda* is a sweet and sour vegetable fry, but I find it equally appetizing as a thick soup.

2 tablespoons olive oil
1 medium onion, chopped
1 10-ounce package frozen
   artichoke hearts, thawed
1 teaspoon nutmeg
1 No. 2 can peas
1 No. 2 can fava beans
1 cup beef stock or bouillon

1 tablespoon tomato paste
3 sprigs fresh mint (or 1
   tablespoon dried)
½ teaspoon salt
¼ teaspoon black pepper
1 tablespoon sugar
1 tablespoon vinegar
2 cups cooked elbow macaroni

In a large saucepan, heat oil and sauté onion until opaque—about 3 minutes. Add artichokes; sprinkle with nutmeg and sauté for 5 minutes. Add peas and fava beans and their liquid, beef stock, tomato paste, mint, salt, pepper, sugar, and vinegar. Stir and simmer for 20 to 25 minutes. Add cooked macaroni and heat through. Correct seasoning if necessary. Let stand 10 to 15 minutes before serving or serve at room temperature.

SERVES: 6

NOTE: *Fritteda* can also be served as a vegetable casserole, leaving out the beef stock and macaroni.

Zuppa di Patate e Uova
POTATO AND EGG SOUP

3 tablespoons olive oil
4 medium potatoes, cubed
1 medium onion, chopped
1 quart water

¼ cup minced parsley
Salt and black pepper
4 eggs

In a large skillet, heat oil and sauté potatoes and onion for 5 minutes. Transfer to kettle. Cover with water, parsley, and salt and pepper to taste. Bring to a boil; cover and boil gently until potatoes are tender—20 to 25 minutes. Lower heat; drop eggs, one at a time, in broth. Cover and poach for 5 minutes.

SERVES: 4

NOTE: It is possible to make this soup in advance, but add and cook eggs just before serving.

Stracciatella con Funghi e Pomodori
EGG-DROP SOUP WITH
MUSHROOMS AND TOMATOES

3 tablespoons olive oil
1 medium onion, chopped
1 clove garlic, cut in half
½ pound mushrooms, thinly
  sliced
2 cups canned whole tomatoes
2 tablespoons fresh rosemary
  (or 2 teaspoons dried)

1 teaspoon salt
¼ teaspoon black pepper
1 quart chicken stock
2 eggs, slightly beaten
4 friselle (bread rusks)
1 cup grated caciocavallo
  cheese

Heat oil in a large skillet; sauté onion and garlic until golden. Add mushrooms and sauté for 3 minutes. Stir in tomatoes, rosemary, salt, and pepper; simmer for 10 minutes. Discard garlic and transfer mixture to a large kettle.

Pour in chicken stock and bring to a boil. Pour in eggs slowly, stirring rapidly with a whisk, until eggs coagulate. Place 1 frisella in each soup bowl and ladle soup over it. Sprinkle with grated cheese and serve immediately.

SERVES: 4

Minestra di Ceci
CHICK-PEA SOUP

2 cups chicken stock or bouillon
1 cup scraped, chopped carrots
1 large tomato, peeled, chopped
1 teaspoon dried or 1 tablespoon fresh rosemary

2 No. 2 cans chick-peas
Salt and freshly ground black pepper
½ cup grated Parmesan cheese

Bring chicken stock to a boil; drop in carrots, tomato, and rosemary, and boil gently until carrots are tender—10 to 15 minutes. Add chick-peas and their liquid and cook 10 minutes longer over medium heat. Salt and pepper to taste. Sprinkle with Parmesan cheese before serving.

SERVES: 4 to 6

Noccioline di Manzo in Brodo
MEATBALL SOUP

MEATBALLS:
1 pound ground beef
1 egg
1 small onion, minced
1 small clove garlic, minced
¼ cup minced parsley
½ cup bread crumbs

⅓ cup grated Romano cheese
½ teaspoon salt
¼ teaspoon black pepper
6 cups beef or chicken stock
8 ounces egg noodles
¾ cup grated Romano cheese

Combine beef, egg, onion, garlic, parsley, bread crumbs, cheese, salt, and pepper. Wet hands with water and shape meat mixture into small balls 1 inch in diameter. Set aside.

Bring beef stock to a boil; drop in meatballs and simmer until meatballs are cooked—8 to 10 minutes. Cook egg noodles according to directions on package. Drain and add to soup. Ladle into warm bowls and sprinkle generously with grated Romano cheese.

SERVES: 4 to 6

Zuppa di Verdura

SEASONAL FRESH VEGETABLE SOUP

1 medium onion, chopped
4 stalks celery, chopped
1 pound zucchini, sliced
¼ cup olive oil
6 cups vegetable bouillon
½ pound fresh fava beans
½ pound fresh string beans
1 cup fresh peas

4 sprigs Italian parsley (flat leaf)
2 bay leaves
1 teaspoon salt
½ teaspoon bruised peppercorns
4 medium ripe tomatoes, skinned, chopped
1 cup grated Parmesan cheese

Brown onion, celery, and zucchini in hot oil for 5 to 8 minutes. Transfer to kettle. Pour vegetable bouillon into kettle; add fava beans, string beans, peas, parsley, bay leaves, salt, and peppercorns. Bring to a boil; cover and boil gently until beans and peas are tender—15 to 20 minutes.

Stir in tomatoes and zucchini and simmer for 10 minutes. Correct seasoning if necessary. Discard parsley, bay leaves, and peppercorns. Serve hot with grated cheese.

SERVES: 6 to 8

NOTE: This recipe may be made with any combination of fresh vegetables in season (carrots, potatoes, squash, peppers, eggplant, leeks, turnips, etc.).

Minestra di Melanzane

EGGPLANT SOUP

¼ cup olive oil
1 small onion, chopped fine
2 stalks celery, chopped fine
1 large green pepper, cut in strips
½ pound eggplant, diced
1 cup skinned, chopped fresh or canned tomatoes

3 leaves fresh basil (or 1 teaspoon dried)
Salt and black pepper
1 quart beef stock or bouillon
½ cup grated Parmesan cheese (optional)

In a skillet, heat oil and sauté onion, celery, pepper, and eggplant for 5 minutes. (Add more oil if vegetables begin to stick.) Stir in tomatoes, basil, and salt and pepper lightly; simmer for 5 minutes.

Transfer mixture to a kettle. Pour beef stock over vegetables and bring to a boil. Cover and boil gently for 10 minutes. Correct seasoning if necessary. Serve as is or with grated cheese.

SERVES: 4

Minestrone di Trippa
TRIPE CHOWDER

This recipe has been simplified to take advantage of our vast selection of fresh vegetables and convenience foods. The flavor, texture, and appearance have, if anything, been improved.

1½ pounds tripe, parboiled	2 medium potatoes, diced
2 thick strips bacon, chopped	16 ounces (2 cups) V-8 juice
2 leeks, chopped (or 1 medium onion)	2 cups beef stock or bouillon
2 stalks celery, chopped	2 tablespoons minced parsley (for garnish)

Rinse tripe well with cold water. Cover with warm water and boil for 1 hour. Drain, rinse well with cold water, and cut in small squares. Set aside.

In a large saucepan, fry bacon for 2 minutes; add leeks, celery, and potatoes, and sauté for 5 minutes. Pour in V-8 juice, beef stock, and tripe. Stir and simmer for 25 minutes. Portion in deep bowls and garnish with minced parsley.

SERVES: 4

PASTA

Over Two Hundred Varieties

It is said that a wealthy nobleman of Palermo who was noted for his love of fine food possessed a cook with a marvelous inventive genius. One day this talented cook created a farinaceous dish and served it with a rich sauce and grated Parmesan cheese in a large bowl. The first mouthful caused the illustrious epicure to shout: *"Cari!"* (the darlings!). With the second mouthful, he emphasized his statement, exclaiming: *"Ma cari!"* (ah, but what darlings!). And as the flavor of the dish grew upon him his enthusiasm rose to even greater heights, and he cried out with joyful emotion: *"Ma caroni!"* (ah, but dearest darlings!). In paying this supreme tribute to his cook's discovery, the nobleman bestowed the name by which this admirable preparation is known today . . . macaroni!

Macaroni and pasta are synonymous generic terms describing egg pastas (thin or broad noodles, lasagna, fettucini, ravioli, cappeletti, agnolotti) or commercially packaged dry pastes (the most popular being spaghetti, rotellini, macaroni, linguini, rigatoni, shells, and elbows). Over two hundred varieties of pasta are made and prepared in favorite ways in every region of Italy. Romans prepare pasta in long strips; in Bologna they prefer flat ribbons; and in Sicily they roll pasta on knitting needles to form a dried spiral. In any shape or form, pasta cannot be dismissed as a mere article of food; it is a feast!

Sicilians are enormous eaters of pasta and masters at preparing it in many variations. In fact, according to a revealing statistic, eighty out of one hundred Sicilian families eat pasta at least once a day. Very often pasta is made fresh in home or restaurant kitchens and served floating in a variety of sauces or soups. They combine pasta with everything: eggplant, cauliflower, broccoli, beans, asparagus, peas, fresh fennel, herbs, anchovies, sardines, ground hamburger, or shredded veal and pork. Sicilians' outstanding passion for pasta is nothing new. Throughout history even though many foreign nations invaded and inhabited Sicily and brought with them their typical cuisines, none managed to dominate or replace the popularity of pasta.

Pasta's popularity and appeal is not peculiar to Sicily alone; everybody loves pasta. Unfortunately, not everybody, even the Sicilians, knows how to cook it properly. It should be cooked in a large kettle filled with rapidly boiling water. If the water is not boiling the pasta will only become soggy. The rapid and continuous boiling keeps the macaroni moving about so it will cook quickly and evenly. If the kettle is too small, the pasta will not have room to expand. Since pasta loves water, it drinks plenty of it, so insufficient water will cause it to be hard and tough. The proportion of water will depend on the amount of pasta cooked, but generally three quarts of water are required for one pound of pasta, and cooking time depends on the size and thickness of the pasta. However, and most important, pasta should be cooked *al dente*. In other words, not soft or mushy, but tender yet resilient to the bite.

Fusilli al Forno
EGGY MEAT AND MACARONI CASSEROLE

Baked macaroni casseroles are excellent for buffet dinners and make-ahead meals. This recipe was Grandmother's creation and a family favorite.

2 tablespoons olive oil
2 pounds ground beef
3 cloves garlic, cut in half
1 large onion, chopped
2 6-ounce cans tomato paste
2 teaspoons salt
½ teaspoon black pepper
4 sprigs fresh basil (or 1
    tablespoon dried)

1½ cups water
1 No. 2½ can whole tomatoes
1 pound fusilli (spirals)
1 cup grated Parmesan cheese
    (reserve ½ cup for serving)
6 eggs, slightly beaten

In a large skillet, heat oil and brown ground beef for 5 minutes. Transfer to a large saucepan. In the same skillet, sauté garlic and onion until onion is soft. Add tomato paste and sauté for 3 minutes.

Transfer to the saucepan and stir in salt, pepper, basil, water, and whole tomatoes. Bring to a boil; cover and simmer slowly for 1 hour. Preheat oven to 350° F.

While sauce is simmering, cook spirals according to directions on package, but reduce cooking time by 3 minutes (spirals should be slightly undercooked since they will be baked in oven). Drain.

In a large casserole or shallow baking pan (9×13 inches), spread ½ cup of the sauce and one third of the spirals; cover with more sauce and grated cheese. Continue layering alternately until all of the ingredients are used, ending with spirals on top. Pour eggs over casserole; use fork to loosen spirals, allowing eggs to run through to bottom layer. Top with sauce and grated cheese. Bake for 20 minutes. Remove and let set for 10 minutes for easy handling and serving. Cut in large squares and serve with additional sauce and grated cheese.

SERVES: 8 to 10

Ziti al Forno

BAKED ZITI AND CHEESE CASSEROLE

1 recipe Meat and Tomato Sauce*	8 ounces mozzarella cheese, sliced
1 pound ziti	¾ cup grated Romano cheese
1 pound ricotta cheese	

Preheat oven to 350° F.

Prepare Meat and Tomato Sauce. While sauce is simmering, cook ziti according to directions on package. Drain. Place some of the ziti in a buttered casserole. Cover with 1 ladle of sauce, tablespoons of ricotta, and a few slices of mozzarella; sprinkle with grated cheese. Continue layering alternately until all ingredients are used, ending with ziti on top. Cover with sauce and grated cheese and bake for 25 to 30 minutes. Remove from oven and serve immediately with additional sauce and cheese.

SERVES: 4 to 6

NEW YEAR'S AND CARNIVAL LASAGNE

1 recipe Meat and Tomato Sauce*	1 teaspoon salt
	Lasagne
1 pound Italian sausage, cut in 1-inch pieces	6 hard-cooked eggs, sliced
1½ pounds ricotta cheese	½ pound mozzarella cheese, diced (1 cup)
4 eggs	¾ cup grated Parmesan cheese
¼ cup minced parsley	

Preheat oven to 375° F.

Prepare Meat and Tomato Sauce. While sauce is simmering, sauté sausage pieces in a hot skillet until golden brown. Combine ricotta cheese with eggs, parsley, and salt and mix well. Refrigerate until ready to use. Cook lasagne according to directions on package. Drain, rinse with cold water, and drain well.

Spread a thin layer of sauce in a 9×13-inch casserole or shallow baking pan. Add alternate layers of lasagne, ricotta mixture, sliced eggs, sausage pieces, diced mozzarella, sauce, and a sprinkling of grated Parmesan cheese. Continue layering until all ingredients are used, ending with lasagne, sauce, and grated cheese on top.

Bake for 40 minutes. Remove from oven and let set for 10 minutes before cutting. (This will prevent it from falling apart in serving.) Cut into large squares and serve with additional sauce and grated cheese.

SERVES: 8 to 10

TIP: When cooking large-cut macaroni, add a little olive oil to boiling water to prevent macaroni from sticking together.

Spaghetti di Quaresima

LENTEN SPAGHETTI

During Lent, Sicilians eat meat only a few times a week. Eggs are an economical substitute providing protein and sustenance. This combination of wholesome ingredients, cooked in a unique way, has made Lenten spaghetti a popular winter's meal.

1 recipe Winter's Tomato
 Sauce*
6 eggs
1 pound spaghetti

EGG CROQUETTES:
6 eggs
1 cup bread crumbs
⅓ cup minced parsley
1 small onion, minced
⅓ cup grated Parmesan cheese
½ teaspoon salt
¼ teaspoon black pepper
¼ cup olive oil for frying

Prepare Winter's Tomato Sauce as directed. While sauce is simmering, hard-cook 6 eggs for 15 minutes in boiling-hot water. Cool, shell, and set aside.

In a bowl, beat 6 eggs with a fork until yolks and whites are mixed. Add bread crumbs, parsley, onions, cheese, salt, and pepper, and mix until ingredients are combined. Drop by rounded table-spoons into hot oil and fry until golden on both sides. (Flatten croquettes slightly with spatula before turning.) Add croquettes and hard-cooked eggs to sauce and simmer slowly for 20 minutes. Croquettes will absorb some of the sauce and almost double in size.

Cook spaghetti according to directions on package. Drain and portion into serving bowls. Cover with sauce and serve with 1 hard-cooked egg and 2 croquettes per person.

SERVES: 4 to 6

Cannelloni a la Valle dei Tempi
CANNELLONI FROM THE VALLEY OF THE TEMPLES

Restaurants nestled in Agrigento's famous Valley of the Temples, feature cannelloni (pasta pipes) filled with tasty spiced meat and smacked with a layer of sauce and spicy cheese.

1 recipe Winter's Tomato
 Sauce*
1 recipe Home-made Pasta*
Water
Salt
1½ pounds beef round
¼ pound pork
2 carrots, peeled, chopped
3 sprigs parsley, chopped

2 stalks celery, chopped
2 bay leaves
1 teaspoon salt
1 teaspoon peppercorns
¼ pound mortadella (Italian
 spiced ham), chopped
½ cup grated caciocavallo
 cheese

Prepare Winter's Tomato Sauce. While sauce is simmering, make pasta. Cut dough in half and roll out on floured board into two thin sheets. Cut into 4×5-inch rectangles. Sprinkle lightly with flour and let dry for 1 hour. Drop rectangles, a few at a time, into rapidly boiling salted water (about 4 quarts) for 5 to 8 minutes. Remove with slotted spoon into a bowl of cold water. When pasta is cool enough to handle, drain on damp towels.

Place beef, pork, carrots, parsley, celery, bay leaves, salt, and peppercorns in a large saucepan. Cover with water (approximately 1½ quarts). Bring to a boil; cover and simmer until meat is tender—1 to 1½ hours. Drain off liquid and discard peppercorns. Grind up meat and vegetables with meat grinder or in blender. Add mortadella and blend. Preheat oven to 400° F.

On lower end of pasta rectangle, spread 2 tablespoons of the meat mixture. Roll, diploma style, and place cannelloni in shallow baking dish which has been lined with a thin layer of sauce. Arrange cannelloni just one layer deep; cover generously with sauce and sprinkle with grated cheese. Bake for 10 to 15 minutes. Serve with additional sauce and cheese.

SERVES: 6 to 8

Vermicelli alla Siracusana

VERMICELLI SYRACUSE STYLE

The Italians have facetiously named *vermicelli*—little worms! Probably because vermicelli (very fine strands of egg noodles) multiply after cooking and simulate worms in density. Syracusians, in all seriousness, have created a colorful and snappy vegetable sauce to complement the tasty, eggy worms.

3 yellow or green peppers
1 1- to 2-pound eggplant
Salt
1½ pounds ripe tomatoes (or 2 cups canned plum tomatoes)
¼ cup olive oil
2 cloves garlic, minced
4 fresh basil leaves (or 1 tablespoon dried)
¼ cup capers
8 black Sicilian olives, pitted, chopped
6 anchovies, chopped
½ teaspoon salt
1 pound vermicelli
½ cup grated caciocavallo cheese

Cut peppers in half; remove and discard stems, seeds, and sponge. Rinse with cold water; dry and broil, skin side up, for 2 minutes. Cool, peel off skins, and cut in strips. Remove and discard stem from eggplant; dice; salt liberally and drain in colander for 15 minutes. Rinse off salt; dry with absorbent paper and set aside. If using ripe tomatoes, plunge in boiling water for 1 to 2 minutes. Remove skins and stems; discard. Chop tomatoes and set aside.

Heat oil in a large skillet; add garlic and brown lightly. Add diced eggplant and pepper strips and sauté for 10 minutes. (Add more oil if vegetables begin to stick.) Stir in tomatoes, basil, capers, olives, anchovies, and salt. Cover skillet and simmer slowly for 5 to 10 minutes.

Cook vermicelli according to directions on package. Drain. Transfer to a warm serving bowl; cover with vegetable sauce and mix well. Sprinkle with grated cheese and serve immediately.

SERVES: 4 to 6

Mille Foglie alla Pirandello

LEAVES OF PASTA ALLA PIRANDELLO

Luigi Pirandello, one of the greatest playwrights of the twentieth century, was born in Agrigento, Sicily. Mille Foglie alla Pirandello is dedicated to him and matches his magnificence. These light, graceful, and tender leaves of pasta are comparable in texture to the famous napoleon pastry.

1 recipe Meat and Tomato Sauce*	½ pound caciocavallo cheese, coarsely grated
1 recipe Home-made Pasta*	½ cup grated Parmesan cheese

Prepare Meat and Tomato Sauce. While sauce is simmering, make Home-made Pasta. Cut dough in half; roll out on floured board into two very thin sheets (⅛ inch thick). Cut sheets into 2½ ×12-inch strips. Sprinkle with flour and drop a few strips at a time into boiling salted water (about 4 quarts) for 5 to 8 minutes. Remove with slotted spoon into bowl of cold water. When pasta is cool enough to handle, drain on damp towels. Preheat oven to 400° F.

In a 9×13-inch shallow baking pan, spread one ladle of sauce. Layer pasta strips alternately with sauce and grated caciocavallo cheese until ingredients are used, ending with sauce and cheese on top. Bake at 400° F. for 15 minutes. Let pasta stand for 5 to 10 minutes before serving. Cut into large squares and serve with additional sauce and grated Parmesan cheese.

SERVES: 8 to 10

TIP: When cooking large-cut macaroni, add a little olive oil to boiling water to prevent macaroni from sticking together.

Gnocculli

GNOCCHI WITH MEAT SAUCE

Gnocchi is a type of pasta made with flour and ricotta cheese or potatoes or cereal. Gnocculli (Sicilian dialect for gnocchi) resemble nuggets of gold and taste like mini-morsels of heaven.

1 recipe Meat and Tomato Sauce*	Pinch of salt
4 cups sifted flour	3 tablespoons salt
1 pound ricotta cheese	1 cup grated Parmesan cheese

Prepare meat and tomato sauce as directed. In a large bowl, combine flour, ricotta, and salt. Mix until dough cleans sides of bowl and forms a ball. Turn onto a lightly floured board and knead until dough is smooth—about 5 to 8 minutes.

Cut dough into 8 sections. Roll each section into long finger-shaped rolls (½ inch in diameter) and cut into ½-inch pieces. With index finger, press each piece in the center, gently but firmly, rolling slightly to form a shell-like shape. Sprinkle with flour and let stand 15 minutes.

Shake off excess flour and drop gnocculli gently into 6 quarts rapidly boiling salted water. Boil until tender—12 to 15 minutes. Drain well; cover with meat and tomato sauce; sprinkle with cheese and serve immediately.

SERVES: 6 to 8

Pasta Fritta
FRIED SPAGHETTI

Pasta Fritta is traditionally served for *il cenone* (Christmas Eve supper). I think it's an unusual and tasty first course for any time of the year.

½ pound spaghettini or
    vermicelli
1 2-ounce can anchovies
¼ cup olive oil

3 eggs
3 tablespoons grated Parmesan
    cheese
Freshly ground black pepper

Cook spaghettini following directions on package. When done, drain well and set aside. Chop anchovies, reserving 3 whole fillets for garnish.

In a large skillet, heat oil and add cooked spaghettini and anchovies. Fry for 8 to 10 minutes over medium heat until spaghettini is golden and crispy on bottom side. Beat eggs slightly with cheese and freshly ground pepper to taste. Pour over spaghettini and cook until eggs are set.

Cover skillet with a plate the same size as the skillet and reverse spaghettini onto plate. Slide back into skillet to cook bottom side for 2 minutes. Slide onto a warm serving plate and garnish with anchovy fillets. Cut into wedges, omelet style, and serve immediately.

SERVES: 4

VARIATION: Substitute a 6-ounce can of Italian-style tuna for anchovies and cook as directed above.

Rotellini al Forno
BAKED WAGON WHEELS

1 recipe Ragù alla Siciliana*
1 pound rotellini (wagon wheels)
½ cup grated Romano cheese

Preheat oven to 400° F.

Prepare Ragù alla Siciliana. While sauce is simmering, cook wagon wheels according to directions on package. Drain. Return to kettle and mix with 2 cups sauce.

Oil small molds (15 to 20 ounces each) for individual servings.

Fill to the top with wagon wheel mixture. Bake for 10 minutes. Remove from oven and let stand for 5 minutes before unmolding. Place serving plates over molds. Reverse and turn out molds onto plates. Top with sauce and grated cheese and serve immediately. SERVES: 4 to 6

Spaghetti alla Carrettiera
COACHMAN'S SPAGHETTI

Sicilian coachmen created Spaghetti alla Carrettiera to have something hot, simple, filling, and inexpensive to eat while working. Long ago, along the main thoroughfares in Sicily, it was common to see these men in their black frocks boiling water over small wooden fires for their daily pastasciutta (pasta coated lightly with herbs and cheese or tomato sauce). Formerly, this specialty was considered a peasant dish, but today it is an epicurean favorite with both rich and poor alike.

1 pound spaghetti	2 cups chopped fresh parsley
¼ cup olive oil	½ cup Romano cheese
2 cloves garlic, minced	Freshly ground black pepper

Cook spaghetti according to directions on package. While spaghetti is cooking, heat oil in a large skillet and sauté garlic for 2 or 3 minutes. Stir in cooked, drained spaghetti, parsley, and cheese, and mix well. Heat together for 2 minutes. Transfer to a warm serving bowl and season with freshly ground pepper to taste.
SERVES: 4 to 6

Pasta di Casa
HOME-MADE PASTA

Pasta is easy and fun to make at home, and the time consumed is well worth the superior product. Nothing commercially sold can match the delicate flavor and light texture of freshly made pasta.

This basic recipe may be used in making fettuccine, ravioli, cannelloni, tagliatelle, capelletti, spaghetti, lasagne, and mille foglie.

3 cups sifted flour
½ teaspoon salt
3 large eggs

1 tablespoon olive oil
⅓ to ½ cup water

In a large bowl, measure the flour and sprinkle the salt over it. Make a well in center; add eggs and oil and mix thoroughly. Pour water in gradually and mix until dough cleans bowl and forms a ball. (A little more or less water may be necessary.)

Turn dough onto a lightly floured board. Knead with back of hand, turning and rolling until dough is smooth and satiny—about 10 minutes. Put dough in a bowl, cover with cloth, and refrigerate for 15 minutes.

Cut dough into four equal pieces and roll into sheets ⅛ inch thick. Cut and/or shape to type of pasta desired.

YIELD: 1½ to 2 pounds pasta

VARIATION: For a delicate accent, add 2 ounces of your favorite fresh minced herb to the flour mixture, and continue as directed.

Linguine in Salsa di Calamari alla Sorella Sara
SISTER SARA'S LINGUINE WITH SQUID SAUCE

Fish lovers! Here is an exotic dish that stirs the soul and thrills the stomach!

2 pounds squid
3 tablespoons olive oil
1 small onion, minced
2 cloves garlic, cut in half
1 No. 2½ can tomato purée

1 teaspoon salt
¼ teaspoon black pepper
4 sprigs parsley, minced
1 pound linguine

Have fishmonger clean squid, removing the flat bone, eyes, ink sac, and intestines. Rinse well with cold water; drain; dry and slice into 1-inch rings.

In a large saucepan, heat oil and sauté onions and garlic until golden. Add squid and sauté until squid begins to curl—about 5 minutes. Pour in tomato purée, salt, pepper, and parsley; stir.

Bring to a boil; lower heat; cover and simmer slowly until squid is tender—about 1 hour. Correct seasoning if necessary.

While sauce is simmering, cook linguine according to directions on package. Drain and mix with sauce. Serve with squid garnishing the top.

SERVES: 4 to 6

NOTE: Grated cheese is never served with fish-and-pasta dishes; its strong aroma and flavor overpowers the delicate flavor of fish.

Maccheroni con le Seppie

"INKY" MACARONI WITH CUTTLEFISH

Alas! Gastronomes, the secret of this mysterious dish is hidden in *le seppie,* or cuttlefish. Cuttlefish are two-gilled cephalopodous mollusks containing ink sacs that give them the power of ejecting indelible ink to darken the water and conceal themselves from pursuit. For culinary purposes, however, the ink sacs serve to color the sauce and macaroni. It's a blueblood recipe! *Non è vero?*

1½ pounds cuttlefish	1½ cups water
3 tablespoons olive oil	½ teaspoon salt
1 medium onion, chopped	1 pound thick spaghetti or
1 7-ounce can tomato paste	macaroni

Remove internal shells, eyes, and intestines from cuttlefish, but do not discard the ink sacs (or have fishmonger clean fish for you). Rinse well with cold water; drain and pat dry. Heat oil in a saucepan and sauté onion until golden. Add cuttlefish and sauté until they begin to curl and turn pink—about 5 minutes. Stir in tomato paste, water, and salt. Cover and simmer until cuttlefish is tender—30 to 40 minutes. Correct seasoning if necessary.

While sauce is simmering, cook spaghetti according to directions on package. Drain. Transfer to a large spaghetti bowl and mix with sauce. Serve with cuttlefish garnishing the top.

SERVES: 4 to 6

Conchiglie con Cavolfiore
SHELLS AND FLOWERS

1 large head cauliflower (2 to 3
    pounds) (or 2 10-ounce
    packages frozen cauliflower)
1 tablespoon salt
1 pound pasta shells

¼ cup olive oil
2 large cloves garlic, minced
⅔ cups grated Romano cheese
Freshly ground black pepper
Salt

Wash cauliflower with cold running water; remove leaves and core. Cut or break cauliflower head into rosettes. Add salt to water and bring to a boil; drop in cauliflower rosettes and cook until tender —15 to 20 minutes. Drain, reserving ½ cup liquid; set aside.

Cook shells according to directions on package. Drain. Heat oil in same kettle and sauté garlic until golden. Add shells, cauliflower rosettes, ½ cup liquid, grated cheese, and freshly ground pepper to taste. Toss until ingredients are thoroughly mixed. Season lightly with salt, if necessary.

SERVES: 4 to 6

Fettuccine di Spinaci con Salsa di Filetto di Pomodoro
SPINACH FETTUCCINE
WITH "BEEFSTEAK" TOMATO SAUCE

Plum tomatoes are referred to as small "beefsteaks" in Italian. Their plump, plum-shaped bodies yield a sweet, light, and savory sauce.

2½ pounds fresh plum tomatoes
    (or 1 No. 3 can plum
    tomatoes)
¼ cup butter
1 small onion, chopped fine
½ pound ham or prosciutto,
    diced

6 sprigs fresh basil (or 1
    tablespoon dried sweet basil)
1 teaspoon salt
¼ teaspoon black pepper
1 pound spinach fettuccine
¾ cup grated Parmesan cheese

If using fresh tomatoes, plunge in boiling water for 1 to 2 minutes. Remove stems and skins; slice and discard seeds. Set aside.

In a large saucepan, melt butter and sauté onion until golden. Add ham and sauté 3 minutes longer. Stir in tomatoes, basil, salt, and pepper to taste. Simmer slowly until excess water from tomatoes has been reduced—20 to 30 minutes.

While sauce is simmering, cook fettuccine according to directions on package. Drain and transfer to a warm serving bowl. Cover with some of the sauce and sprinkle with grated cheese. Serve with additional sauce and grated cheese.

SERVES: 4 to 6

Pasta cca Muddica

ANGEL'S HAIR WITH BREAD CRUMBS

Capelli d'angelo is the very thinnest of spaghetti—so thin and fine that it is named "angel's hair." It requires just a quick dousing in boiling water for a few minutes to bring out its fine flavor.

1 recipe Anchovy Sauce*   Freshly ground black pepper
1 cup bread crumbs
1 pound uncooked capelli
   d'angelo or vermicelli

Prepare Anchovy Sauce as directed. Spread bread crumbs on a baking sheet and toast in a preheated oven at 350° F. until golden brown—10 to 15 minutes. Cook capelli d'angelo according to directions on package. Drain and mix with anchovy sauce. Serve with toasted bread crumbs and freshly ground pepper to taste. A dish fit for angels!

SERVES: 4 to 6

NOTE: Capelli d'angelo is an imported product and is sold at Italian groceries or gourmet shops.

Ravioli di Carne e Spinaci

MEAT AND SPINACH RAVIOLI

1 recipe Home-made Pasta*   1 pound ground beef
2 10-ounce packages frozen   1 teaspoon salt
   chopped spinach   ¼ teaspoon black pepper
¼ cup minced onions   1 egg, slightly beaten
2 tablespoons olive oil

Prepare Home-made Pasta as directed. Cook spinach according to directions on package; drain and squeeze out excess liquid with hands. Brown minced onions in hot oil. Add ground beef and sauté for 5 minutes, turning meat with spatula to brown evenly.

Combine spinach with meat mixture and season with salt and pepper. Cool for 5 minutes; add egg and mix thoroughly. Fill, shape, and cook as directed for Mama's Ravioli.* Serve with hot tomato sauce and grated cheese.

SERVES: 6 to 8

VARIATION: Serve ravioli with salsa besciamella (white sauce) accented with a splash of tomato sauce and grated cheese.

Pasta con le Sarde
GREEN AND SILVER SPAGHETTI

Pasta con le Sarde is the most distinguished of Sicilian specialties, and a dish of the people. Its hearty combination of fresh and salted sardines, fennel leaves, currants, and pine nuts is intermixed with thick strings of chewy spaghetti. Toasted bread crumbs were orginally sprinkled over the top instead of cheese for economy's sake, and today the practice continues since they add a rather crispy texture and nutty flavor to the dish.

1 medium onion, minced
2 tablespoons pine nuts
¼ cup olive oil
1 pound fennel leaves, chopped (2 cups)
1 8-ounce can tomato purée
2 tablespoons currants
Salt and black pepper

½ pound fresh sardine or smelt fillets, cut in 1-inch pieces
4 to 6 salted sardines, rinsed and cut in 1-inch pieces
1 pound perciatelli (thick macaroni)
1 cup toasted bread crumbs

In a large saucepan, brown onion and pine nuts in hot oil for 3 minutes. Stir in fennel, tomato purée, currants, and salt and pepper to taste. Simmer slowly for 10 minutes. Add pieces of fish and continue simmering for 10 minutes.

Cook perciatelli according to directions on package. Drain; return to kettle and pour half the sauce over it. Mix and heat together for 3 minutes. Portion into deep bowls; cover with more sauce and top

with salted sardine pieces. Serve with toasted bread crumbs. (Toast crumbs in a moderate oven or brown carefully in a heavy skillet.)
SERVES: 4 to 6

NOTE: Making this recipe from fresh ingredients as suggested results in a superb dish. However, it is possible to purchase Complete Seasoning for Pasta con le Sarde in tins, and salted sardines, from Italian groceries or gourmet shops. The seasoning has to be heated and mixed with spaghetti as directed.

Ravioli Casalinghi
MAMA'S RAVIOLI

CHEESE FILLING:

2 pounds fresh ricotta cheese
¼ cup minced fresh mint (or 1 tablespoon dried)
½ teaspoon salt
3 eggs
1 recipe Home-made Pasta*

2 eggs, slightly beaten
1 recipe Meat and Tomato Sauce*
1 cup grated Parmesan cheese (for serving)

Combine ricotta, mint, salt, and 3 eggs together in a large bowl. Refrigerate.

Prepare Home-made Pasta. On a lightly floured board, roll each dough piece into 4×12×⅛-inch rectangles. Place fully rounded tablespoons of ricotta mixture 1 inch apart on lower half of dough. Brush the other halves with slightly beaten eggs and adjust dough over cheese filling, pressing gently with fingertips around each mound of filling. Dip a 2-inch ravioli or biscuit cutter in flour; place over cheese mound and cut out like a cookie or biscuit. Flour ravioli lightly and let stand ½ hour.

When ready to cook, brush off excess flour and carefully drop a few at a time into 4 quarts salted boiling water. (Water should be constantly boiling while ravioli are cooking.) Remove from boiling water with slotted spoon and drain in colander. Keep cooked ravioli warm while the rest are cooking. Serve with hot Meat and Tomato Sauce* and grated Parmesan cheese.
SERVES: 6 to 8

NOTE: Ravioli freeze well. When ready to use, thaw at room temperature for 1 hour before cooking.

Crosetti

ZUCCHINI AND MEAT PIE

¼ cup olive oil
1½ pounds zucchini, cut in
    ½-inch slices
1 large onion, chopped
2 cloves garlic, minced
2 stalks celery, chopped fine
2 tablespoons olive oil
1½ pounds stewing veal
1 No. 2½ can plum tomatoes
    in purée

3 sprigs fresh basil (or 1
    tablespoon dried)
2 sprigs parsley, chopped
1 teaspoon salt
¼ teaspoon black pepper
1 pound mafalda (broad
    noodles) or lasagne
1 cup coarsely grated
    caciocavallo cheese

In a large skillet, heat ¼ cup olive oil and brown zucchini lightly.
Set aside. In same skillet, sauté onions, garlic, and celery until
golden—about 5 minutes. Transfer to a large saucepan. Add 2
tablespoons oil to skillet and brown veal lightly on all sides. Transfer
to saucepan. Stir in tomatoes, basil, parsley, salt, and pepper, and
simmer slowly until meat is tender—about 1 hour. Remove meat;
cool; shred and return to sauce. Preheat oven to 350° F.

Cook mafalda according to directions on package. Drain, rinse
with cold water, and drain. Pour a ladle of sauce into a 10-inch round
spring-form pan. Layer mafalda (overlapping layers), zucchini,
sauce, and cheese. Continue layering until all ingredients are used,
ending with mafalda on top. (Cut top layer to fit pan.) Cover with
sauce and cheese and bake in a moderate oven at 350° F. for 30
minutes. For easy handling, cool for 10 minutes before serving. Cut
in wedges and serve with additional sauce and cheese.

SERVES: 6 to 8

RIGATONI DONNAFUGATA

Donnafugata is the lovely town that houses the Salina estate in *The
Leopard*. If food and literature can be compared, Rigatoni Donnafugata, created at the Fico d'India restaurant in Palermo, is equal
to Tomasi di Lampedusa's masterpiece.

1 tablespoon olive oil
¼ cup chopped salt pork
5 scallions, chopped fine
¼ pound prosciutto (ham), chopped
¼ pound cooked veal, shredded†
3 tablespoons tomato paste
¼ cup sherry
½ cup liquid from peas
½ teaspoon salt

1 10-ounce package frozen artichoke hearts (or 1 No. 2 can), quartered
¼ pound mushrooms, sliced thin
1 cup canned early peas (reserve ½ cup liquid)
1 cup heavy cream (½ pint)
1 pound rigatoni (macaroni)
½ cup grated Parmesan cheese (for serving)

Heat oil in a large skillet; add salt pork and sauté for 5 minutes. Add scallions, prosciutto, and shredded veal and sauté for 5 minutes. Add tomato paste, sherry, liquid from peas, salt, and artichokes and simmer slowly for 10 minutes. Stir in sliced mushrooms and peas; simmer for 5 minutes. Stir in cream and heat through. Correct seasoning if necessary.

While sauce is simmering, cook rigatoni according to directions on package. Drain. Portion into bowls; top with sauce and a sprinkling of grated cheese. Serve immediately.

SERVES: 4 to 6

† Cook veal in chicken stock with 2 sprigs parsley, 1 carrot, 1 bay leaf, and 1 small onion. Cook until meat is tender—35 to 40 minutes.

SPAGHETTI ALLA NORMA

Spaghetti alla Norma is a culinary accolade to the famous composer Vincenzo Bellini, for his incredibly beautiful opera *Norma*. Bellini, a native son of Catania, Sicily, is remembered and honored with sumptuous gardens, monuments, and *Spaghetti alla Norma*.

2 tablespoons olive oil
2 cloves garlic, cut in half
1 medium onion, minced
1 No. 2½ can plum tomatoes
1 6-ounce can tomato paste
1 tablespoon dried basil
1 teaspoon salt
¼ teaspoon black pepper

1 large eggplant (about 2 pounds)
Salt
¼ cup olive oil
1 pound spaghetti
1 cup grated ricotta salata cheese

Heat 2 tablespoons olive oil in a large saucepan and sauté garlic and onions until golden. Add plum tomatoes, tomato paste, basil, salt, and pepper. Bring to a boil, cover, and simmer slowly for 1 hour.

Remove stem from eggplant and discard. Cut in ½-inch slices; salt liberally and drain in colander for 30 minutes. Rinse off salt; dry slices with absorbent paper. Fry in ¼ cup hot oil until crisp. (Add more oil if necessary.) Drain on absorbent paper; keep warm and set aside.

Cook spaghetti according to directions on package. Drain. Portion spaghetti in warm serving bowls; layer with eggplant slices, sauce, and grated cheese. Serve immediately.

SERVES: 6

Pasta Tiano
EGGPLANT, MEAT, AND MACARONI CASSEROLE

Named in dialect after the ceramic dish in which it is baked, this casserole is savory and satisfying and intrigues a crowd.

3 tablespoons olive oil
1½ pounds beef, cut in 2-inch squares
1 large onion, chopped
3 cloves garlic, cut in half
1 7-ounce can tomato paste
1 can water
1 No. 2½ can whole tomatoes

3 sprigs basil (or 1 tablespoon dried)
1½ teaspoons salt
½ teaspoon black pepper
1 eggplant (about 2 pounds)
¼ cup olive oil
1 pound elbow macaroni
1 cup grated Romano cheese

In a large skillet, heat 3 tablespoons oil and lightly brown beef squares. Transfer to a large saucepan. Brown onion and garlic in same skillet until onion is soft. Transfer to saucepan and stir in tomato paste, water, whole tomatoes, basil, salt, and pepper. Bring to a boil, cover, and simmer slowly until meat is very tender—about 1½ hours. Discard garlic and correct seasoning if necessary. Remove meat, cool, shred, and return to sauce.

Remove stem from eggplant and peel skin from top to bottom. Cut in thin slices, salt liberally, and let stand in colander for ½ hour. Rinse off salt, pat slices dry, and fry in ¼ cup oil until slices are crisp. (Eggplant absorbs a lot of oil; add as needed.) Drain on absorbent paper and set aside. Preheat oven to 400° F.

Cook elbow macaroni according to directions on package. Drain. Ladle ½ cup sauce in shallow baking dish (9×13 inches); layer some spaghetti, eggplant slices, meat sauce, and grated cheese. Continue layering until all of the ingredients are used, ending with spaghetti, sauce, and cheese on top. Bake for approximately 20 minutes. For easy cutting and handling, let casserole stand for 10 to 15 minutes before serving. Cut in large squares and serve with additional sauce and cheese.

Serves: 8 to 10

RICE SPECIALTIES

Strangely enough, rice was first introduced to European gastronomy by the Sicilians. In the ninth century, the Arabs brought rice plants from India and planted the first European rice fields in Sicily. Unfortunately, the methods of cultivation in those times were rudimentary and the terrain produced sparse crops. Hence, the price was high and rice was served only on the tables of the wealthy. In the centuries following, the situation became progressively worse and the planting of rice was completely abandoned.

However, as soon as any foreigner arrives in Sicily, his first encounter with the cuisine will be with rice croquettes, called *arancini*. They are sold everywhere, in fry stands on the beach, in cafes, and in bars serving hot food (*tavola calda*). This contradiction is easy to explain: the love of this particular dish remained even though the product was not readily available, and today most of the rice comes from the mainland of Italy.

When people from the provinces came to the city on daily business, rather than buying dinner and in order to save money, they would buy several *arancini* to appease their hunger and reserve their appetite for a large plate of pasta awaiting them at home.

Sicilian rice dishes are not many in number, but they are very different in composition and flavor.

Arancini

RICE CROQUETTES

2 cups uncooked long-grain rice	3 tablespoons softened butter
1 quart chicken stock or bouillon	4 egg yolks
1 teaspoon saffron	1 cup grated Parmesan cheese

Combine rice, chicken stock, and saffron in a large kettle. When chicken stock begins to boil, turn heat down low; stir rice once; cover kettle tightly and simmer until all liquid is absorbed—about 15 minutes. (Rice should be soft and slightly sticky so that it will hold together.) Set rice aside to cool. Add softened butter, egg yolks, and Parmesan cheese to cooled rice; stir well. Refrigerate.

FILLING:

¼ cup olive oil
¼ cup chopped onions
¼ teaspoon chopped celery
½ pound veal, beef, or pork
1 6-ounce can tomato paste

1 can water
½ teaspoon salt
¼ teaspoon black pepper
⅓ cup canned or frozen peas

In a saucepan, heat oil and sauté onions and celery until golden —about 5 minutes. Add meat and brown. Stir in tomato paste, water, salt, and pepper. Cover and simmer until meat is tender— about 1 hour. Add peas and cook for 5 minutes longer. Remove meat and cool. When cool enough to handle, shred and return to sauce. Set aside.

FRYING CROQUETTES:

4 egg whites, slightly beaten
2 cups bread crumbs
1 quart vegetable oil for deep-frying

While oil is heating in deep-fat fryer to 370° F. (1-inch bread cube will brown evenly in 1 minute), shape rice mixture into round balls (about ½ cup each). With index finger on chopstick, make a hole in rice ball; add 1 tablespoon filling and cover hole with more rice. Dip croquettes in egg whites and roll in bread crumbs until thoroughly coated. Drop carefully into heated oil, a few at a time, and fry until golden, turning once. Remove with slotted spoon and drain on absorbent paper. Serve warm or at room temperature.

SERVES: 6 to 8

VARIATION: Shape croquettes in triangular form and fill centers with *salsa besciamella* (white sauce) instead.

Insalata di Riso con Pomodori e Olive

COLD RICE RING

2 cups uncooked long-grain rice
4 cups water
2 teaspoons salt
2 tablespoons butter
¼ cup olive oil

2 fresh or canned tomatoes, skinned, seeded, chopped
½ cup black olives, pitted, sliced
1 tablespoon minced sweet basil
Parsley

Cover rice with the water; add salt and butter and bring to a boil. Stir with fork; lower heat and cover. Simmer until the water has been absorbed—25 to 30 minutes.

Stir in oil, tomatoes, olives, and basil and mix well. Pour into a 2-quart ring mold and press down lightly with fork. Let stand at room temperature until ready to serve. Unmold by reversing onto a serving plate. (Shake mold to loosen rice.) Garnish with parsley.

SERVES: 6 to 8

VARIATION: For tomatoes, substitute 1 6-ounce jar roasted red peppers, chopped. Garnish with lemon wedges and parsley.

Riso e Melanzane alla Palermitana

RICE AND EGGPLANTS PALERMO STYLE

2 large eggplants
Salt
2 tablespoons olive oil
2 cups uncooked long-grain rice
1 quart chicken stock (or bouillon)
¼ cup olive oil
2 large green peppers, cut in strips
1 medium onion, chopped

2 tablespoons olive oil
1 No. 2½ can tomato purée
1 tablespoon fresh minced basil (or 1 teaspoon dried)
1 teaspoon salt
¼ teaspoon black pepper
1 cup grated caciocavallo cheese (reserve ⅓ cup for serving)

Remove and discard stems from eggplants; cube. Sprinkle liberally with salt and let drain in colander for 30 minutes. Then, rinse with cold water; drain; dry with absorbent paper. Set aside.

Heat 2 tablespoons olive oil in a saucepan; pour in rice and toast lightly for 3 to 5 minutes. Pour in chicken stock and bring to a boil. Stir with fork; cover and simmer slowly for 20 minutes. (Rice should be slightly undercooked.) Drain and set aside. Preheat oven to 350° F.

In a large skillet, heat ¼ cup olive oil. Sauté peppers and eggplants until lightly browned—about 10 minutes. (Add more oil if necessary.) Set aside.

Sauté onions in 2 tablespoons hot oil until golden. Pour in tomato purée, basil, salt, and pepper. Stir and simmer for 15 minutes.

In a large oiled casserole, layer rice, eggplants and peppers, sauce, and grated cheese alternately until ingredients are used, ending with rice, sauce, and cheese on top. Bake for approximately 20 minutes. Serve with additional rice and cheese.

SERVES: 4 to 6

Riso ai Carciofini e Olive

RICE WITH ARTICHOKES AND OLIVES

2 tablespoons olive oil
1 medium onion, chopped
1 10-ounce package frozen
  artichoke hearts, thawed, cut
  in half
2 cups whole tomatoes, chopped
1 teaspoon marjoram

½ teaspoon salt
¼ teaspoon black pepper
2 anchovies, chopped
6 black olives, pitted, chopped
1 cup uncooked long-grain rice
½ cup grated Romano cheese

In a saucepan, heat oil and brown onion for 2 minutes. Add artichoke hearts and sauté for 5 minutes. Stir in tomatoes, marjoram, salt, and pepper and simmer for 15 minutes. Add anchovies and olives and simmer for 5 minutes.

Cook rice according to directions on package. Drain and place in serving bowl. Cover with sauce and sprinkle with grated cheese. Serve hot.

SERVES: 4

Risotto alla Pescatora

RICE FISHERMAN STYLE

2 tablespoons olive oil
1 medium onion, chopped
2 cloves garlic, cut in half
1 pound squid, cleaned, sliced
1 No. 2½ can tomato purée
½ cup clam juice
½ cup water

4 sprigs parsley
1 pound fresh shrimp, shelled
2 dozen fresh clams, scrubbed
Salt
2 cups uncooked long-grain rice
3 tablespoons minced parsley

In a saucepan, heat oil and brown onion, garlic, and squid for 5 minutes. Pour in tomato purée, clam juice, water, and sprigs of parsley. Stir and simmer until squid is tender—20 to 25 minutes. Add shrimp and clams and simmer until clams steam open—5 to 8 minutes. Salt to taste. Discard garlic and parsley.

Cook rice according to directions on package. Drain and place in serving bowl. Cover with fisherman's sauce and sprinkle with minced parsley. Serve hot.

SERVES: 4 to 6

Pasticcio di Riso
RICE, CHEESE, AND MEAT TORTE

SAUCE:
- 1 medium onion, chopped
- 2 cloves garlic, crushed
- 2 tablespoons olive oil
- 1 No. 2½ can tomato purée
- 1 tablespoon dried basil
- 4 sprigs fresh parsley
- 1 teaspoon salt
- ¼ teaspoon black pepper
- 3 cups water
- 1 2-pound frying chicken, whole (with giblets)
- 1 recipe meatballs (from Meatball Soup*)
- 2 tablespoons olive oil

RICE:
- 2½ cups uncooked long-grain rice
- 3½ cups chicken stock or bouillon
- 1 cup tomato sauce (from this recipe)
- 3 tablespoons butter
- 3 eggs, slightly beaten
- 1 cup Parmesan cheese

CHEESE FILLING:
- 1 pound ricotta cheese
- 8 ounces mozzarella cheese, chopped
- 2 tablespoons fresh mint (or 1 tablespoon dried)
- ½ teaspoon salt
- ¼ teaspoon black pepper

Sauté onion and garlic in hot oil for 3 to 5 minutes. Pour in tomato purée, basil, parsley, salt, pepper, and water; stir. Bring to a boil; add chicken and giblets; cover and boil gently. Prepare and shape meatballs. Brown in 2 tablespoons hot oil for 3 to 5 minutes. Add to sauce and simmer until chicken is tender—about 45 minutes.

Remove chicken and cool. When cool enough to handle, remove and discard skin and bones. Shred chicken and set aside. Discard garlic and parsley.

Cover rice with chicken stock, tomato sauce, and butter. Bring to a boil; stir with fork; lower heat; cover and simmer slowly for 20 to 25 minutes. Rice should be slightly undercooked. Drain; combine with eggs and cheese. Cool. Preheat oven to 350° F.

Combine ricotta, mozzarella, mint, salt, and pepper; mix well. Brush 10-inch spring-form pan with oil; spread with 1 layer of rice. Cover with a layer of cheese filling, shredded chicken, meatballs, and sauce. Continue layering until all the ingredients are used, ending with rice and sauce on top. Bake for 30 to 40 minutes. Let stand at room temperature 10 minutes before removing spring form. Slice cake style and serve with additional sauce and cheese.

SERVES: 6 to 8

THE SICILIAN
EGG BASKET

Eggs have always been popular in Sicilian cookery, but they are also indispensable for their nutritional and economic values. Sicilians have known for centuries that eggs carry in their golden hearts every food element the human body needs. Whenever anyone in my family caught cold, Mama ran to the kitchen to make an eggnog for *sustanza* (strength). Or she would mix two egg yolks with a little sugar and stir them into her morning coffee if she was not feeling up to par.

Although eggs are eaten often in Sicily, they are never eaten for breakfast. But they are frequently added to soups and are the main ingredient in some entrée dishes and desserts. Until recently, most religious holidays exempted meat from the diet, so eggs and fish were the usual protein alternatives.

Most Southern Italians prefer to have their eggs cooked in olive oil rather than butter. Fried eggs and omelets are the most popular ways of preparing eggs in all of Italy.

Omelets, or *froscia,* as they are called in Sicilian, are the theme of most light suppers and appear unfailingly on antipasto tables in restaurants. Substantial in composition, they stand two to six inches high and are cooked on both sides.

Frittatone alla Campagnola
HAM OMELET CAKE

This omelet is not a dessert, but it is as high and round as a layer cake. It's served hot as a light luncheon or supper dish. Often it is served at room temperature as an appetizer.

2 tablespoons olive oil	½ cup bread crumbs
1 small onion, minced	¼ cup grated Parmesan cheese
1 cup chopped prosciutto or ham	2 tablespoons minced parsley
8 large eggs	¼ teaspoon white pepper

Heat oil in an 8-inch skillet and sauté onions for 3 minutes. Add chopped ham and brown lightly. Beat eggs slightly and combine with bread crumbs, cheese, parsley, and pepper. Pour over ham and onions and cook over low heat. Pull eggs along sides with spatula, spilling egg liquid onto bottom of skillet. Continue until eggs do not run any longer.

Slip omelet onto a plate (same size as skillet). Turn over onto another plate and slip back in skillet to cook other side (about 2 minutes). Serve hot or at room temperature.

SERVES: 2 to 4

Froscia Ripiena al Forno
RICOTTA OMELET IN TOMATO SAUCE

CHEESE FILLING:

1 pound ricotta cheese, drained	8 large eggs
4 tablespoons grated Parmesan cheese	2 tablespoons water
	Salt and black pepper
¼ teaspoon white pepper	¼ cup butter
1 teaspoon nutmeg	1 cup Winter's Tomato Sauce*

Combine cheese filling ingredients and set aside.

Beat eggs with water and salt and pepper to taste. Melt butter in a large skillet; raise heat and pour in eggs. Stir, bringing in eggs from sides of pan to the center. Do this quickly and shake pan with other hand so that eggs will not stick to the bottom. Keep on lifting and stirring the eggs until all the liquid runs under and coagulates. Preheat oven to 325° F.

Spread ricotta filling over omelet. Roll, diploma style, and close open end with toothpicks; place in a buttered casserole and pour tomato sauce over it. Bake for 10 minutes.

SERVES: 2 to 4

Froscia di Asparagi
ASPARAGUS OMELET

1 10-ounce package frozen asparagus	2 tablespoons water
	Salt and black pepper
6 large eggs	2 tablespoons olive oil

Cook asparagus according to directions on package. Drain well and set aside.

Beat eggs with water and salt and pepper to taste. Heat oil in a skillet, add asparagus, and sauté for 3 minutes. Pour eggs over asparagus, keeping heat constant and low. Pull omelet along sides with a spatula, spilling egg liquid onto bottom of skillet. Continue until eggs do not run any longer.

Slip omelet onto a plate (same size as skillet). Turn over onto another plate and slip back in skillet to cook other side—about 1 or 2 minutes. Serve hot.

SERVES: 2 to 3

NOTE: If using fresh asparagus, cut or snap off lower tough white part of stems. Stand asparagus up and tie in bundle. Place, standing up, in bottom of double boiler. Add boiling water to come halfway up stems. Bring· to a boil; cover with inverted upper part of double boiler. Cook over high heat until asparagus is fork-tender—8 to 10 minutes. Drain and cut into small pieces. Continue as directed above.

Froscia di Spinaci e Formaggio

SPINACH-CHEESE OMELET

1 10-ounce package frozen spinach
6 large eggs
¼ cup grated Parmesan cheese
¼ teaspoon black pepper
Butter
3 tablespoons grated Parmesan cheese

Cook spinach according to directions on package. Drain well and set aside.

Beat eggs with ¼ cup grated Parmesan cheese and pepper. Melt 2 tablespoons butter, raise heat, and pour in egg mixture. Pull in sides of omelet with fork and stir in center; continue until all liquid runs to the bottom and coagulates.

Place spinach over omelet and dot with butter. Fold over edge one third (edge closest to you) and then other edge over one third, with both edges meeting at center. Turn omelet over onto heated platter and sprinkle with grated cheese.

SERVES: 2

Uova Strapazzate al Pomodoro

SCRAMBLED EGGS AND TOMATOES

2 tablespoons olive oil	½ teaspoon salt
1 medium onion, minced	¼ teaspoon black pepper
1½ cups canned or chopped fresh tomatoes	½ teaspoon sugar
1 teaspoon dried mint	8 large eggs, slightly beaten

In a large skillet, heat oil and sauté onion for 2 minutes. Stir in tomatoes, mint, salt, pepper, and sugar and simmer for 8 to 10 minutes. Stir in eggs; let eggs set for 2 minutes. Scramble and cook until eggs have coagulated. Serve over hot buttered toast.

SERVES: 4

Mozzarella Fritta con Uova

MOZZARELLA OMELET

per person:	2 large eggs	2 tablespoons butter
	Salt and black pepper	1 slice mozzarella cheese

Beat eggs slightly with salt and pepper to taste. Melt butter in a small skillet. Raise heat, pour in eggs, and scramble with fork until eggs are semicoagulated—about 30 seconds. Center cheese slice over eggs; fold one edge over one third and the other edge over one third with both edges meeting at center. Turn omelet over onto warm plate. Continue making individual omelets for as many people as are present.

Uova in Camicia al Pomodoro

POACHED EGGS IN TOMATO SAUCE

2 tablespoons olive oil	1 teaspoon salt
1 medium onion, minced	¼ teaspoon black pepper
1 No. 2½ can whole tomatoes, chopped	6 to 8 eggs
1 teaspoon dried basil (or 4 fresh leaves)	¼ cup grated Parmesan cheese

In a large skillet, heat oil and sauté onion for 3 minutes. Stir in tomatoes, basil, salt, and pepper. Simmer for 10 minutes. Break eggs, one at a time, into a saucer. Slip each egg from saucer onto tomato sauce; cover; lower heat and poach until whites coagulate —3 to 5 minutes. Sprinkle eggs with cheese and place under hot broiler for just long enough to toast cheese—about 1 minute.

SERVES: 4

Crocchette di Uova
EGG CROQUETTES

6 large eggs, slightly beaten
⅓ cup grated Romano cheese
1 cup bread crumbs
¼ cup minced parsley

1 small onion, minced
Salt and black pepper
Olive oil

Combine eggs, cheese, bread crumbs, parsley, onion, and salt and pepper to taste; mix well. Heat oil, ½ inch deep, in a large skillet. Drop croquettes by round tablespoons into hot oil; fry until golden brown, turning once. Serve as an hors d'oeuvre, as a first course, or in place of potatoes.

SERVES: 4 to 6

Froscia di Peperoni, Patate, e Uova
PEPPERS, POTATOES, AND EGGS

2 large green peppers, seeded, cut in strips
¼ cup olive oil
1 large onion, sliced

2 medium potatoes, boiled, sliced
10 large eggs, slightly beaten
2 tablespoons water
Salt and black pepper

In a large skillet, sauté peppers in hot oil for 5 minutes. Add onion and potatoes and sauté for 5 to 8 minutes longer. Beat eggs slightly with water and salt and pepper to taste. Pour over vegetables and cook over low heat. Pull eggs along sides with spatula, spilling egg liquid onto bottom of skillet. Continue until eggs do not run any longer.

Slip omelet onto a plate (same size as skillet). Turn over onto another plate and slip back in skillet to cook other side—about 2 minutes. Serve hot.

SERVES: 3 to 4

THE CHEESES
OF SICILY

Sicilians adore cheese, and there is hardly a dish made without it. They sprinkle it generously over pasta, soup, and pizza, combine it with meat or vegetables, sweeten it for desserts, and even cook it as a replacement for meat and fish.

Sicily, like other regions of Italy, makes and consumes many kinds of Italian cheeses. However, those listed on the chart below originated on the island of Sicily:

NAME	COLOR AND SHAPE	CHARACTERISTICS
Caciocavallo	Pale yellow. Often shaped like coupled gourds or round or oblong pears with a short neck topped with a ball.	Hard, tangy, and full-bodied. Its name, meaning "horse cheese," is derived from the custom of hanging it in pairs on horseback (over a stick). Made from cow's milk. Delicate and sweet when used in cookery —also eaten as a table cheese. When aged, it is sharp and tangy and excellent for grating.
Incanestrato	White, round, basket shape.	Sharp cheese, taking its name from the basket it's placed in for aging. Eaten with bread, fruit, and wine.
Manteca	Pale yellow, round ball.	Made in every province of Italy, but the Sicilian variety is particularly delicious. Enclosed in the hard outer wrapping of cheese is a yolk of butter, which remains surprisingly fresh. (The cheese resembles a hard-cooked egg in composition.) Other names for this cheese are *burrini, burri,* and *butirri.* An excellent table cheese.

NAME	COLOR AND SHAPE	CHARACTERISTICS
Pecorino Siciliano	White or straw-colored, compact, cake shape.	The rind bears the marks of the basket in which the cake was pressed. Made from whole sheep's milk. Typically sharp in taste; used as a table or grating cheese after ripening for at least four months.
Pepato	White, round basket shape.	The same as *incanestrato*, but with whole black peppercorns for accent in color and flavor. Delicious with crusty bread and dry red wine.
Ragusano	Straw-colored, finely textured. Rectangular shape with rounded angles; dark-brown rind.	Made from whole cow's milk. Made sweetish and delicate for the table quality; sharp and tasty for grating quality.
Ricotta salata (salted ricotta)	Snow-white, round.	Cured with salt and dried in the air, this cheese is semihard and semisalty. Used in salads, for snacks, and in cooking. When aged, used for grating.

FISH

From the Waters
of the Mediterranean

The warm, blue waters of the Mediterranean provide Sicily with an enormous selection of seafood: swordfish, tuna, squid, sardines, anchovies, whiting, mackerel, dogfish, shad roe, shrimp, lobster, mussels, cuttlefish, oysters, clams, and octopus. Whether or not Sicilians believe fish is brain food is questionable, but they have been smart enough to know that fish and shellfish are both healthy and economical. Hence, seafood is heavily consumed and is as popular as meat.

It is possible in many cities to go to the wharf and choose one's dinnertime delicacies from the day's catch. How ideal, yet cooking seafood requires a special ability. And Sicilians have the ability to cook seafood properly and also imaginatively in so many ways. Necessity, plus a pinch of knowhow, enabled them to learn the two secrets of seafood cookery: seafood cooks quickly, and therefore it needs a short cooking time; and seafoods are tender and juicy before they are cooked—there is no connective tissue that needs tenderizing, and cooking should simply bring out the flavor and coagulate the protein.

Squid, octopus, salted and dry cod, fresh tuna, fresh sardines, and anchovies are available when in season in Italian fish markets; and in New York and San Francisco, squid and octopus are always available in Chinese markets.

Calamari Ripieni al Sugo
STUFFED SQUID IN TOMATO SAUCE

2 pounds medium squid	¼ cup chopped parsley
1½ cups bread crumbs	¼ teaspoon black pepper
¼ cup grated Romano cheese	1 recipe Winter's Tomato Sauce*
1 small onion, minced	

Remove outer skins, insides, eye sacs, ink sacs, and backbones of squid, or purchase already cleaned. Rinse well with cold water; drain and dry with absorbent paper.

Combine bread crumbs, cheese, onion, parsley, and pepper. Fill squid cavities two thirds full with bread crumb mixture. Close open ends with toothpicks or sew with coarse thread. Cook in prepared tomato sauce until squid is tender—30 to 40 minutes. Discard toothpicks or thread. Serve with spaghetti.

SERVES: 4 to 6

Cozze alla Marinara
STEAMED MUSSELS SAILOR STYLE

2 tablespoons olive oil	½ cup dry white wine
1 medium onion, chopped	½ teaspoon salt
2 cloves garlic, crushed	⅓ cup chopped parsley
1 No. 2½ can whole tomatoes	4 dozen mussels

In a saucepan, heat olive oil and sauté onion and garlic for 3 minutes. Pour in tomatoes, wine, salt, and parsley. Cover and simmer for 10 minutes.

Scrub mussels under cold running water; remove and discard beards. Drain. Add mussels to sauce and steam until mussels open —5 to 10 minutes. Discard unopened mussels and garlic.

Serve in soup bowls with crusty bread or over spaghetti.

SERVES: 4

Crocchette di Sarde
SARDINE CROQUETTES

1 pound sardines or smelts	¼ cup minced parsley
2 eggs	Salt and freshly ground black
½ cup bread crumbs	pepper
¼ cup grated Parmesan cheese	2 tablespoons olive oil

Remove heads, tails, fins, backbones, and skin from sardines. Rinse with cold water and dry with absorbent paper. Grind fish to a pulp in blender or with meat grinder. Transfer to a bowl and combine with eggs, bread crumbs, cheese, parsley, and salt and pepper to taste. Shape into 1-inch balls and fry in hot oil until golden on all sides. Serve with a salad, home fries (potatoes), and Eggplant-Cheese Quartet.*

SERVES: 4

VARIATION: Brown sardine croquettes lightly in hot oil. Add to 2 cups Winter's Tomato Sauce* and simmer for 15 minutes. Serve with spaghetti.

Calamari Ripieni al Forno in Salsa di Acciughe
BAKED STUFFED SQUID IN ANCHOVY SAUCE

SQUID:
1½ cups bread crumbs
1 medium onion, minced
¼ cup minced parsley
¼ teaspoon salt
¼ teaspoon black pepper
2 pounds medium squid, cleaned

SAUCE:
½ cup butter
¼ cup olive oil
6 cloves garlic, sliced paper-thin
1 2-ounce can anchovies, chopped
Black pepper

Preheat oven to 350° F. Combine bread crumbs, onion, parsley, salt, and pepper. Fill squid cavities two thirds full with bread crumb mixture and close open ends with toothpicks or sew with coarse thread. Place in a shallow baking pan.

Over moderate heat, melt butter (do not brown). Add olive oil, garlic, anchovies, and pepper to taste; blend until anchovies are dissolved. Pour sauce over squid and bake, basting occasionally, until squid is tender—about 40 minutes. Serve with linguine and a mixed salad.

SERVES: 4 to 6

Sarde a Beccaficu
SARDINE BUTTERFLIES

2½ pounds fresh sardines or smelts
Flour
1½ cups bread crumbs
⅓ cup grated Parmesan cheese

2 tablespoons minced parsley
5 scallions, chopped
¼ teaspoon salt
¼ teaspoon black pepper
4 tablespoons olive oil

Remove heads, tails, fins, and backbones from sardines, or purchase drawn. Rinse well with cold water; drain and dry with absorbent paper. Split bellies open so that each sardine is in one flat piece (butterfly style). Dredge in flour on skin sides only.

Combine bread crumbs, cheese, parsley, scallions, salt, pepper, and 2 tablespoons of the olive oil. Spread bread crumb mixture over insides of half of the sardines. Cover with remaining sardines, sandwich style.

Heat 2 more tablespoons olive oil in a large skillet. Lift sardine butterflies with pancake turner and place in hot oil. Fry golden on one side for 3 to 5 minutes; turn carefully and fry on other side until golden. (Sardines will not fall apart in frying if carefully handled.)

Serve with Delicate-sharp Artichoke Pie* and Cucumber Salad.*

SERVES: 6 to 8

Piscistoccu a Missinisa

CODFISH MESSINA STYLE

2 pounds fresh codfish, cut in 3-inch pieces
Flour
5 tablespoons olive oil
1 medium onion, chopped
2 stalks celery, chopped
1 No. 2½ can whole tomatoes, chopped

2 large potatoes, thinly sliced
½ cup pitted and chopped Sicilian green olives
¼ cup capers
½ teaspoon salt
¼ teaspoon black pepper
1 pound zucchini, thinly sliced

Dredge fish in flour and brown lightly in 3 tablespoons of the hot olive oil. Set aside. In a large saucepan, brown onion and celery in remaining 2 tablespoons hot oil. Add tomatoes, potatoes, olives, capers, salt, and pepper. Stir and simmer for 20 minutes. Add zucchini and codfish and simmer for 15 minutes longer.

SERVES: 6

NOTE: This recipe is made authentically with dried or salted codfish, but for the sake of expediency, it is made here with fresh cod.

Insalata di Frutti di Mare
COLD SEAFOOD SALAD

SALAD:
1 medium onion, quartered
2 stalks celery, with tops
1 large lemon, quartered
3 quarts water
1 pound squid, drawn, cut in rings
1 pound octopus, cut in pieces
1 pound fresh shrimp

SALAD DRESSING:
½ cup olive oil
Juice of 2 lemons
¼ cup chopped parsley
½ teaspoon salt
Freshly ground black pepper

Put onion, celery, lemon, and water in a large kettle. Bring to a boil; plunge in squid and octopus and boil gently until seafood is tender—40 to 50 minutes. Drop in shrimp and boil until shrimp turns pink—about 5 minutes. Drain, cool, and shell shrimp. Discard onion, celery, and lemon and chill seafood in refrigerator.

Blend salad ingredients together and mix with seafood. Let stand at room temperature for 30 minutes before serving. Serve with crusty bread for an appetizer or luncheon dish.

SERVES: 4

Nasello al Forno in Salsa di Semi di Sesamo
BAKED WHITING IN SESAME SAUCE

4 pounds whiting
1 medium onion, sliced
6 sprigs parsley, chopped
2 lemons, cut in wedges
Parsley

SESAME SAUCE:
½ cup white dry wine
¼ cup olive oil
¼ cup sesame seeds
¼ teaspoon crushed red pepper
½ teaspoon salt
1 clove garlic, minced

Preheat oven to 350° F. Remove and discard bones, fins, and scales from fish. Do not remove heads or tails. Rinse well with cold water and drain. Place whole fish in a shallow oiled baking pan.

Blend sesame sauce ingredients together and pour over fish. Cover with sliced onion and parsley.

Bake in oven until fish flakes at touch of fork and white flesh is opaque—30 to 40 minutes. Baste fish during baking. Arrange fish on a heated platter. Discard onion and parsley. Pour sauce over fish. Garnish with lemon wedges and parsley.

SERVES: 4 to 6

Baccalà Con Olive in Umido

CODFISH STEW

Here is another popular dish that's inexpensive, savory, and so inviting. Its preparation is somewhat time-consuming, but it's well worth it.

FISH:
2½ pounds dried boned codfish
Water
Flour
Salt and black pepper
4 tablespoons olive oil
2 large onions, chopped
½ pound Italian black olives

SAUCE:
1 tablespoon olive oil
1 7-ounce can tomato paste
1 tablespoon orégano
½ teaspoon salt
¼ teaspoon black pepper
3 tomato-paste cans water

Cover codfish with cold water and soak for 2 days, changing water three or four times. Drain; cover fish with warm water and bring to a boil. Simmer until fish is tender but firm—about 1 hour. Drain well and dry with absorbent paper. Dredge fish in flour; salt and pepper lightly. Brown lightly in 2 tablespoons of the hot oil. Remove to a heated platter and keep warm.

In a saucepan, heat 1 tablespoon olive oil; pour in tomato paste, orégano, salt, and pepper. Stir and sauté for 3 minutes. Pour in water; stir and simmer for 10 minutes.

Heat remaining 2 tablespoons olive oil and brown onions and olives for 5 minutes. Pour in tomato sauce; add fish and cover. Simmer until all flavors are blended and fish is fork-tender—about 30 minutes.

SERVES: 6 to 8

Triglia al Forno

BAKED ROLLED MULLET FILLET
IN ORANGE SAUCE

1 large navel orange	¼ cup golden raisins (sultanas)
1½ pounds mullet fillets	¼ cup pignoli (pine nuts)
Flour	2 tablespoons minced parsley
¼ cup butter	¼ teaspoon salt
½ cup dry white wine	⅛ teaspoon white pepper
1 cup bread crumbs	¼ cup butter

Preheat oven to 350° F. Grate rind from orange; peel and section. Set aside. Dredge fillets in flour. Brown lightly in ¼ cup melted butter (about 3 to 5 minutes). Transfer to buttered casserole; pour wine over fillets.

Combine bread crumbs, raisins, pine nuts, parsley, salt, pepper, and orange rind. Spread over fish. Dot with ¼ cup butter and orange sections. Bake until fish is opaque and bread crumb topping is toasted—20 to 30 minutes.

SERVES: 4

NOTE: If mullet is unavailable, use pompano or sole.

Pesce Spada alla Marinara

SWORDFISH SAILOR STYLE

⅓ cup onions, chopped	4 fresh basil leaves (or 1
2 tablespoons olive oil	teaspoon dried)
1 No. 2½ can whole tomatoes	⅓ cup capers
1 teaspoon salt	2 pounds swordfish
¼ teaspoon black pepper	

In a large skillet, sauté onion in hot oil for 3 minutes. Stir in tomatoes, salt, pepper, basil, and capers. Cover and simmer for 15 minutes. Correct seasoning if necessary.

Place swordfish in sauce and poach until fish flakes at touch of fork and looks opaque—about 5 minutes on each side. Arrange swordfish on a heated platter and spoon sauce over it. Serve with Coachmen's Spaghetti* and Cousin Theresa's Cheese and Salami Salad.*

SERVES: 4

Braciole di Pesce Spada al Pomodoro

SWORDFISH ROLLS IN TOMATO SAUCE

1½ cups bread crumbs
¼ cup capers
¼ cup chopped parsley
¼ cup grated Parmesan cheese
6 black Italian olives, minced
¼ teaspoon black pepper

2 pounds swordfish
  or sole fillets
Olive oil
Flour
Quick Sauce Sailor Style*

Combine bread crumbs, capers, parsley, cheese, olives, and pepper. Spread over fillets; sprinkle with olive oil; roll and secure open ends with toothpicks or tie with thread. Dredge rolls in flour and brown lightly in 2 tablespoons hot oil.

Place fish rolls in prepared Quick Sauce and simmer until fish is opaque and fork-tender—10 to 15 minutes. Remove toothpicks or thread. Arrange on a heated platter; spoon sauce over fish and serve with Rice Croquettes* and a green salad.

SERVES: 6

Sarde Crude Marinate

MARINATED RAW-COOKED SARDINES

Eating raw fish may not appeal to most, but the sardines in this recipe are "cooked" in the marinade. The citric acid present in lemon juice chemically changes the composition of the fish so that it tastes cooked. Try it. It's simple to make, and so nourishing and refreshing as an appetizer or light luncheon dish.

1 pound fresh sardines or
  smelts
½ cup olive oil
Juice of 3 large lemons

5 or 6 sprigs fresh mint
  (or 1 tablespoon dried)
Salt and freshly ground black
  pepper

Fillet sardines, removing heads, tails, fins, backbones, and skin. Rinse with cold water; drain and dry with absorbent paper. Place fillets in a deep dish and cover with olive oil, lemon juice, mint, and salt and freshly ground pepper to taste. Marinate in refrigerator for 3 to 4 hours. Serve fillets over a bed of Boston lettuce and let stand at room temperature for 30 minutes before serving.

SERVES: 4

Sarde Fritte con Semi di Finocchio

FENNEL-FRIED SARDINES

2 pounds fresh sardines or smelts
Flour
Salt and freshly ground black pepper

¼ cup olive oil
2 cloves garlic, minced
1 teaspoon fennel seeds

Remove heads, tails, fins, and backbones from sardines, or purchase drawn. Rinse well with cold water; drain and dry with absorbent paper. Dredge in flour; salt and pepper lightly.

Heat oil in a large skillet and brown garlic and fennel seeds for 3 minutes. Place sardines in skillet and fry until golden—3 to 4 minutes on each side.

SERVES: 4

Zuppa di Pesce alla Siracusana

FISH STEW SYRACUSE STYLE

1 medium onion, minced
2 cloves garlic, crushed
2 stalks celery, minced
¼ cup olive oil
1 6-ounce can tomato paste
2 cans water
½ cup dry white wine
2 bay leaves
4 sprigs parsley

1 teaspoon salt
¼ teaspoon black pepper
2 pounds cuttlefish, sliced
1 dozen mussels, scrubbed, with beards removed
1 pound bass, cut in 3-inch pieces
1 pound codfish, cut in 3-inch pieces

Brown onion, garlic, and celery in hot oil. Stir in tomato paste, water, wine, bay leaves, parsley, salt, and pepper; simmer for 10 minutes. Add cuttlefish and simmer for 30 minutes. Add mussels, bass, and codfish and simmer until fish flakes at touch of fork and looks opaque—about 15 minutes. Discard unopened mussels, garlic, parsley, and bay leaves.

Serve in soup bowls with crusty rusks of bread for soaking up the sauce.

SERVES: 4 to 6

Pesce Spada alla Griglia con Rosmarino

ROSEMARIED BROILED SWORDFISH

4 swordfish steaks (about 2   Fresh or dried rosemary
    pounds)   1 recipe Lemon Sauce*
Olive oil

Preheat broiler for 10 minutes or prepare charcoal fire in advance so that coals are ash-colored when fish is placed on oiled grill. Brush swordfish steaks with oil; sprinkle with rosemary to taste. Broil or grill until fish flakes easily—8 to 10 minutes on each side. Arrange on a heated platter and pour sauce over fish. Serve hot.

SERVES: 4

Fritto Misto di Pesce

COMBINATION FISH FRY

Fritto Misto di Pesce is any combination of fish of one's preference, cut into bite-size pieces, dipped in batter and deep-fat fried. The batter and method of cooking compliments the delicate flavor and texture of the fish.

BATTER:
1 teaspoon active dry or
    compressed yeast
¼ cup warm clam juice or
    warm water
2 cups flour
1 teaspoon salt
¼ teaspoon white pepper
¼ cup olive oil
1½ cups beer
3 egg whites, beaten stiff

FISH:
About 1½ quarts vegetable oil
    for deep-frying
2 pounds fresh shrimp, shelled
2 pounds squid, sliced,
    parboiled for 20 minutes
2 pounds halibut, cut in small
    pieces
2 lemons, cut in wedges

Soften yeast in warm clam juice; set aside for 5 minutes. Sift flour, salt, and pepper together. Add yeast mixture, oil, and beer to sifted dry ingredients. Beat until smooth. Fold in egg whites and blend well. Let batter rest for 15 mintues.

Heat oil to 370°F. (1-inch bread cube browns evenly in 1 minute). Dip fish in batter; hold against side of bowl for 5 seconds and drop carefully into hot oil. Fry in deep fat until golden brown

—about 2 to 3 minutes on each side. Remove with slotted spoon and drain on absorbent paper. Keep cooked fish warm while frying the remainder. Serve hot with lemon wedges.

SERVES: 6 to 8

Nasello Fritto
GOLDEN FRIED WHITING

3 pounds whiting, drawn
Flour
2 egg whites, slightly beaten

Olive oil
Salt and freshly ground black pepper

Slice whiting into 2-inch pieces. Dredge in flour, dip in egg whites, and fry in 1 inch of oil until golden—about 3 minutes on each side. Salt and pepper to taste and serve immediately.

SERVES: 4 to 6

Tonno in Salsa Agrodolce
SWEET AND SOUR TUNA

2 pounds fresh tuna steaks
Flour
Olive oil
2 large onions, sliced
½ cup wine vinegar

1 tablespoon sugar
¼ cup fresh mint (or
  1 tablespoon dried)
Salt

Dredge fish in flour and brown lightly in ¼ cut hot oil for 2 minutes on each side. Set aside and keep warm. In the same skillet, heat 2 tablespoons olive oil and sauté onions for 3 minutes. Pour in vinegar; sprinkle sugar, mint, and salt to taste over onions and mix well.

Return fish to skillet; cover and simmer with onion sauce for 8 to 10 minutes. Let stand 5 to 10 minutes before serving.

SERVES: 4 to 6

Calamari Ripieni di Ricotta al Forno

RICOTTA-STUFFED SQUID CASSEROLE

SAUCE:

1 small onion, chopped
1 tablespoon olive oil
2 cups whole tomatoes, chopped
6 sprigs parsley
½ cup dry white wine
½ teaspoon salt
¼ teaspoon black pepper

FISH:

1 pound ricotta cheese
2 eggs
¼ cup grated Parmesan cheese
¼ cup minced parsley
2 pounds medium squid, cleaned
2 tablespoons olive oil

Preheat oven to 350° F. Brown onion in hot oil for 2 minutes. Stir in tomatoes, parsley, wine, salt, and pepper and simmer for 15 minutes.

Combine ricotta with eggs, cheese, and parsley. Fill squid cavities two thirds full with ricotta mixture. Secure open ends with toothpicks or sew with coarse thread. Brown squid in hot oil for about 5 minutes. Transfer to casserole and pour sauce over fish. Cover and bake at 350° F. until squid is tender—about 45 minutes.

SERVES: 4 to 6

Lumache in Umido

SNAIL STEW

4 dozen snails (in their shells)
1 medium onion, chopped
2 cloves garlic, cut in half
2 tablespoons olive oil

1 No. 2½ can whole tomatoes
4 sprigs parsley
1 teaspoon salt
¼ teaspoon black pepper

Wash snails with cold running water until thoroughly clean. Turn snails over to drain in colander. Brown onion and garlic in hot oil for 3 minutes. Add tomatoes, parsley, salt, pepper, and snails; stir; cover and simmer slowly for 15 to 20 minutes. Correct seasoning if necessary. Discard garlic and parsley. Serve with crusty bread or over spaghetti.

SERVES: 4

Insalata di Tonno
TUNA SALAD

2 7-ounce cans Italian-style tuna
1 medium onion, minced
4 stalks celery, chopped
Juice of 2 medium lemons
Salt and freshly ground black
  pepper

1 head romaine lettuce, cored,
  washed
2 tomatoes, cut in wedges

Place tuna with its oil in a medium bowl, and break fish up into small pieces. Add onion, celery, lemon juice, and salt and pepper to taste; mix well. Serve over crisp lettuce leaves and garnish with tomato wedges.

SERVES: 4

Nasello in Umido
STEWED WHITING

3 pounds whiting, drawn
3 to 4 tablespoons olive oil
1 large onion, chopped
2 large ripe tomatoes,
  skinned, sliced, seeded

⅓ cup chopped parsley
1 cup clam juice
Salt and freshly ground black
  pepper

Cut whiting into 3-inch pieces. Rinse with cold water, drain, and dry with absorbent paper. Brown lightly in hot oil and set aside.

In same skillet, sauté onion in hot oil for 3 minutes. Add tomato slices and parsley and sauté for 3 minutes. Return whiting to skillet; pour in clam juice and salt and pepper to taste. Cover and simmer slowly until fish flesh is opaque and fork-tender—10 to 15 minutes.

SERVES: 4 to 6

MEAT AND POULTRY

Thank Sicily
for the Meatball!

Cattle were scarce in Sicily and the only animals available for consumption were heifers and those slaughtered because they were too old. Unlike the French, Sicilians had no knowledge of butchery and would cut what beef they had in any manner. The result was tough, stringy, and not very edible. Nevertheless, Sicilians soon discovered a way to make meat tender: they ground it up. So be it—Sicilians invented the meatball! Meatballs of every size and variation were created: colossal, large, medium, small, flat, filled, fried, baked, stewed, and even tiny ones to be added to soup.

Although cattle were scarce, pigs were plentiful. Fed with what Mother Nature provided—acorns and figs of India (prickly pears)—they cost nothing to maintain. Pork became a mainstay of the cuisine and was prepared in innumerable ways, the most popular being sausage. Even though sausage is very simply made with ground pork, pieces of cheese, salt, fennel seeds, and a little red pepper, it can nevertheless be cooked in a variety of ways: fried, broiled, steamed, grilled, stewed, baked, and even dried. The different methods of cooking sausage affects this basic food and results in a variety of dishes.

Veal, chicken, and variety meats are popular favorites also. These meats are cheaper than beef and more plentiful; therefore, they appear frequently on home and restaurant tables. *Involtini di vitello ripieni* (stuffed veal rolls), grilled chicken basted with a tangy lemon sauce, boiled or baked *milza* (spleen) covered with sharp grated cheese, and liver smothered with onions, fresh mint, and vinegar are regular listings on Sicilian menus. Each is simply but imaginatively cooked and all are much in demand.

Scaloppine di Vitello alla Messinese
VEAL CUTLETS MESSINA STYLE

2 pounds veal cutlets, ⅛ inch
  thick
2 tablespoons olive oil
3 slices salt pork, chopped
1 medium onion, minced
2 stalks celery, minced
1 carrot, chopped
2 slices ham, chopped
2 cups whole canned tomatoes,
  chopped

2 yellow peppers, cut in strips
1 teaspoon sage
1 tablespoon minced parsley
Salt and freshly ground black
  pepper
8 slices white bread
¼ cup olive oil

Preheat oven to 350° F.

In a large skillet, brown cutlets lightly on each side in 2 table-spoons hot oil. Transfer to a shallow oiled baking pan. Set aside.

In same skillet, brown salt pork for 3 minutes. Add onion, celery, and carrots and sauté for 5 minutes. Stir in ham, tomatoes, peppers, sage, parsley, and salt and pepper to taste; cover and simmer for 5 minutes. Pour mixture over veal slices and bake for approximately 30 minutes.

Remove crusts from bread. Heat ¼ cup oil in a large skillet until it begins to sizzle. Add bread and fry until lightly browned on both sides. Serve veal cutlets with vegetable topping over *pain carré* (fried bread).

SERVES: 6 to 8

Costolette di Vitello alla Siciliana
BREADED VEAL CUTLETS SICILIAN STYLE

1½ cups cracker crumbs
½ cup grated Romano cheese
¼ cup minced parsley
½ teaspoon salt
¼ teaspoon freshly ground
  black pepper

1½ pounds veal cutlets,
  ⅛ inch thick
3 large eggs, slightly beaten
3 tablespoons olive oil
2 lemons, cut in wedges

Combine cracker crumbs with cheese, parsley, salt, and pepper. Dip veal cutlets first in eggs, then in cracker crumb mixture, coating well.

Heat oil in a large skillet; add cutlets and fry until golden— 2 to 3 minutes on each side. Add more oil if necessary.

Serve with lemon wedges, Broccoli Affogati,* and Arugula and Little Beefies Salad.*

SERVES: 4 to 6

NOTE: About 30 small crackers yield 1½ cups cracker crumbs.

Vitello Glacé alla Motta

SAVORY VEAL ROAST ALLA MOTTA

The Motta family of Catania, Sicily, takes pride in serving this roast with Cheesed Zucchini,* Eggplant Quails,* and Seasame-seed Rolls.*

1 3- to 4-pound veal pot roast (shoulder)	½ cup warm water
Olive oil	½ cup dry white wine
Butter	4 sprigs fresh basil
1 large onion, chopped	(or 1 tablespoon dried)
2 carrots, chopped	Salt and freshly ground black
4 stalks celery, chopped	pepper

In a large saucepan, brown veal in 1 tablespoon olive oil and 2 tablespoons butter. Remove and set aside.

In same saucepan, add 1 tablespoon olive oil and 3 tablespoons butter and sauté onion, carrots, and celery for 5 minutes. Pour in water and wine; return roast to pan. Season with basil and salt and pepper to taste. Cover and simmer slowly until veal is tender— about 2 hours—basting occasionally.

Remove veal from pan and cool for 20 minutes. Slice thinly and arrange on a heated platter. Crush vegetables with fork and simmer for 5 to 8 minutes. Pour down center of veal slices and serve.

SERVES: 6

Arrosto di Vitello al Latte

ROSEMARIED VEAL ROAST

3 to 4 pounds boneless veal roast (leg)
3 cloves garlic, cut in half
¼ cup butter
2 teaspoons rosemary

Salt
1 cup milk
Juice of 2 lemons
Parsley

Rub veal with garlic. In a large saucepan, brown veal lightly in heated butter. Sprinkle with rosemary and salt to taste. Pour milk in bottom of pan. Cover and simmer slowly until veal is tender —about 2 hours—basting occasionally.

Cool 20 minutes before slicing. Slice thinly and arrange on heated platter. Squeeze lemon juice over veal slices and garnish with parsley. Serve with Capunatina* and a tossed salad.

SERVES: 6 to 8

Polpettone di Manzo, Maiale, e Vitello

THREE-MEATS MEATLOAF

1 small eggplant (about ½ pound)
Salt
¼ cup olive oil
1 pound ground beef
½ pound ground pork
½ pound ground veal

1 cup bread crumbs
½ cup grated Parmesan cheese
1 medium onion, minced
2 cloves garlic, minced
3 eggs
2 teaspoons salt
1 teaspoon black pepper

Preheat oven to 350° F.

Remove stem and skin from eggplant and discard. Dice pulp; salt liberally and drain in colander for 15 minutes. Rinse salt off with cold water; drain and dry with absorbent paper. Sauté eggplant in hot oil until lightly browned—5 to 8 minutes. Set aside.

In a large bowl, combine all remaining ingredients. Mix in eggplant. Pour into an oiled standard loaf pan and bake for 1½ hours. Cool for 10 to 15 minutes before slicing. Serve with Rice-stuffed Tomatoes* and Peperonata.*

SERVES: 6 to 8

Costolette di Maiale con Salsa al Vermut

TIPSY PORK CHOPS

2 pounds loin pork chops, ¾
  inch thick
Flour
Salt and freshly ground black
  pepper
½ cup shallots, minced
2 cloves garlic, minced
2 tablespoons olive oil

½ cup vermouth
½ cup beef stock or bouillon
½ pound mushrooms, sliced
  lengthwise
6 sprigs parsley, minced
2 tablespoons olive oil
¼ cup butter

Dredge pork chops in flour; salt and pepper to taste. Brown shallots and garlic in 2 tablespoons hot oil for 3 minutes. Add pork chops and fry until well browned on both sides. Add vermouth and beef stock; cover and simmer slowly for 15 to 20 minutes, turning once or twice.

In another skillet, sauté mushrooms and parsley in 2 tablespoons olive oil and the butter until well browned—5 to 8 minutes. Salt and pepper to taste. Combine with chops and simmer together for 3 minutes. Arrange chops in a line down center of heated serving platter; pour sauce, mushrooms, and parsley over them and serve immediately.

SERVES: 4 to 6

Involtini di Manzo con Vino Rosso

BEEF BIRDS IN WINE SAUCE

1 pound beef tenderloin, thinly
  sliced
Flour
½ cup bread crumbs
⅓ cup grated Parmesan cheese
¼ cup chopped shallots or
  scallions
2 cloves garlic, minced

¼ cup chopped celery
¼ cup chopped parsley
¼ teaspoon salt
¼ teaspoon black pepper
Olive oil
2 cups beef stock
1 cup dry red wine
1 bay leaf

Pound meat slices thin with meat mallet or flat side of cleaver. Dredge in flour and set aside.

Combine bread crumbs, cheese, shallots, garlic, celery, parsley, salt, and pepper. Spread 1 rounded tablespoon of bread crumb mixture over each tenderloin slice. Sprinkle with olive oil to moisten bread crumbs. Roll, jelly-roll fashion, and tie with thread or fasten ends with toothpicks.

Brown beef birds in 2 tablespoons hot oil. Pour in beef stock, wine, and bay leaf. Bring to a boil; lower heat; cover and simmer until meat is tender—about 30 minutes. If sauce is too thin, raise heat up high and cook for 5 minutes to reduce liquid. Serve beef birds and sauce over buttered noodles with Stuffed Mushroom Capfuls* and a mixed salad.

SERVES: 4

Bistecca Impanata alla Griglia
BREADED AND BROILED SICILIAN STEAK

MARINADE:
- 1 cup olive oil
- ½ cup wine vinegar
- 6 basil leaves (or 1 tablespoon dried)
- 2 cloves garlic, minced
- 1 teaspoon salt
- ½ teaspoon freshly ground black pepper
- 4 boned sirloin steaks or shell steaks, 1 inch thick

BREADING:
- 1½ cups bread crumbs
- ½ cup grated Parmesan cheese
- 1 tablespoon orégano

Blend oil, vinegar, basil, garlic, salt, and pepper together. Place steaks in marinade and marinate for 2 hours or overnight, turning occasionally.

Preheat broiler. Combine breading ingredients. Dip steaks in breading, coating both sides well. Place on an oiled broiler pan 3 inches from flame. Broil to desired rareness and serve immediately on warm plates.

SERVES: 4

Bistecca alla Palermitana

SIRLOIN STEAK PALERMO STYLE

2 tablespoons bread crumbs
2 tablespoons grated Parmesan
cheese
6 anchovies, chopped
1 large tomato, skinned, chopped
¼ cup capers

6 boneless sirloin steaks, ½ inch
thick
2 tablespoons olive oil
Salt and freshly ground black
pepper

Combine bread crumbs, cheese, anchovies, tomato, and capers; set aside.

Pan-fry steaks in hot oil to desired rareness. Arrange on an ovenproof platter and sprinkle with bread crumb mixture. Salt and pepper to taste. Place under a hot broiler for 2 to 3 minutes to crisp topping. Serve immediately.

SERVES: 6

Farsumagru in Salsa di Pomodoro

ROLLED BEEF IN TOMATO SAUCE

Farsumagru is an extraordinary Sicilian word meaning "false-lean." It describes this dish perfectly—lean meat lined with a rich filling and cooked in a rich tomato sauce—*ottimo* (excellent) for a dinner party!

1 1½-pound round steak
1½ pounds ground beef
1 small onion, chopped
¼ cup bread crumbs
¼ cup grated Romano cheese
1 egg
½ teaspoon salt
¼ teaspoon black pepper
2 hard-cooked eggs, cut in half
⅓ cup olive oil

TOMATO SAUCE:
1 medium onion, chopped
2 cloves garlic, cut in half
3 6-ounce cans tomato paste
3 cups water
1 tablespoon basil
1½ teaspoons salt
½ teaspoon black pepper

Pound steak thin with meat mallet or flat side of cleaver. Combine ground beef, onion, bread crumbs, cheese, egg, salt, and pepper. Spread evenly over round steak. Place hard-cooked eggs, yolk side down, along lower end of meat. Roll, jelly-roll fashion, and tie securely with thread or fasten with meat bracelets.

In a large skillet, brown meat roll well in hot oil. Remove and set aside. Brown onions and garlic in same oil for 3 minutes. Stir in tomato paste, water, basil, salt, and pepper. Bring sauce to a boil; lower heat; add meat roll and simmer slowly until meat is tender— about 2 hours. Discard garlic.

Remove meat roll from sauce and cool for 1 hour before slicing. Discard thread or remove bracelets. Cut in ½-inch slices and arrange in rows on a warm serving platter. Spoon hot sauce down middle of slices and serve. Farfalle (butterflies or bows), Romaine and Fennel Salad,* and crusty bread complete the meal. (Remaining sauce is sufficient for 1 pound of farfalle.)

SERVES: 6 to 8

VARIATION: *Alternate Filling*—Combine 1 cup bread crumbs, ¼ cup grated Parmesan cheese, ¼ cup minced parsley, 2 tablespoons seedless raisins, 2 tablespoons pine nuts, ⅓ cup chopped onions, 2 cloves garlic (minced), ½ teaspoon salt, ¼ teaspoon black pepper, and ¼ cup minced salt pork. Spread mixture evenly over meat and roll, jelly-roll fashion. Tie securely and continue as directed above.

Fegato di Maiale alla Griglia
BROILED PORK LIVERS

8 bay leaves	8 slices bacon
8 medium pork livers	Salt and black pepper
(about 1½ pounds)	

Place 1 bay leaf over each pork liver. Wrap with bacon slices and secure with toothpicks. Salt and pepper to taste. Broil in a preheated broiler, 4 inches from flame, for 6 to 8 minutes on each side. Discard toothpicks and serve hot.

SERVES: 4

Bistecca alla Pizzaiola

BEEFSTEAKS IN SPICY TOMATO SAUCE

1 medium onion, chopped
2 cloves garlic, minced
2 tablespoons olive oil
4 chuck fillet steaks, 1 inch thick
1 No. 2½ can whole tomatoes
1 teaspoon salt
¼ teaspoon black pepper
¼ teaspoon crushed red pepper
1 tablespoon orégano

BAKED POLENTA:
2 cups water
1 cup polenta
½ teaspoon salt
2 tablespons butter

Preheat oven to 350° F.

In a large skillet, sauté onion and garlic in hot oil for 3 minutes. Add steaks and brown for 2 minutes on each side. Pour in tomatoes and crush lightly with fork. Stir in salt, black and red pepper, and orégano. Bring to a boil; lower heat; cover skillet and simmer slowly until meat is tender—1½ to 2 hours.

Bring water to a boil; pour in polenta, stirring rapidly. Cook until polenta has thickened like cereal. Stir in salt and butter. Pour in a greased loaf pan and bake for 15 to 20 minutes. (Insert toothpick in center of loaf; if it comes out clean, polenta is done.) Cool; cut in ½-inch slices.

Serve steaks with sauce and slices of baked polenta.

SERVES: 4

Fegato di Vitello con la Salvia

SAGED CALF'S LIVER

Powdered sage
1½ pounds calf's or steer liver,
    thinly sliced
Salt and freshly ground black
    pepper

¼ cup butter
¼ pound caciocavallo cheese,
    coarsely grated

Rub sage liberally on liver slices and season with salt and freshly ground pepper to taste. Sauté in butter for 1 to 2 minutes on each side. (Do not cook longer or liver will toughen.) Arrange on a heated serving platter and sprinkle with grated cheese. Serve immediately.

Involtini di Vitello in Salsa di Pomodoro
VEAL ROLLS IN TOMATO SAUCE

1 recipe Winter's Tomato Sauce*
1½ pounds veal cutlets (about 8)
Mozzarella cheese
Minced fresh or dried sweet basil
¼ cup butter

Prepare Winter's Tomato Sauce as directed.

Pound veal slices thin with meat mallet. Place 1 slice mozzarella cheese over each cutlet and sprinkle with basil to taste. Roll and secure ends with toothpicks or skewers. Brown in melted butter on all sides for 3 to 5 minutes. Place in tomato sauce and simmer for 30 minutes. Remove toothpicks or skewers before serving.

SERVES: 4 to 6

Bollito di Manzo
BOILED BEEF DINNER

This simple hot and cold dinner is cooked in one pot. The soup is served hot, the meat and potato salad entrée cold. Savory garlic bread and chilled rosé wine add the finishing touches to this easy and substantial meal.

1 2-pound piece beef (top round)
1 onion, quartered
2 carrots, chopped
2 stalks celery, chopped
4 sprigs parsley
1 teaspoon salt
3 peppercorns, bruised
Water
1 whole tomato, skinned, chopped
2 medium potatoes
1 cup uncooked egg noodles

SALAD DRESSING:
¼ cup olive or salad oil
¼ cup wine vinegar
⅓ cup chopped celery
¼ cup chopped parsley
1 large onion, sliced, separated into rings

In a large kettle, place beef, onion, carrots, celery, parsley, salt, peppercorns, and tomato. Cover with water to 4 inches above meat-and-vegetable mixture. Bring to a boil; skim; cover and boil gently for 1 hour. Then add potatoes and boil gently until potatoes and meat are tender—about 30 minutes longer. Remove potatoes and meat and set aside to cool. Discard onion and parsley.

Add noodles to soup and boil gently until noodles are soft— about 5 minutes. When meat is cool enough to handle, shred apart. Slice potatoes thinly. Blend salad ingredients together; pour over meat and potatoes and toss until ingredients are mixed. Serve over a bed of crisp iceberg lettuce.

SERVES: 4 to 6

Scaloppine di Maiale al Marsala
PORK CUTLETS IN MARSALA WINE

1½ pounds pork cutlets, ⅛ inch thick
Flour
Salt and black pepper

⅓ cup chopped salt pork
2 cloves garlic, cut in half
1 cup dry Marsala wine
8 slices prosciutto (Italian ham)

Pound cutlets thin with meat mallet. Dredge in flour mixed with salt and pepper to taste. Set aside.

Fry salt pork in skillet with garlic for 5 minutes. Add cutlets and fry for 5 minutes on each side. Discard excess grease. Stir in wine and simmer for 10 minutes. Cover each cutlet with 1 slice ham; cover and simmer 5 minutes longer. Discard garlic.

Arrange meat on a warm serving platter and pour sauce down center of meat. Serve immediately.

SERVES: 4 to 6

Bistecca Piccante
PIQUANT SHELL STEAK

2 cloves garlic, minced
1 tablespoon olive oil
4 shell steaks, 1 inch thick
1 tablespoon minced sweet basil

Salt and freshly ground black pepper
1 tablespoon wine vinegar

In a skillet, brown garlic in oil for 3 minutes. Add steaks, basil, and salt and pepper to taste. Cover and cook for 5 minutes. Sprinkle with vinegar and cook over very low heat for 5 minutes longer. Serve with zucchini and Snow Topped Tomato Salad.*

SERVES: 4

Fettine di Vitello alla Garibaldi
VEAL SCALLOPS ALLA GARIBALDI

This dedication is in tribute to Giuseppe Garibaldi, a great soldier and patriot, who led one thousand Red Shirt troops in the liberation of Sicily in 1860.

2 pounds veal scallops, thinly sliced
Flour
Salt and freshly ground black pepper
¼ cup olive oil

6 shallots, minced
1 No. 2 can artichoke hearts, drained, cut in half
½ cup dry white wine
1 No. 2 can early peas

Dredge veal in flour mixed with salt and pepper to taste. Brown lightly in hot oil for 1 minute on each side. Set aside. In same skillet, sauté shallots and artichokes for 5 minutes. Add wine, peas, and their liquid and simmer for 5 minutes. Push vegetables aside; return veal to skillet and simmer for 3 minutes. Arrange veal slices on a heated platter with peas and sauce over them. Place artichokes around meat.

SERVES: 4 to 6

Fettine di Vitello al Forno
VEAL CUTLET PIZZA

2 pounds veal cutlets
Olive oil
½ can anchovies, chopped
¼ cup grated Romano cheese

1½ cups fresh or canned tomatoes, chopped
1 tablespoon orégano
Freshly ground black pepper

Preheat oven to 400° F.

Pound cutlets flat with meat mallet or flat side of cleaver. Pour ¼ cup olive oil in shallow baking pan; arrange cutlets in a single layer in pan. Sprinkle with anchovies, cheese, tomatoes, orégano, pepper to taste, and oil. Bake for 10 minutes. Serve with crusty bread and Grandma Greco's Stuffed Artichokes.*

SERVES: 6 to 8

Lenticchie con Salsicce al Forno

BAKED SAUSAGES OVER PEBBLES

Pebbles, or lentils, are an excellent base for juicy, spicy, cheesy sausages. Their combination lends an international flavor to a buffet party with a minimum of effort and expense, as befits the times.

1 recipe Lentil Soup*
1½ cups fresh or canned
    tomatoes, chopped

2 cloves garlic, minced
1½ pounds Italian sausage
    (or 12 links Sausage Tiranno*)

Cook Lentil Soup as directed, but use only 6 cups warm water instead of 2 quarts. Bring to a boil, cover, and simmer for 40 minutes. Preheat oven to 400° F.

Remove lentils from heat; stir in tomatoes and garlic. Transfer to a large casserole; cover with sausages and bake until sausages are cooked, browned, and bubbling—about 20 minutes.

SERVES: 6 to 8

Bonata

STUFFED SPINACH AND BEEF LOAF

2 packages active dry yeast
¼ cup lukewarm water
5 cups sifted flour
1½ teaspoons salt
1½ cups water
Oil or melted butter

FILLING:
2 10-ounce packages frozen
    chopped spinach
1 large onion, chopped
2 tablespoons olive oil
1 pound ground beef
Salt and freshly ground black
    pepper
Garlic salt

Dissolve yeast in the water; let stand in a warm place for 5 minutes. Measure sifted flour and salt in a large bowl; make a well in center and pour in yeast mixture and water. Mix until dough cleans sides of bowl and forms a ball. (Add extra water if necessary.) Turn onto a lightly floured board and knead 8 to 10 minutes. Place dough into a greased bowl and brush top with oil or melted butter. Cover with cloth and let rise in a warm place (85° F.) free from drafts until double in bulk—about 1 hour.

While dough is rising, cook spinach according to directions on package. Drain and press out water. In a large skillet, sauté onions in hot oil for 3 minutes. Stir in ground beef and sauté until meat is lightly browned—5 to 8 minutes. Season with salt, pepper, and garlic salt to taste. Add drained spinach and mix well. Set aside. Preheat oven to 400° F.

After dough has doubled in bulk, punch it down and turn onto floured board. Knead it for 5 minutes. Roll dough into a 12×18× ¼-inch rectangle. Brush with oil and spread meat and spinach mixture evenly over rectangle. Roll, jelly-roll fashion, and place (open end at bottom) on an oiled baking pan. Bake until dough is browned and cooked through—30 to 40 minutes. Cool and cut into 1-inch slices. Serve with Lucia's String Bean Salad* and Mushroom Capfuls.*

SERVES: 6 to 8

VARIATION: *Convenience Dough*—Mix 4 cups Bisquick with ¾ cup milk. Turn onto a well-floured board, dust with flour, and roll into a 12×18×½-inch rectangle. Continue as directed above.

Arrosto di Agnello alla Mama Lucia
MAMA LUCIA'S LAMB ROAST

1 3- to 4-pound leg of lamb	2 tablespoons instant minced
3 cloves garlic, cut in slivers	onion
¼ cup chopped fresh mint (or	Sea salt and freshly ground
1½ tablespoons dried)	black pepper
¼ cup chopped parsley	

Preheat oven to 350° F.

With a sharp knife or larding needle, make holes or slits over entire roast. Fill holes with garlic, mint, and parsley at random. Sprinkle with instant minced onion, and freshly ground sea salt and pepper to taste.

Place roast in an oiled baking pan, fat side up. Roast until lamb is tender and medium rare—1½ to 2 hours.

SERVES: 6 to 8

NOTE: To get the full flavor and succulence of lamb, it should be served medium rare with its natural juices running from the delicate pink meat. Americans are unaccustomed to eating lamb this way, but after trying this recipe I'm sure they will never eat it any other way.

Involtini di Maiale

PORK ROLL-UPS

Involtini is a term for cutlets (pork, veal, beef, or chicken) spread with a bread crumb mixture, rolled, braised or grilled in sauce, or broiled.

1½ pounds pork cutlets
1 cup bread crumbs
⅓ cup chopped parsley
1 tablespoon rosemary
Salt and freshly ground black
  pepper

Garlic salt
Olive oil
1 bunch scallions, sliced
  lengthwise

Preheat broiler for 10 minutes.

Flatten cutlets with meat mallet or flat side of cleaver. Combine bread crumbs, parsley, rosemary, and salt, pepper, and garlic salt to taste. Moisten bread crumb mixture with 2 tablespoons olive oil. Spread 1 to 2 tablespoons of bread crumb mixture over each cutlet. Place 2 to 3 scallion slices at lower end of cutlets; roll, jelly-roll fashion, and fasten open ends with toothpicks or skewers.

Arrange pork roll-ups in a broiler pan with 2 tablespoons olive oil. Place pan 3 inches below flame and broil until meat is well done—4 to 6 minutes on each side. If grilling over a charcoal fire, place meat directly over fire and grill until meat is well browned and sizzling.

SERVES: 6

VARIATION: Substitute beef, chicken, or veal cutlets and prepare in the same manner. If desired, use orégano, tarragon, or basil instead of rosemary.

Arrosto di Manzo
RED WINE SIRLOIN ROAST

1 3- to 4-pound boneless beef
   sirloin roast
2 cloves garlic, cut in half
2 tablespoons olive oil
Orégano
Monosodium glutamate (MSG)
Sea salt and freshly ground
   black pepper

2 medium onions, chopped
1 bunch Car-ettes,† peeled
8 small potatoes
2 bay leaves
1 cup dry red wine

Preheat oven to 300° F.

Rub entire roast with garlic; reserve garlic. Brown roast well in hot oil. Sprinkle with orégano, MSG, and sea salt and pepper to taste. Place in baking pan with onions, Car-ettes, potatoes, bay leaves, wine, and reserved garlic. Cover and bake at 300° F. for 1½ hours, basting occasionally.

Remove cover, baste roast and vegetables with drippings, and continue roasting for 30 minutes longer. Remove and cool roast 20 minutes before slicing. Arrange slices on a heated platter with Car-ettes and potatoes. Discard garlic and bay leaves, heat drippings and onions, and pour over sirloin slices. Serve immediately with a crisp salad and hot rolls.

SERVES: 6 to 8

† Car-ettes are young, small carrots; if unavailable, use regular carrots, cut in half.

Spiedini alla Siciliana
BEEF ROLL-UPS

1½ cups bread crumbs
1½ cups grated Parmesan
cheese
Salt and freshly ground black
pepper
1 pound beef (eye round),
cut in ⅛-inch slices
Olive oil
Bay leaves

FILLING:
1 large onion, chopped
2 tablespoons olive oil
1 cup canned whole tomatoes,
chopped
⅓ cup minced parsley
Remaining bread crumb mixture

Preheat broiler for 10 minutes.

Combine bread crumbs, cheese, and salt and pepper to taste. Set aside. Pound meat slices thin with meat mallet or flat side of cleaver. Brush with oil on both sides, dredge in bread crumb mixture, and set aside.

Sauté onion in 2 tablespoons olive oil until tender—about 5 minutes. Add tomatoes and parsley and sauté for 3 minutes. Remove from flame and stir in remaining bread crumb mixture.

Spread 1 to 2 tablespoons filling over each beef slice. Roll, jelly-roll fashion, and place 1 bay leaf over every open end. Secure ends and bay leaves with skewers. Arrange in a shallow broiler pan to which 2 tablespoons oil has been added. Broil 3 inches from flame until meat is cooked—5 to 8 minutes on each side.

SERVES: 4

Costolette di Vitello alla Griglia
HERBED VEAL CHOPS

6 loin veal chops, 1 inch thick
Olive oil
Rosemary
Sea salt

Freshly ground black pepper
2 lemons, cut in wedges
Fresh rosemary or parsley

Preheat broiler for 10 minutes.

Brush veal chops with oil; sprinkle with rosemary and freshly ground sea salt and pepper to taste. Brush broiler pan with oil; arrange chops on pan 4 inches from flame. Broil to desired doneness—about 10 minutes on each side. Arrange on a warm platter with lemon wedges and garnish with fresh rosemary or parsley sprigs.

SERVES: 6

Costolette di Maiale alla Griglia
ORÉGANOED PORK CHOPS

6 loin pork chops, ¾ inch thick   Onion salt
Orégano   Freshly ground black pepper
Garlic salt   Vegetable oil

Preheat broiler for 10 minutes.

Sprinkle pork chops with orégano, garlic salt, onion salt, and pepper to taste. Brush broiler pan with oil; arrange chops on broiler pan 4 inches from flame. Broil until done—10 to 15 minutes on each side. Serve hot.

SERVES: 4 to 6

Scaloppine di Vitello al Marsala
VEAL CUTLETS WITH MARSALA WINE

1½ pounds veal cutlets, thinly   ¼ pound prosciutto (Italian
  sliced   ham), chopped
Flour   ⅓ cup olive oil
Salt and freshly ground black   ½ cup dry Marsala wine
  pepper
½ pound mushrooms, sliced
  lengthwise

Pound cutlets thin with meat mallet or flat side of cleaver. Dredge in flour and sprinkle with salt and pepper to taste. Set aside.

Sauté mushrooms and ham in 3 tablespoons of the olive oil until tender—about 5 minutes. Set aside.

Pour remaining oil in skillet and fry cutlets lightly for 1 to 2 minutes on each side. Pour in wine, mushrooms, and ham and cook over high heat for 3 minutes.

Arrange meat on warm serving platter. Pour mushrooms, ham, and wine sauce over meat. Serve immediately.

SERVES: 6

Fegato di Vitello in Salsa Agrodolce
TANGY CALF'S LIVER

1 pound calf's liver, thinly sliced
Olive oil
2 large onions, sliced
⅓ cup wine vinegar

Salt and freshly ground black
pepper
5 fresh basil leaves (or 1
tablespoon dried)

Sauté liver slices in 2 tablespoons hot oil until lightly browned
—1 to 2 minutes on each side. Remove and set aside.

In same skillet, add 3 tablespoons olive oil; when hot, sauté
onions until soft and transparent. Pour in vinegar and sprinkle with
salt and pepper to taste; add basil. Simmer for 5 minutes.

Push onions to one side; return liver to skillet and cover with
onions. Cook for 2 to 3 minutes. Serve immediately.

SERVES: 4

Costolette di Vitello in Casseruola
VEAL CHOP CASSEROLE

Veal chop casserole is an example of real home cooking. One would
hardly think it's Sicilian; but it is! Try it—it's *gustoso* (savory)!

1½ cups bread crumbs
½ cup grated Romano cheese
Salt
Freshly ground black pepper
6 rib veal chops, 1 inch thick
4 stalks celery (inner stalks with
  leaves), cut in 2-inch pieces

1 large potato, thickly sliced
1 large onion, thinly sliced
3 tablespoons olive oil
¼ cup warm water

Preheat oven to 400° F.

Combine bread crumbs with cheese, and salt and pepper to taste.
Coat veal chops, celery, potato, and onion with bread crumb
mixture. Heat oil in a shallow casserole. When hot, add meat and
vegetables and brown for 5 minutes on each side. Pour in warm
water; cover baking pan and bake until meat is tender—45 minutes
to 1 hour.

SERVES: 6

Stufato di Agnello Primavera
SPRING-LAMB STEW

2 medium zucchini (about 1½ pounds), sliced
⅓ cup olive oil
1 medium onion, chopped
2 pounds stewing lamb

2 cups water
1 teaspoon salt
¼ teaspoon black pepper
2 sprigs fresh mint (or 1 tablespoon dried)

In a large skillet, sauté zucchini in hot oil until lightly browned—3 to 5 minutes. Remove and set aside. In same skillet, sauté onion until opaque—about 3 minutes. Add lamb and brown lightly on all sides. Transfer onion and lamb to a large kettle. Pour in water, salt, pepper, and mint; bring to a boil. Cover; lower heat and simmer slowly until meat is tender—about 1 hour. Add zucchini and simmer 10 to 15 minutes longer. Serve with boiled parsleyed potatoes and crusty whole wheat bread.

SERVES: 6 to 8

SAUSAGE TIRANNO

Johnnie Tiranno of Buffalo, New York, is one of the best butchers in the world. This is his Sicilian sausage recipe, and it's first rate.

3½ pounds pork loin
1½ pounds beef
5 teaspoons salt
1½ cups minced Italian parsley (flat leaf)
3 tablespoons fennel seed
¾ cup coarsely grated Romano cheese

¾ cup coarsely grated Parmesan cheese
1 teaspoon freshly ground black pepper
1 cup water
½ pound sausage casings†

Grind pork with beef, using medium blade on grinder, or have butcher do this for you. Combine ground meat with salt, parsley, fennel seed, Romano cheese, Parmesan cheese, and pepper. Mix until all ingredients are well blended. Pour in water slowly (mixture may take a little less or a little more) and mix until all ingredients are bound together. Correct seasoning if necessary.

† Casings may be ordered through your butcher or purchased at pork stores.

Place sausage casings in a bowl of cold water. Open one end of casing and run cold water through entire casing. Cut 2 feet of casing; tie one end; thread open end onto funnel tube (either hand or machine funnel). Push sausage mixture through funnel and tube into casing. Tie open end and twist filled casing into sausage links. Repeat process until mixture is finished. Fry, grill, broil, or bake as suggested in recipe, or freeze sausage for future use.

YIELD: Approximately 40 links.

VARIATION: *Sausage Patties*—Prepare sausage mixture as directed, but do not use casings. Instead, shape mixture into 2½-inch rounds and fry or grill until brown and crispy in texture.

This sausage mixture makes excellent stuffing for poultry, meal rolls (braciole), and vegetables (i.e., peppers, zucchini, escarole).

Salsicce: Fritte, alla Griglia, ed al Forno

SAUSAGE: FRIED, GRILLED, AND BAKED

The rich cheesy flavor of Sicilian sausages needs no assistance or compliments from sauces or vegetables. They're perfectly delicious simply fried, grilled, or baked.

Frying: Let sausages stand at room temperature for 30 minutes. Brush a large skillet with oil and preheat skillet. When skillet is hot, add sausages and fry until golden brown on all sides, 10 to 15 minutes.

Grilling: Start fire in advance; let sausages stand at room temperature for 30 minutes. When coals are ash-colored, place sausages over an oiled grill. Grill until sausages are golden brown, sizzling, and crispy.

Broiling: Let sausages stand at room temperature for 30 minutes; brush broiler pan with oil; preheat broiler. Place sausages on pan 4 inches from flame and broil until sausages are golden brown and sizzling—5 to 8 minutes on each side. For a crispy texture on both sides, split sausages open and broil for 5 minutes on split sides.

Baking: Place sausage links in a casserole; cover and bake in a preheated oven at 400° F. for 10 to 15 minutes. Then, place casserole under a preheated broiler until sausages are browned and crisp—about 5 minutes. Serve immediately or cover and keep warm in oven (250° F.) until ready to serve.

Hors d'oeuvre: Cut sausage links into 1-inch pieces. Broil as directed. Sprinkle with lemon juice; insert toothpicks and serve hot.

Milza Ripiena
BAKED STUFFED VEAL SPLEEN

1 whole veal spleen	1 large clove garlic, minced
½ cup chopped fresh mint	Salt
¼ cup chopped parsley	¼ cup olive oil
½ teaspoon crushed red pepper	¼ cup wine vinegar

Remove skin from spleen and rinse well with cold water; dry with absorbent paper. Cut a deep pocket in spleen and fill with mint, parsley, crushed pepper, garlic, and salt to taste. Close open end of pocket with toothpicks or skewer. Heat oil and sauté spleen for 20 minutes. Remove and place on chopping block to cool. Cut spleen in thin slices and return to skillet. Pour vinegar over slices; cover and cook until spleen is tender—about 30 minutes.

SERVES: 4

Agnello alla Cacciatora con Riso e Patate
LAMB, RICE, AND POTATOES, HUNTERS' STYLE

Here's another all-in-one dinner that's not only delicious but saves on the budget and dishwashing, too!

1 large onion, chopped	½ teaspoon black pepper
2 cloves garlic, cut in half	1 tablespoon dried mint (or 4 sprigs fresh)
2 stalks celery, chopped	
2 carrots, chopped	1 cup uncooked rice
2 tablespoons olive oil	3 medium potatoes, thinly sliced
2 pounds stewing lamb	¼ pound ricotta salata or Romano cheese cut in slivers
1 No. 2½ can whole tomatoes	
1 teaspoon salt	

In a large saucepan, brown onion, garlic, celery, and carrots in hot oil for 5 minutes. Add lamb and brown on all sides. Stir in tomatoes, salt, pepper, and mint. Cover and simmer slowly for approximately 1½ hours. Discard garlic.

Make a well in center and pour in rice; scatter potatoes and cheese around stew. Cover and simmer, stirring occasionally, until rice and potatoes are cooked—about 30 minutes longer.

SERVES: 4 to 6

Polpette de Carne Fritte
SPICY FRIED MEATBALLS

1½ pounds ground beef	2 eggs
1 medium onion, chopped	1½ teaspoons salt
1 cup bread crumbs	1 teaspoon freshly ground
⅓ cup grated Romano cheese	black pepper
½ cup chopped parsley	3 tablespoons olive oil

Combine beef, onion, bread crumbs, cheese, parsley, eggs, salt, and pepper; blend. Shape mixture into thick 2½-inch rounds and fry in hot oil until well browned on one side—3 to 5 minutes. Flatten meatballs slightly with pancake turner; turn and fry for 3 to 5 minutes on other side.

Serve with string bean salad and tomatoes, crusty bread and home fries.

SERVES: 4 to 6

Polpette di Carne alla Griglia
NUTTY BROILED HAMBURGERS

1½ pounds ground beef	½ cup chopped parsley
1 medium onion, chopped	2 eggs
1 large clove garlic, minced	1½ teaspoons salt
1 cup bread crumbs	1 teaspoon freshly ground black
⅓ cup Romano cheese	pepper
4 ounces pignoli (pine nuts)	Oil

Preheat broiler.

Combine beef, onion, garlic, bread crumbs, cheese, pine nuts, parsley, eggs, salt, and pepper; blend well. Shape mixture into thick 2½-inch rounds.

Brush broiler pan or grill with oil and broil 3 inches from flame until hamburgers are well browned and crispy—about 5 minutes on each side.

SERVES: 4 to 6

Vastieddi
CHEESE AND SPLEEN SANDWICHES

Palermitanos snack on cheese and spleen sandwiches for a quick lunch or in between meals. They are sold exclusively from fry stands, *friggitorie*. Vastieddi may sound a bit bizarre, but they are rather mild in flavor, high in protein, easy on the pocketbook, and very tasty indeed.

1 whole calf's or lamb's spleen	½ pound ricotta cheese
2 quarts water	4 rolls with sesame seeds
1 teaspoon salt	¼ pound caciocavallo cheese,
Juice of 1 lemon	coarsely grated
1 cup olive oil or melted lard	

Boil spleen in 2 quarts salted water and lemon juice (put skins in, too) until tender—1 to 1½ hours. Drain and cool. Remove skin and cut into ⅛-inch slices.

Heat oil in skillet; place spleen slices in carefully and heat through for 5 minutes. Spread ricotta ¼ inch thick on bottom halves of rolls. Cover with 2 or 3 spleen slices and sprinkle with cheese. Serve immediately.

SERVES: 4

Companatto o Soffritto di Frattaglie
HASLET STEW

Haslet stew is another dish of the people popularized for its low cost and first rate protein. A haslet is the lungs, heart, and liver of an animal, in combination. It's sold from variety-meat specialty stores in Italian districts or may be ordered from your butcher. Today gourmets consider variety meats a delicacy, whereas Sicilians have been thriving on them for centuries.

1 lamb haslet
1 lemon
2 tablespoons olive oil
1 medium onion, chopped
1 No. 2½ can whole tomatoes, chopped
6 sprigs fresh mint (or 1 tablespoon dried)
6 sprigs fresh basil (or 1 tablespoon dried)
Juice of 1 lemon
1 teaspoon salt
¼ teaspoon black pepper

Soak haslet in 2 quarts cold water with juice and skins of 1 lemon for 1 hour. Drain and dry with absorbent paper. With sharp kitchen shears, snip lungs into small pieces; chop heart and cube liver with a sharp knife.

Sauté lungs and heart in hot oil for 3 minutes. Stir in onion and sauté 2 minutes longer. Pour in tomatoes, mint, basil, lemon juice, salt, and pepper. Simmer for 1 hour. Add liver and simmer until it loses its red color—5 to 8 minutes. Serve over boiled rice with a green salad.

SERVES: 4

Pollo al Marsala
CHICKEN WITH MARSALA WINE

1 3½-pound frying chicken, quartered
Flour
Salt and black pepper
2 tablespoons olive oil
1 small onion, chopped
1 stalk celery, chopped
2 tablespoons melted butter
½ cup Marsala wine
1 cup chicken stock or bouillon
1 teaspoon tomato paste
1 teaspoon rosemary
½ pound mushrooms, thinly sliced
¼ cup minced Italian (flat leaf) parsley
¼ cup melted butter

Dredge chicken in flour; season with salt and pepper to taste. Sauté in hot oil until chicken is golden, turning once. Transfer to a large saucepan.

In same skillet, brown onion and celery in 2 tablespoons melted butter for 3 minutes. Transfer to saucepan with wine, chicken stock, tomato paste, and rosemary. Stir well; cover; and simmer until chicken is tender—about 1 hour.

While chicken is simmering, sauté mushrooms and parsley in ¼ cup melted butter for 5 to 8 minutes. Add to saucepan 10 minutes before chicken is done.

SERVES: 4

Pollo alla Messinese

CHICKEN WITH TUNA SAUCE, MESSINA STYLE

Pollo alla Messinese is an exceptional entrée that can be made in advance and refrigerated until serving time. Its combination of tender chicken dressed with a creamy tuna sauce will undeniably be the star attraction on any buffet table or at any company meal.

1 3½-pound broiling chicken, cut into serving pieces	2 anchovies, chopped
1 medium onion	½ cup chopped celery
2 stalks celery, chopped	⅓ cup capers
2 carrots, scraped	Salt and black pepper
3 sprigs parsley	1 head iceberg lettuce, shredded, chilled
1 teaspoon salt	2 ripe tomatoes, cut in wedges
2 quarts water	Parsley
1 cup mayonnaise	
1 3-ounce can tuna (Italian style), drained	

Place chicken pieces, onion, celery, carrots, parsley, and salt in a large kettle. Cover with water; bring to a boil. Cover kettle and boil gently until chicken is tender—about 1 hour. Drain, reserving broth for first course. Cool chicken; when cool enough to handle, remove and discard skin. Set aside.

Put mayonnaise, tuna, anchovies, and chopped celery in blender. Blend until mixture is smooth. Stir in capers and salt and pepper to taste. Arrange chicken over shredded lettuce. Spoon sauce over chicken; garnish platter with tomato wedges and parsley.

SERVES: 4 to 6

Pollo Marinato alla Griglia

LEMON-BROILED CHICKEN

2 3-pound broiling chickens,
    quartered
2 onions, thinly sliced
10 sprigs parsley

1 cup olive oil
Garlic salt
Freshly ground black pepper
4 large lemons, quartered

Place chicken in a shallow broiler pan. Cover with onions, parsley, oil, and garlic salt and pepper to taste. Squeeze lemons over chicken and leave skins in pan. Marinate for 2 hours, turning occasionally.

Preheat broiler for 10 minutes. Place chicken and marinade under hot broiler, 4 to 5 inches from flame. Broil 10 to 15 minutes on each side basting occasionally. Discard parsley (if charred) before serving.

SERVES: 6 to 8

Pollo Fra Diavolo

DEVILED CHICKEN

Olive oil
1 3½-pound broiling chicken,
    cut into serving pieces
½ cup finely chopped shallots
2 cloves garlic, cut in half
1 No. 2½ can whole tomatoes
    in purée

1 cup dry white wine
⅓ cup chopped parsley
1 teaspoon salt
¼ teaspoon freshly ground black
    pepper
¼ teaspoon crushed red pepper
1 pound spinach fettuccine

In a large skillet, heat 2 tablespoons olive oil and brown chicken until golden. Transfer to a large casserole.

In same skillet, sauté shallots and garlic for 3 minutes. (Add more oil if necessary.) Stir in tomatoes, wine, parsley, salt, and black and red pepper. Simmer for 10 minutes. Pour sauce over chicken and bake 350° F. until chicken is tender—about 1 hour.

While chicken is baking, cook fettuccine according to directions on package. Drain. Serve chicken and sauce over fettuccine.

SERVES: 4 to 6

Cappone Ripieno con Salsiccia al Forno

BAKED GOLDEN CAPON
WITH SAUSAGE STUFFING

1 5-pound capon, with giblets
1 small onion, minced
⅓ cup chopped celery
¼ cup butter
4 links sweet Italian sausage,
  chopped (casings removed)

1 No. 2½ can whole chestnuts,
  drained, chopped
Salt and black pepper
Softened butter

Preheat oven to 350° F.

Wash capon with cold water; drain and dry with absorbent paper (dry cavity very well). Chop giblets and set aside.

Sauté onion and celery in heated butter for 3 minutes. Add sausages, giblets, and chestnuts; sauté for 5 to 8 minutes, stirring well. Salt and pepper to taste.

Pull back the skin of the neck over the neck opening; fasten with skewer. Fill body cavity lightly with stuffing. Sew or skewer opening closed; truss capon. Rub well with softened butter and sprinkle with salt. Place in roasting pan and roast until golden brown and tender—about 1½ hours.

SERVES: 6

Coniglio in Agrodolce

SWEET AND SOUR RABBIT

MARINADE:

1½ cups dry red wine
1½ cups water
1 medium onion, thinly sliced
2 bay leaves
1 teaspoon whole cloves
1 teaspoon salt
3 peppercorns, crushed

2 to 3 pounds rabbit, cut into
  serving pieces
Flour
⅓ cup chopped salt pork
5 or 6 shallots, minced
⅓ cup golden raisins (sultana)
¼ cup (2 ounces) pignoli (pine
  nuts)
2 tablespoons wine vinegar
2 tablespoons sugar
1 tablespoon instant flour

Combine marinade ingredients in a saucepan and bring to a boil. Remove from heat and let cool until tepid. Place rabbit pieces in a large china bowl and pour marinade over them. Marinate for 2 to 4 hours or overnight.

Remove rabbit from marinade and drain on absorbent paper; pat dry. Dredge in flour and set aside. In a large saucepan, sauté salt pork for 3 minutes. Add shallots and sauté until golden. Add rabbit and brown well—about 5 minutes on each side. Strain marinade over rabbit and bring to a boil. Cover and simmer for 30 minutes. Stir in raisins, nuts, vinegar, and sugar. Cover and simmer until rabbit is tender—about 30 minutes longer. Turn off heat. If sauce is thin, blend in instant flour (blend with ½ cup sauce before adding to saucepan); cover and let sauce thicken (in its own heat) for 2 to 3 minutes. Serve over rice or buttered fettuccine.

SERVES: 4 to 6

Pollo alla Cacciatora

CHICKEN CACCIATORE

1 3½-pound broiling chicken, cut into serving pieces
Flour
Olive oil
1 large onion, thinly sliced
1 clove garlic, minced
1 No. 2 can whole tomatoes, chopped
1 bay leaf
2 tablespoons tomato paste
½ cup dry white wine
1 teaspoon marjoram
Salt and freshly ground black pepper
2 large green peppers, cut in strips
½ pound mushrooms, thinly sliced

Dredge chicken in flour and brown lightly in a skillet in 2 tablespoons hot olive oil. Transfer to a large saucepan. In same skillet, brown onion and garlic in 1 tablespoon hot oil for 3 minutes. Transfer to saucepan with tomatoes, bay leaf, tomato paste, wine, marjoram, and salt and pepper to taste. Stir and simmer for 40 minutes.

Sauté peppers in 3 tablespoons hot oil for 3 minutes. Add mushrooms and sauté for 5 minutes longer. Transfer to saucepan and simmer until chicken is tender—about 10 minutes. Correct seasoning if necessary. Discard bay leaf and serve over wide noodles (tagliatelle).

SERVES: 4 to 6

Zuppa di Pollo
CHICKEN IN THE POT SICILIAN STYLE

2 2-pound frying chickens, cut into serving pieces
2 quarts water
1 medium onion, quartered
4 stalks celery, chopped
2 carrots, chopped
3 sprigs parsley
½ cup whole tomatoes
1 walnut-size piece Romano cheese
1 tablespoon salt
¼ teaspoon black pepper
1 cup uncooked vermicelli
1 cup grated Romano cheese

Place chicken, water, onion, celery, carrots, parsley, tomatoes, piece of cheese, salt, and pepper in a large kettle. Bring to a boil and skim surface. Cover and simmer until chicken is tender—about 1 hour.

Discard onions and parsley. Bring soup to a boil and add vermicelli; boil until vermicelli are tender—about 5 minutes. Transfer to a warm tureen and serve with grated cheese.

SERVES: 6 to 8

Pollo con Melanzane
CHICKEN WITH EGGPLANT

Salt
1 medium eggplant (about 1 pound), peeled, chopped
1 3-pound broiling chicken, cut into serving pieces
2 tablespoons olive oil
2 cups chicken stock or bouillon
2 tablespoons tomato paste
1 tablespoon orégano
¼ cup olive oil
1 large onion, sliced
2 large green peppers, cut in strips
2 cups fresh or canned tomatoes, skinned, chopped
Freshly ground black pepper

Salt eggplant liberally and drain in colander for 30 minutes. Rinse off salt; drain and dry with absorbent paper.

In a large saucepan, brown chicken in 2 tablespoons hot oil. Pour in chicken stock, tomato paste, and orégano and simmer for 40 minutes.

While chicken is simmering, heat ¼ cup olive oil in a large skillet. Add onion, peppers, and eggplant and sauté for 10 minutes (add more oil if necessary). Add tomatoes and salt and pepper to taste and simmer for 5 minutes longer. Transfer to saucepan and simmer until chicken is tender—about 10 minutes. Correct seasoning if necessary.

SERVES: 4 to 6

Pollo in Salsa di Capperi
CHICKEN IN CAPER SAUCE

1 3- to 4-pound frying chicken, cut into serving pieces	½ teaspoon salt
Olive oil	¼ teaspoon black pepper
2 large onions, chopped	⅓ cup capers
4 stalks celery, chopped	2 tablespoons vinegar
4 tablespoons tomato paste	1 tablespoon sugar
1 cup water	½ cup pitted green Sicilian olives

Brown chicken lightly in 2 tablespoons hot olive oil. Transfer to large saucepan.

Brown onions and celery in 2 tablespoons hot oil until soft and lightly browned—8 to 10 minutes. Add tomato paste, water, salt, pepper, capers, vinegar, and sugar; simmer for 5 minutes. Pour over chicken; cover saucepan and simmer until chicken is tender—about 1 hour. Add olives and simmer 10 minutes longer. Take off heat and cool for 20 minutes before serving. (The sweet and sour sauce will be too piquant if served hot.)

SERVES: 4 to 6

NOTE: Chicken in Caper Sauce is a headliner at the Foccaceria, a modest luncheonette-type restaurant in New York City that specializes in Sicilian specialties.

Involtini di Pollo
ELEGANT STUFFED CHICKEN BREASTS

6 chicken breasts
Flour
Salt and black pepper
6 slices (¼ pound) prosciutto
6 slices (8 ounces) mozzarella
cheese
¼ cup butter

1 cup chicken stock or bouillon
1 cup Marsala wine
⅓ cup butter
2 tablespoons olive oil
½ pound mushrooms
⅓ cup minced Italian (flat
leaf) parsley

Bone chicken breasts or purchase boned. Dredge in flour mixed with salt and pepper to taste. Layer each chicken breast with 1 slice prosciutto and 1 slice mozzarella. Roll and close open ends with skewers or toothpicks.

In a large skillet, brown chicken breasts lightly in ¼ cup heated butter. Pour in chicken stock and wine. Cover skillet and simmer slowly until chicken breasts are tender—about 30 minutes.

In another skillet, heat ⅓ cup butter and the olive oil together. Add mushrooms and sauté until crisp—about 8 minutes. Stir in parsley and sauté 3 minutes longer. Add to chicken 5 minutes before it is done. Remove skewers or toothpicks before serving. Serve over saffron rice or buttered noodles.

SERVES: 6

BREAD

The Staff of Life

Senza pane, non mangiare! (Without bread, one cannot eat!)
Every Sicilian practices this motto daily. Bread is a way of life for
every Sicilian whether he be rich or poor. It carries the lore of
centuries, the color of the Mediterranean sun, and the fragrances
of an exotic island.

The art of Sicilian bread baking is as old as the history of man.
The method of hand-molding every variety is still practiced and
baking them in open hearths results in a delicious hard crust.
Bastoni cimminati (long crusty-brown seeded loaves), golden whole
wheat loaves, *foccace* (sesame-seed hard rolls), and *tupe* (large
rings of crusty bread with artichoke patterns decorating the tops)
are just a few basic breads. Special holiday breads and breads that
are meals in themselves are also important in the Sicilian repertoire.
Special mention must be made of the incomparable and popular
appetizer or snack bread called pizza.

Pizza in Sicily is very different from the classical thin-crusted
pies (Neapolitan style) that everyone relishes here. Sicilian pizza
is more breadlike, laden heavily with anchovies, chopped onions,
orégano, tomatoes, olive oil, pepper, and grated cheese. Sicilian
pizzerias are different too. Instead of using large commercial ovens,
Sicilians bake their pizzas on an open hearth, next to the coals,
until the light crust is golden in color. Not only does this method
produce delicious results, but it also lends a warm and decorative
air to these establishments. Sfincione* and Pizza Catanian Style*
are unusual variations worth noting.

Frittelline della Festa
HOLIDAY FRITTERS

Bite-size fruit and vegetable fritters add sparkle to any holiday meal. Try the selection suggested or improvise with your own favorite combination.

1 cup sifted flour	1 quart vegetable oil
½ teaspoon baking powder	1 large apple, peeled, cored,
1 tablespoon sugar	cut into eighths
1 egg	8 dried figs, cut in half
½ cup milk	8 cauliflowerets, cooked
1 tablespoon melted butter	

In a large bowl, sift dry ingredients together. Combine egg, milk, and melted butter in another bowl. Pour liquid mixture over dry ingredients, stirring well until batter is smooth—about 2 minutes.

Heat oil to 370° F. (1-inch bread cube browns evenly in 1 minute). Dip apple pieces, figs, and cauliflowerets in batter; drop carefully in hot oil, a few at a time, and fry until golden brown, turning once. Remove from oil with slotted spoon and drain on absorbent paper. Serve hot.

YIELD: 2 dozen

NOTE: Fritters may be warmed at 250° F. for 5 or 6 minutes when ready to serve.

Pizza Espresso
INSTANT PIZZA

All wise homemakers keep an emergency shelf stocked with convenience foods and extras for unexpected guests or for when time runs short. Instant pizza is made with stored staples that produce very tasty results indeed.

INSTANT PIZZA DOUGH:
3 cups Bisquick
½ to ¾ cup milk
Olive oil

PIZZA SAUCE:

2 tablespoons instant onions (or
1 small onion, chopped)

½ teaspoon instant minced
garlic (or 1 clove garlic,
minced)

2 tablespoons olive oil

1 8-ounce can tomato purée

½ teaspoon salt

⅛ teaspoon black pepper

2 teaspoons orégano

PIZZA TOPPING:

1 medium onion, chopped

½ can anchovies, drained,
chopped

½ pound pepperoni (dried
sausage) thinly sliced

½ cup grated Romano cheese

6 to 8 fresh mint leaves,
chopped (or 1 tablespoon
dried)

Measure Bisquick into a bowl; pour in milk gradually and mix until a soft dough has formed. Turn onto a well-oiled 10×15-inch rectangular baking pan; flatten and spread to fit pan. Brush with olive oil.

In a small saucepan, sauté onions and garlic in hot oil for 3 minutes. Pour in tomato purée, salt, pepper, and orégano; cover and simmer for 15 minutes.

Spread sauce on top of dough.

Cover with topping ingredients.

Bake in a preheated oven at 400° F. for 15 to 20 minutes. Serve hot or at room temperature.

SERVES: 6 to 8

Pane con Formaggio e Pepe al Forno
PEPPER-SPECKLED CHEESE BREAD

1 loaf Italian bread, fresh or
day-old

¼ to ⅓ cup olive oil

⅔ cup grated Romano or
Parmesan cheese

Freshly ground black pepper

Preheat oven to 400° F.

Split loaf in half lengthwise. Brush halves liberally with oil; cover with grated cheese and pepper to taste. Place on a baking sheet and bake until cheese is toasted—8 to 10 minutes. Cut into wedges; serve hot.

SERVES: 3 to 6

PIZZA MUFFOLETTO

My name, Muffoletto, is also the name of a pizza—a specialty of the Palermo province. Pizza Muffoletto (Muffolettu in Sicilian dialect) is made from an ancient recipe using fresh tomato sauce, salted sardines, and a sprinkling of bread crumbs instead of cheese. It's a dish of the people—filling, inexpensive and tasty. In other locales, it is named Sfinciuni Salati, Sciavazza or Sfincinuni di Santa Vitu.

PIZZA DOUGH:
1¼ cups sifted flour
½ teaspoon salt
1 teaspoon sugar
1 tablespoon shortening

½ cup hot water
½ package active dry yeast
   (1½ teaspoons)
Olive oil

PIZZA SAUCE:
2 to 4 tablespoons olive oil
1 large onion, chopped
4 large ripe tomatoes, skinned, chopped, seeded
¼ cup parsley, minced
½ teaspoon salt

PIZZA TOPPING:
10 salted sardines or anchovies
   (available in Italian markets)
½ cup bread crumbs or grated cheese
Olive oil
Freshly ground black pepper

Sift flour, salt, and sugar together. Melt shortening in the hot water; cool to lukewarm. Add yeast to lukewarm liquid and let stand for 5 minutes. Combine liquid and dry ingredients (except olive oil); mix until dough cleans sides of bowl and is smooth. Gather up with fingers and form a ball. Place in an oiled bowl; turn to oil top. Cover with cloth; let rise in a warm place (85° to 90° F.), free from drafts, until doubled in bulk—about 35 to 45 minutes. (Prepare pizza sauce and topping while dough is rising.)

When dough has doubled, punch down and turn onto a lightly floured board. Roll out and flatten into a well-oiled 10×15-inch rectangular baking pan. Brush with olive oil. Preheat oven to 450° F.

In a saucepan, heat oil and sauté onion for 3 minutes. Stir in tomatoes, parsley, and salt and simmer for 5 to 8 minutes. Spread sauce over pizza dough.

Rinse sardines with cold water; dry with absorbent paper and cut into small pieces. Distribute them evenly over pizza with bread crumbs, a sprinkling of oil, and pepper to taste. Bake at 450° F. for 20 to 30 minutes. Cut in large squares and serve hot.

SERVES: 6 to 8

Fanfarichi

DAD'S SPECIAL LITTLE BIRTHDAY CAKES

On Dad's birthday, Mother always made *fanfarichi* (anchovy fritters) instead of birthday cake. They were his favorite "special little birthday cakes"!

1 package compressed or active dry yeast	1 2-ounce can anchovies, drained, chopped
1 cup lukewarm water	1 to 2 cups vegetable oil
3 cups sifted all-purpose flour	

Crumble yeast and dissolve in lukewarm water; let stand for 5 minutes. Measure sifted flour into a large bowl; make a well in center and pour in yeast mixture. Mix with wooden spoon or electric mixer until air bubbles appear and batter is thick and smooth—5 to 7 minutes. Cover with cloth and put in a warm place (85° F.) free from drafts for 1 hour.

Turn dough onto a lightly floured board. Dust with flour and punch down. Knead anchovies into dough. Continue kneading until dough is smooth and satiny—about 5 minutes. Cut dough into 2-inch pieces. Flatten pieces by hand or rolling pin so that they are only ¼ inch thick.

In a large skillet, pour in oil 1 inch deep and heat to 370° F. (a small piece of bread browns evenly in 1 minute). Place fritters, a few at a time, in hot oil. Fry until golden brown, turning once. Remove from skillet with slotted spoon and drain onto absorbent paper. Serve hot.

YIELD: Approximately 2½ dozen

VARIATION: Substitute 1 cup chopped cooked shrimp for anchovies.

NOTE: Anchovy fritters are popular during the Lenten season, when meatless recipes are at a premium. They are a good substitute for bread, potatoes, or dumplings.

Pizza ai Quatro Gusti

PIZZA WITH FOUR TOPPINGS

Pizza with Four Toppings is not only appealing to the eye, but stirs up the olfactory and taste senses too!

Use pizza sauce and dough from Pizza Muffoletto.* Roll and shape dough into a 13-inch circle. Place on a well-oiled baking sheet or round pizza pan. Brush lightly with oil. Preheat oven to 450° F.

Select any four of the listed toppings and arrange each over one fourth of the dough. What a nice way to share a pizza. One may eat just the quarter he prefers or sample another section.

TOPPINGS:

½ cup chopped prosciutto or ham
5 marinated artichoke hearts, cut in half
1 dozen fresh shucked mussels or clams
1 green pepper, cut in 2-inch strips
1 to 2 Italian sausages, cut in 1-inch pieces
½ cup mushrooms, thinly sliced
4 to 6 cooked meatballs, quartered
1 cup ricotta, crumbled

After selecting and sectioning toppings, cover entire pie with:

8 ounces mozzarella cheese, chopped
2 cups fresh or canned tomatoes, peeled, chopped
6 to 8 fresh basil leaves, chopped (or 1 tablespoon dried)
Light sprinkling of olive oil
Salt and freshly ground black pepper to taste

Bake in a hot over at 450° F. until done—20 to 25 minutes. Slice pie-fashion and serve hot.

SERVES: 6 to 8

Scacciata
PIZZA CATANIA STYLE

1 envelope active dry yeast
¼ cup lukewarm water
1 cup lukewarm water
¼ teaspoon salt
3½ cups sifted flour
Olive oil
⅔ pound caciocavallo cheese, sliced

1 2-ounce can anchovies, drained, chopped
1 medium onion, chopped
8 Sicilian black olives, pitted, chopped
½ cup grated Romano cheese
Freshly ground black pepper

Preheat oven to 450° F.

Dissolve yeast in ¼ cup lukewarm water; let stand for 5 minutes. Pour 1 cup lukewarm water and salt into a large bowl. Stir in yeast mixture and 2½ cups of the sifted flour. Beat well; add remaining flour. Mix until dough is smooth and cleans sides of bowl. Gather up with fingers and form into ball. Turn onto a lightly floured board and knead until dough is smooth and elastic and does not stick to hands—8 to 10 minutes. Place in a greased bowl, turn to grease top, and cover with a cloth. Let set in a warm place (85° to 90° F.) free from drafts until dough doubles in size—approximately 1 hour. Punch down, turn onto a lightly floured board, and knead for 5 minutes. Roll out and flatten to fit two 9-inch oiled pie plates. Brush tops with oil.

Sprinkle caciocavallo cheese, anchovies, onion, olives, Romano cheese, oil, and pepper to taste over both pies. Bake in a hot oven (450° F.) for 20 to 30 minutes. Slice pizza-pie-fashion and serve hot or at room temperature.

SERVES: 10 to 12

VARIATIONS: Shape dough to fit 12×18-inch oiled rectangular baking pan. Arrange pieces of ham, mozzarella cheese, drained cooked spinach, and chopped onions over dough. Sprinkle with oil and grated Parmesan cheese. Bake as directed above.

For Individual Pizzas: Shape dough into 6-inch circles. Brush with oil and cover with pizza sauce, cooked eggplant slices, salami pieces and grated Parmesan cheese. Bake at 450° F. for 15 to 20 minutes.

Calzoni

BAKED SANDWICH SURPRISE

The Italians put their humor to work in naming, this recipe. The shape of the sandwich suggests a trousers leg, so the Italians flippantly named it "trousers," or *calzoni*. It is a specialty of Southern Italy, and the Sicilian version is given here and now.

DOUGH: Prepare dough as directed in Pizza Catania Style.* Roll dough into thin sheets and cut into 6-inch circles (makes about 12 circles). Brush tops with oil.

> FILLING: 6 slices prosciutto or boiled ham, cut in half
> 12 slices ricotta salata cheese (1 pound)
> Freshly ground black pepper
> 1 egg, slightly beaten
> 1½ to 2 quarts vegetable oil

On one half of circles, place ham and cheese slices; grind pepper to taste over filling. Fold circles, turnover style, and seal with beaten egg, pressing edges together with fingertips.

Heat oil to 370° F. (a small piece of bread browns evenly in 1 minute). Drop calzoni carefully into hot oil (a few at a time) and fry until golden brown—8 to 10 minutes. Remove with slotted spoon and drain on absorbent paper.

YIELD: 1 dozen

Panini Rustici

SASSY CARNIVAL ROLLS

1 pound ricotta cheese
2 eggs
½ teaspoon salt
8 ounces mozzarella, diced
¼ pound salami, chopped
¼ pound prosciutto (ham), chopped
¼ pound mortadella (spiced ham), chopped
6 sesame-seed hard rolls, cut in half
½ cup grated Parmesan cheese
Freshly ground black pepper
¼ cup butter

Preheat oven to 350° F. Combine ricotta, eggs, salt, mozzarella, salami, prosciutto, and mortadella. Using a palette knife, spread cheese mixture over halves of rolls. Sprinkle tops with cheese, pepper, and butter (1 teaspoon per roll).

Place rolls on baking sheet and bake at 350° F. for 10 to 15 minutes. Remove from oven and put under hot broiler long enough to toast grated cheese—2 to 3 minutes. Serve hot as a first course or luncheon dish. If cut into quarters, *Panini Rustici* becomes a savory canape.

YIELD: 12 halves

Pane di Monreale

ARTICHOKE-SHAPED BREAD OF MONREALE

Monreale, famous for its outstanding gold mosaic cathedral, also harbors fine outdoor restaurants specializing in buffets and spit-roasted meats. They're absolutely charming and so fragrantly fetching. One evening, while dining in Monreale at La Botte (the Wine Barrel), I sought to follow one rather delicate and exotic aroma. My well-trained nose led me to a large basket of freshly baked bread on the buffet table. Its permeating aroma was created by mahlepi—an unusual Syrian spice widely used in Greece and Middle Eastern countries. I was told by the *patrona* (owner) that it was a local bread made nearby. After a little research, I concluded that it probably came from Piano del Albanese, a Greek community and Monreale's neighboring town.

2 packages active dry yeast	1 teaspoon ground mahlepi
2 teaspoons salt	(available in Greek and
1 tablespoon sugar	gourmet stores)
2 tablespoons shortening	1 tablespoon olive oil
1 cup warm milk	1 egg, slightly beaten
5 cups unsifted flour	

Preheat oven to 400° F. Grease a baking sheet.

In a small bowl, mix yeast, salt, sugar, shortening, and warm milk together. Let stand for 5 minutes. In a large bowl, measure flour and mix with ground mahlepi. Make a well in center; pour in yeast mixture and mix well until dough is smooth. Gather up with fingers and form into ball.

Turn onto lightly floured board and knead in olive oil until dough is smooth and satiny—about 5 minutes. (Dough may be a little sticky—do not add extra flour.) Place in a greased bowl; turn to grease top. Cover with cloth and let rise in a warm place (85° F.) free from drafts for 1 hour. After dough has doubled in bulk, punch down; turn onto lightly floured board and knead for 5 minutes.

To shape artichoke: Roll dough into one long rope, 30×2½ inches. Cut rope into three varying lengths: long, medium, and short. Wind each rope loosely to form coil. Arrange graduating coils, one on top of the other, on greased baking sheet. Cover with cloth and let rise in a warm place for 1 hour or until double in bulk.

With kitchen shears, cut slits 1 inch apart around each coil and spread apart slightly. Brush with egg and bake in a hot oven at 400° F. or until golden brown—about 40 minutes. (Insert toothpick or cake tester in center of loaf, if dry when removed, bread is done.)

Focacce

SESAME-SEED ROLLS

2 packages active dry or
  compressed yeast
2½ cups warm water
1 tablespoon salt
1 tablespoon melted shortening
  or butter

7 cups unbleached flour, unsifted
1 egg, slightly beaten
2 tablespoons cold water
½ cup sesame seeds

Preheat oven to 400° F. Grease two baking sheets.

In a large bowl, combine yeast, water, salt, and shortening. Let stand for 5 minutes. Add flour and stir until blended (dough will be sticky). Transfer to a large bowl and turn to grease top. Cover with cloth and let rise in a warm place (85° F.) free from drafts until double in bulk—about 1 hour.

Punch dough down and turn onto lightly floured board; knead for 5 minutes. Cut dough into 24 equal pieces. Shape into rounds and place on greased baking sheets, 2 inches apart. Cover with cloth and let rise until double in bulk—about 1 hour. With kitchen shears, cut slits on roll tops, criss-cross fashion. Brush rolls with egg mixed with cold water and sprinkle liberally with sesame seeds. Bake until rolls are browned—about 25 minutes. Cool on wire racks.

YIELD: 2 dozen

Treccia Dorata

GOLDEN BRAID

A crusty and impressive-looking loaf. Make it for a holiday meal or company dinner.

1 cup warm water	5 cups sifted flour
2 tablespoons shortening	1 cup water
2 teaspoons salt	1 tablespoon oil
1 tablespoon sugar	1 egg, beaten
2 packages active dry or compressed yeast	½ cup sesame seeds

In a small bowl, combine warm water, shortening, salt, sugar, and yeast. Let stand 5 minutes. Measure 5 cups sifted flour into a large bowl; make a well in flour and pour in liquid mixture. Stir with a spoon or electric mixer until all ingredients are thoroughly blended. Add additional cup water gradually and mix until dough cleans bowl and forms a ball. (A little more or less water may be necessary.)

Turn out onto a lightly floured board. Knead with back of hand, turning and rolling, for about 5 minutes. Add 1 tablespoon olive oil and knead for an additional 3 to 5 minutes, until dough is smooth and satiny. Place dough in a greased bowl, turning to grease top. Cover bowl with a dish towel and let rise in a warm place (85° F.) free from drafts until double in bulk—about 1 hour.

Punch dough down by placing fist in center; pull in edges; turn onto a lightly floured board. Knead for 3 to 5 minutes. Cut dough into 3 pieces. Roll each piece of dough into a 20-inch rope. Twist ropes together, loosely, stretching slightly until opposite ends are brought together. Lift braid onto a greased baking sheet. Cover and let rise for a second time in a warm place for approximately 45 minutes to 1 hour.

Poke finger in dough; if indentation remains, dough is ready to be baked. Brush sides and tops of bread with beaten egg. Sprinkle with sesame seeds. Bake in a preheated oven at 400° F., for approximately 1 hour or until bread has a deep golden glaze. Remove from baking sheet and cool on a wire rack. Serve sliced. Try toasting slices for breakfast—they're delicious.

VARIATION: Rolls can be made instead by cutting dough into 4-inch strips and braiding as directed above.

STORAGE TIPS: Bread remains fresh for a week if stored in a tightly sealed plastic bag. Freeze if desired in plastic bags or aluminum foil. If foil is used, thaw without unwrapping at 350° F. for 20 to 30 minutes.

VEGETABLES
AND SALADS
REIGN SUPREME

Vegetables and salads are the pillars and beams of Sicilian cooking. They give structure and balance to meals while also providing eye and palate appeal. *Verdura,* or greens, are not only popular for their natural goodness, but because they are nutritious, economical, and filling. Salads and cooked greens are usually eaten twice daily, for dinner and supper. They're cooked in soups or combined with pasta, or served as companions to meat and fish; very often they are the whole meal.

The artichoke is a composite plant of the aster family, somewhat resembling the thistle and cultivated for its thick, fleshy receptacle supporting the flower. This beautiful olive-green vegetable with its tulip-shaped leaves is cooked whole in a variety of ways, or the heart is culled, cooked and served as an appetizer, in salads, or with the entrée.

Burdocks are akin to the artichoke and also resemble it in flavor. Rough-leaved, sometimes called cardoon, this perennial plant is now considered a delicacy by the Italians, Spanish, and French. It can be found in season during the spring and fall at Italian green-groceries. The Japanese have tinned the root and it may be purchased in Japanese markets all year long.

Sicilians are particularly partial to cauliflower and zucchini, often combining them with pasta or frying them in olive oil. Sometimes they sauté or bake them with onions and cheese. Zucchini is often prepared in a sweet and sour marinade and served at room temperature.

Heavenly food, royal in color, smooth to the touch, full-bodied and delicious, eggplant reigns supreme for both the rich and the poor in Sicily. Next to pasta, eggplant is highest in popularity. It keeps well, needs no special storage, is plentiful and inexpensive, filling and satisfying—no wonder eggplant is served religiously in Sicilian homes. Also, it is listed in every eating establishment as a tempting appetizer, an elaborate entrée, a mixed salad, and a special vegetable. It is cooked whole, thinly sliced, chopped, stuffed, baked, fried and stewed. But the *pièce de résistance* is when this vegetable is made into a salad. The most popular and famous salad is Capunatina. Try it for a unique culinary experience.

Redder than all reds, sweet as honey, round or plum-shaped, tomatoes are the nectar, wine and base of Sicilian cooking. During July and August you can still see women spreading cooked tomatoes on large boards to dry in the strong summer sun. After a few hours of drying, the tomatoes are transformed into a concentrated paste and scooped into ceramic crocks to be used throughout the winter months, when tomatoes are expensive. This crude method of making tomato paste has gone on for centuries and continues today, even though tinned paste is available in groceries throughout Sicily.

Cavolfiore Fritto con Olive alla Catanese

BLACK AND WHITE CAULIFLOWER ROSETTES, CATANIA STYLE

2 10-ounce packages frozen
  cauliflower
Flour
3 egg whites, slightly beaten
¼ cup olive oil

8 black Italian or Greek olives,
  pitted, chopped
Salt and freshly ground black
  pepper

Cook cauliflower according to directions on package. Drain and cool. Dredge in flour and dip in egg whites. In a large skillet, heat oil and fry cauliflower until golden brown on one side. Drop in olives; stir. Turn cauliflower over; fry golden brown on other side. Salt and pepper to taste before serving.

SERVES: 6 to 8

NOTE: If time permits, use fresh cauliflower instead. Cut or break 1 large head into rosettes; cover with salted water and boil until tender—about 15 minutes. Drain; cool and continue as directed.

Peperoni Strascinati in Padella

EGGPLANT AND PEPPER MEDLEY

1 large eggplant (2 to 3 pounds)
Salt
6 large frying peppers
Olive oil

1 large onion, chopped
6 stalks celery, chopped
Freshly ground black pepper

Remove stem from eggplant and chop eggplant into 1-inch pieces. Salt liberally and drain for 30 minutes to 1 hour. Rinse off salt and dry with absorbent paper; set aside.

Remove stems and seeds from frying peppers. Rinse, dry, and cut peppers in 1-inch slices.

In a large skillet, heat ¼ cup olive oil and sauté peppers, onion, and celery for 8 to 10 minutes. Add eggplant (adding more oil as needed), and sauté until eggplant is soft and golden—about 20 minutes. Salt and pepper to taste. Serve hot or at room temperature as an appetizer, salad, or cooked vegetable.

SERVES: 6 to 8

Melanzane Primavera

SPRINGTIME EGGPLANT

1 large eggplant (2 to 3 pounds)	Fresh basil leaves
Salt	Salt
Olive oil	Freshly ground black pepper
1 bunch scallions, peeled, chopped	¼ to ⅓ cup grated Romano cheese
2 cups fresh tomatoes, skinned, chopped	

Remove stem from eggplant; pare away skin, from top to bottom, every other inch. Cut into ½-inch slices and salt liberally on all sides. Place on absorbent paper; weight down with a heavy bread board or platter; drain for 1 hour.

In a saucepan, heat 2 tablespoons olive oil and sauté scallions until golden. Add tomatoes, 5 or 6 basil leaves, and salt and pepper to taste. Simmer for 15 to 20 minutes. Set aside.

Rinse off salt from eggplant slices and dry with absorbent paper. In a large skillet, heat ¼ cup olive oil and fry slices golden brown on each side (add oil as needed to prevent sticking and burning). Drain on absorbent paper. Keep cooked slices warm while remainder are being fried. Arrange slices on a heated platter, overlapping them slightly. Pour sauce down center of slices; sprinkle with grated cheese and garnish with fresh basil leaves. Keep warm but wait 5 to 10 minutes before serving to allow the flavor of the sauce to be absorbed. Serve as an appetizer or vegetable.

SERVES: 6

NOTE: Eggplants are extremely watery and contain bitter juices. Therefore, their flesh is always sprinkled liberally with salt to draw out the water and juices, making them more palatable and better for frying.

Fette di Melanzane Ripiene
BREADED EGGPLANT SANDWICHES

1 large eggplant (about 2 pounds)	½ pound mortadella (spiced ham), thinly sliced
Salt	½ pound provolone cheese, thinly sliced
1½ cups bread crumbs	2 eggs, slightly beaten
⅓ cup grated Parmesan cheese	¼ cup olive oil
¼ teaspoon salt	
⅓ cup chopped parsley	

Remove and discard stem from eggplant; cut in ½-inch slices. Salt liberally; weight down with heavy plate; drain for 1 hour. Rinse salt off slices and dry with absorbent paper. Set aside. Preheat oven to 350° F.

Combine bread crumbs, Parmesan cheese, salt, and parsley. Set aside. Put 1 or 2 slices mortadella and 1 slice provolone between 2 eggplant slices. Dip eggplant sandwiches in beaten eggs, then in bread crumb mixture.

Pour olive oil in a shallow baking pan; heat in oven for 5 minutes. Place eggplant sandwiches in pan and bake for 15 minutes on each side. Serve hot or at room temperature.

SERVES: 4 to 6

VARIATIONS: Prepare and cook as directed, using these substitutes:

> meatballs
> prosciutto and mozzarella slices
> anchovies and salami slices

Melanzane al Forno
INDIVIDUAL MEAT-STUFFED EGGPLANTS

1 pound ground beef
2 eggs
1 onion, chopped
2 tablespoons minced parsley
1 cup bread crumbs

⅓ cup grated Parmesan cheese
½ teaspoon salt
¼ teaspoon black pepper
6 small oval eggplants
Olive oil

Combine ground beef, eggs, onions, parsley, bread crumbs, grated cheese, salt, and pepper.

Cut tops (1 inch deep) off eggplants and *do not discard*. Using a grapefruit knife and spoon, hollow centers of eggplants, leaving ½-inch shells. Chop pulp and sauté in ¼ to ⅓ cup hot oil until lightly browned. Add to meat mixture. Preheat oven to 350° F.

Fill eggplants with meat mixture and brush shells with oil. Place in an oiled casserole; cover with eggplant tops. Bake until eggplants are cooked through—30 to 40 minutes. Serve with Cucumber Salad* and crusty Golden Braid.*

SERVES: 6

Cipolle Ripiene alla Palermitana
STUFFED ONIONS, PALERMO STYLE

6 large onions
½ pound ground beef
1 egg
1 tablespoon minced parsley
3 tablespoons grated Parmesan
  cheese

¼ teaspoon salt
⅛ teaspoon pepper
6 slices (8 ounces) mozzarella
6 salami slices

Hollow onions with grapefruit knife, leaving ½-inch shells. Chop onion centers and combine with ground beef, egg, parsley, Parmesan cheese, salt, and pepper. Preheat oven to 350° F.

Fill onions with meat mixture and cover with 1 slice mozzarella cheese and 1 slice salami, pressing salami around onion tops. Place in a shallow oiled casserole and bake until onions are tender—30 to 40 minutes.

SERVES: 6

Carciofi alla Nanna Greco

GRANDMA GRECO'S STUFFED ARTICHOKES

My beautiful and sweet grandmother made the best stuffed artichokes this side of the Mediterranean. This recipe is over two hundred years old.

1½ cups bread crumbs	¼ cup chopped parsley
¼ pound Romano cheese, coarsely grated	Salt
	¼ teaspoon black pepper
1 medium onion, chopped	6 large artichokes
2 cloves garlic, minced	Olive oil

Combine bread crumbs, cheese, onion, garlic, parsley, ½ teaspoon salt, and pepper. Set aside.

Trim stalks at base of artichokes; cut away 1 inch across the tops and discard. Remove discolored leaves; snip off ends of leaves with kitchen shears. Wash with cold water and drain. Spread leaves apart and fill with bread crumb mixture; sprinkle with olive oil.

Place stuffed artichokes in a large kettle. Fill with water halfway up artichokes (about 1½ quarts). Add ½ teaspoon salt and 2 tablespoons oil to water. Bring to a boil; cover and simmer slowly until artichokes are tender—30 to 40 minutes. (Pierce artichoke base with fork; if soft, artichokes are done.) Remove artichokes from water and serve hot or at room temperature.

SERVES: 6

Scarola e Cannellini in Umido

STEWED ESCAROLE AND CANNELLINI BEANS

1 head escarole (about 1½ pounds)	1 cup fresh or canned tomatoes, skinned, chopped
1 teaspoon salt	1 No. 2 can cannellini beans
2 tablespoons olive oil	Salt and freshly ground black pepper
1 clove garlic, minced	

Remove core from escarole and wash under cold running water until thoroughly cleaned. Discard discolored and tough outer leaves. Place in a large kettle with salt and cover with water. Bring to a boil; cover; lower heat and boil gently for 10 to 15 minutes. Drain.

In same kettle, heat oil and sauté garlic for 3 minutes. Add tomatoes and cannellini beans with half of its liquid and simmer for 5 minutes. Stir in escarole and simmer until escarole is tender— 8 to 10 minutes. Salt and pepper to taste. Serve as a thick soup or vegetable.

SERVES: 4 to 6

Fave del Re
ROYAL FAVA BEANS

2 cloves garlic, minced	¼ cup chopped parsley
2 tablespoons olive oil	Salt
2 No. 2 cans fava beans	Freshly ground black pepper

Sauté garlic in hot oil for 3 minutes. Pour in fava beans and their liquid, parsley, salt, and pepper to taste. Stir and cook for 8 to 10 minutes. Serve as a thick soup or vegetable.

SERVES: 4 to 6

VARIATIONS: Serve Fave del Re cold. Garnish with lemon wedges and chopped onions. Minestrone: Drain liquid from 1 No. 2 can sliced carrots; add with 2 cups cooked elbow macaroni to basic recipe. Correct seasoning.

Insalata di Finocchi e Lattuga
SWEET FENNEL AND LETTUCE SALAD

1 head iceberg lettuce	1 No. 2 can sliced beets, drained
2 stalks fennel, chopped	⅓ cup olive oil
Leaves from 1 bunch fennel, chopped	3 tablespoons wine vinegar
	Salt and freshly ground pepper

Remove core and wash lettuce with cold water; drain. Section and dry leaves. Tear leaves into bite-size pieces and mix with fennel stalks and leaves. Just before serving, add beets, oil, vinegar, and salt and pepper to taste. Toss until ingredients and dressing are blended.

SERVES: 6

Insalata di Cavolfiore
CHILLED CAULIFLOWER SALAD

1 large head cauliflower (2 to
   3 pounds)
Salt
⅓ cup olive oil

Juice of 1 to 2 lemons
1 clove garlic, minced
⅓ cup chopped parsley
Freshly ground black pepper

Remove leaves and trim base from cauliflower. Soak, head down, in cold salted water for 15 to 20 minutes. Drain. Break into flowerets; place in a kettle; cover with water and 1 teaspoon salt. Bring to a boil and boil gently until flowerets are tender—10 to 15 minutes. Drain.

Combine oil, lemon juice, garlic, parsley, and salt and pepper to taste. Place flowerets in a salad bowl; while they are still warm, pour salad dressing over them. Chill and serve as a salad or vegetable. Excess dressing should be poured off before serving.

SERVES: 4 to 6

TIP: Cooked vegetables absorb the full flavor of dressing better if it is poured over them while they are still warm.

Insalata di Cetrioli e Pomodori
CUCUMBER SALAD

4 cucumbers, peeled, thinly
   sliced
1 medium onion, chopped
2 tomatoes, quartered
¼ cup fresh chopped basil (or
   1 teaspoon dried)

¼ cup olive or salad oil
Juice of 1 lemon
Salt and freshly ground black
   pepper

Place cucumbers, onion, tomatoes, and basil in a salad bowl. Chill. Just before serving, pour oil, lemon juice, and salt and pepper to taste over vegetables. Toss until vegetables and salad dressing are well blended.

SERVES: 4 to 6

VARIATIONS: Dill or parsley may be substituted for basil.

Insalata con Formaggio e Salame alla Cugina Teresa

COUSIN THERESA'S CHEESE AND SALAMI SALAD

1 head iceberg lettuce, cut in
  bite-size pieces
2 tomatoes, quartered
2 stalks celery, chopped
¼ pound provolone cheese, cut
  in slivers

4 salami slices, chopped
1 cucumber, chopped
½ cup olive oil
3 to 4 tablespoons vinegar
Salt and freshly ground black
  pepper

Place lettuce, tomatoes, celery, cheese, salami, and cucumbers in a large salad bowl. Chill. Just before serving, pour oil, vinegar, and salt and pepper to taste over ingredients; toss untill dressing and ingredients are well blended.

SERVES: 6 to 8

Quaglie di Melanzane

EGGPLANT QUAILS

Small oval eggplants are sliced in fans and deep-fried. The result looks like quails in size, shape, and color. They're as eye-appealing and mellow as a Sicilian sunset.

6 *very small* oval eggplants
Salt
Flour

1½ quarts vegetable oil
Onion and garlic salt
Parsley

Cut 1 inch from stem end of eggplants and discard. Starting at other end, pare off skins with a sharp knife, to within 1 inch of stem ends. Lay eggplants on their sides; starting directly below remaining 1 inch of skin, slice through lengthwise, sectioning every ¼ inch (leave sections attached to stem end). Spread sections apart and sprinkle liberally with salt; drain in colander for 30 minutes. Squeeze eggplants gently to extract as much water as possible; rinse with cold water and dry thoroughly. Dredge in flour and set aside.

Heat oil in frying kettle to 370° F. (a small piece of bread browns evenly in 1 minute). Shake excess flour from eggplants and drop carefully into hot oil. Deep-fry, turning frequently, until golden in color and crisp—8 to 10 minutes. Drain on absorbent paper and sprinkle lightly with onion and garlic salt. Arrange on a warm platter and garnish with parsley.

SERVES: 6

Insalata di Pomodori e Formaggio
SNOW-TOPPED TOMATO SALAD

Ricotta salata cheese is as white as snow; when grated over thin slices of tomatoes, it resembles fresh-fallen snow.

4 ripe medium tomatoes, thinly
  sliced
2 inner stalks celery with tops,
  chopped
Olive oil

Freshly ground black pepper
⅓ cup grated ricotta salata
  cheese
Fresh mint

Arrange tomato slices on serving plate, overlapping them slightly. Sprinkle with celery, oil, and pepper to taste. Cover with cheese and garnish with fresh mint.

SERVES: 4 to 6

Insalata di Uova e Pomodori
EGG AND TOMATO SALAD SUPREME

Special mention goes to this salad for its nourishing yumminess. It's also great as a sandwich filling with whole wheat or pumpernickel bread.

4 hard-cooked eggs, quartered
2 medium tomatoes, quartered
5 scallions, chopped
5 or 6 basil leaves, chopped (or
  1 teaspoon dried)

2 tablespoons olive oil
1 tablespoon vinegar
Salt and freshly ground black
  pepper

Toss eggs, tomatoes, scallions, and basil together with olive oil and vinegar. Salt and pepper to taste. Serve on a bed of romaine or iceberg lettuce.

SERVES: 2 to 4

Funghi Arrosto con Pignoli

BAKED MUSHROOMS AND PINE NUTS

2 pounds extra-large mushrooms
1 lemon, cut in half
Olive oil
2 cloves garlic, minced

¼ to ⅓ cup pine nuts (pignoli)
Freshly ground sea salt
Freshly ground black pepper

Preheat oven to 400° F. Hand-pick mushrooms, selecting the very largest available. Remove stems and reserve for use in another recipe. Wash caps well and carefully with cold water. Drain and rub outside skins with lemon.

Place mushrooms (insides facing up) in an oiled shallow baking pan. Sprinkle with garlic, pine nuts, and sea salt and pepper to taste. Bake for 10 minutes. Place pan under hot broiler for 2 minutes.

SERVES: 4 to 6

Broccoli Affogati

SMOTHERED CAULIFLOWER

Cauliflower in Sicily is the same as in the United States, except that another variety, pale green in color, is also cultivated. This variety is sometimes called *broccoli* in Italian.

Olive oil
1 small bunch scallions, chopped
2 10-ounce packages frozen
  cauliflower, thawed
⅓ cup Romano cheese, cut in
  slivers

⅓ cup minced parsley
1 cup Italian-style bread
  crumbs
6 anchovies, chopped
¼ cup dry, red wine

In a heavy saucepan, heat 2 tablespoons olive oil and sauté scallions until lightly browned—about 3 minutes. Remove and set aside.

Add a layer of cauliflower to same saucepan and sprinkle with some cheese, parsley, bread crumbs, anchovies, and scallions. Continue layering until all ingredients are used. Cover and cook slowly, over moderate heat, for 10 minutes. Pour in wine; cover and cook 10 minutes longer. All liquid should be evaporated; if not, raise heat for a few minutes to do so. Do not stir cauliflower during cooking.

SERVES: 6 to 8

Zucchine in Agrodolce
SWEET AND SOUR ZUCCHINI

3 tablespoons olive oil	Salt and black pepper
2 cloves garlic, crushed	1 tablespoon vinegar
4 medium zucchini, thinly sliced	¼ cup water
3 tablespoons pine nuts (pignoli)	
2 tablespoons golden Sultana raisins, softened in water, drained	

In a large skillet, heat oil and sauté garlic for 2 minutes. Add zucchini and sauté on both sides until golden. Sprinkle with pine nuts, raisins, and salt and pepper to taste and simmer for 3 minutes.

Mix vinegar with water and pour into skillet; cover and simmer slowly until zucchini is tender—about 10 minutes. Discard garlic; cool and serve at room temperature.

SERVES: 4

Panelle Croccre
CHICK-PEA CROQUETTES

Panelle croccre, sold in Palermo exclusively, are shouted from fry stands like outbursts of joy. These flat and crispy croquettes are made with chick-pea flour, water, and salt. They require skill and are rather time-consuming to make, but a tastier facsimile can be made easily with canned chick-peas and seasonings. In Palermo, *panelle* are sold sandwiched between crusty rolls, but I like to serve them as an *hors d'oeuvre* or accompanying fish and meat dishes.

1 No. 2 can chick-peas	2 tablespoons flour
1 small onion, chopped fine	¼ cup olive oil
4 sprigs parsley, minced	1 lemon
½ teaspoon salt	Freshly ground black pepper

Drain chick-peas, reserving 2 tablespoons liquid. Blend or mash chick-peas with liquid until smooth. Add onion, parsley, salt, and flour and stir until well mixed.

Heat oil in a large skillet; slip rounded tablespoons of chick-pea mixture into hot oil (push mixture off spoon with spatula). Fry until golden—about 3 minutes on each side. Drain on absorbent paper and keep warm while remainder are frying. Squeeze lemon over croquettes and season with freshly ground pepper. Serve hot or at room temperature.

SERVES: 4 to 6

Peperoni Gialli e Rossi Ripieni
STUFFED SUNSET PEPPERS

3 large green peppers	1 small onion, minced
3 large red peppers	1 clove garlic, minced
1 pound ground beef	1 tablespoon orégano
1 cup bread crumbs	1 teaspoon salt
1/3 cup grated Parmesan cheese	1/4 teaspoon black pepper
2 eggs	Olive oil

Remove and discard stems, seeds, and sponges from peppers. Rinse with cold water; drain; set aside. Preheat oven to 350° F.

Combine ground beef with bread crumbs, grated cheese, eggs, onion, garlic, orégano, salt, and pepper. Fill peppers with meat mixture.

Brush skins of peppers with oil and place in a casserole with 2 tablespoons olive oil. Bake until peppers are tender—30 to 40 minutes. Serve hot or at room temperature.

SERVES: 6

VARIATION: Dice a small eggplant (about 1 pound); salt and drain for 15 minutes. Wash off salt and dry with absorbent paper. Sauté in 1/4 cup hot oil until brown and crispy. Fill peppers with eggplant and 1 cup chopped mozzarella cheese. Bake as directed above.

Insalata di Fagiolini alla Lucia
LUCIA'S STRING BEAN SALAD

1 pound fresh string beans	1 medium red onion, sliced,
1/4 cup olive oil	separated into rings
Juice of 1 large lemon	
Freshly ground sea salt and	
black pepper	

Snap off and discard stem ends of string beans. Rinse well with cold water. In a kettle, bring 1½ quarts water to a boil; drop in string beans; cover and boil gently until string beans are tender but firm—10 to 15 minutes. Drain; while string beans are still warm, pour oil and lemon juice over them; grind salt and pepper to taste. Cool at room temperature.

When ready to serve, add onion rings and toss until ingredients are intermixed. Serve at room temperature or chill.

SERVES: 4

Peperoni Ripieni con Salciccia alla Fratello Vincenzo
BROTHER VINCENT'S SAUSAGE-STUFFED PEPPERS

4 large green peppers
Olive oil
6 to 8 Italian sausage patties or links
1 medium onion, chopped fine

1 No. 2 can whole tomatoes, chopped
Freshly ground sea salt and black pepper

Remove and discard stems, seeds, and membranes from peppers. Rinse with cold water and dry with absorbent paper. Set aside.

In a skillet, heat 2 tablespoons olive oil; break up sausage patties or links (remove casings) and brown lightly on all sides—about 5 minutes. Stuff peppers with sausage meat.

In same skillet, sauté onions in 2 tablespoons oil for 3 minutes. Add peppers and brown lightly on all sides. Cover and simmer for 10 minutes. Pour tomatoes over peppers; salt and pepper to taste and stir. Simmer for 10 to 15 minutes. Serve hot or at room temperature.

SERVES: 4

Zucchine con Formaggio al Forno
BAKED CHEESE ZUCCHINI

3 small zucchini
6 tablespoons softened butter
6 tablespoons grated Parmesan cheese

Salt and freshly ground black pepper

Preheat oven to 400° F.

Remove and discard stems from zucchini. Wash with cold water; drain. Slice zucchini in half, lengthwise. With palate knife, spread 1 tablespoon butter on each half. Sprinkle with cheese (about 1 tablespoon per half), salt lightly, and add pepper to taste.

Bake in a hot oven at 400° F. until zucchini are tender—15 to 20 minutes.

SERVES: 6

Cipolline all'Origano
HERBED ONION PEARLS

12 small white onions	¼ teaspoon white pepper
Dried orégano	3 tablespoons butter, melted
½ teaspoon salt	

Peel onions carefully and remove cores. Place in a heavy saucepan and sprinkle with 1 teaspoon orégano, salt, and pepper. Cover with water and boil, uncovered, over medium heat, until onions are tender but firm—15 to 20 minutes. Drain. Small particles of orégano will adhere to onions; do not remove. Blend ½ teaspoon orégano with melted butter and add to onions, stirring gently. Serve hot as a side vegetable. Orégano and butter give a mild and lingering flavor to these large edible pearls.

SERVES: 4

Fagiolini Casalinghi al Pomodoro
HOME-STYLE STRING BEANS AND TOMATOES

1½ pounds fresh string beans	1 tablespoon fresh minced basil
1 medium onion, chopped	(or 1 teaspoon dried)
¼ cup olive oil	1 teaspoon salt
2 cups fresh or canned tomatoes, chopped	¼ teaspoon black pepper

Snap off and discard string bean stems. Rinse beans well with cold water and drain. In a saucepan, sauté onion in hot oil for 5 minutes. Add string beans, tomatoes, basil, salt, and pepper; stir. Bring to a boil, cover, lower heat, and simmer slowly until beans are tender but firm—25 to 30 minutes. Serve hot or at room temperature.

SERVES: 4 to 6

Involtini di Prosciutto e Scarola
HAM AND ESCAROLE ROLL-UPS

1 head escarole (about 1½ pounds)	¼ cup grated Parmesan cheese
	2 tablespoons minced parsley
2½ cups water	½ teaspoon salt
1 teaspoon salt	¼ teaspoon black pepper
4 slices prosciutto or boiled ham	Olive oil
1 cup bread crumbs	1 clove garlic, minced

Wash escarole well and place in kettle. Cover with water and salt and boil gently until escarole is tender—20 to 30 minutes. Drain and reserve ½ cup liquid. When cool, cut into quarters; remove core from each quarter. Place escarole quarters on prosciutto slices.

Combine bread crumbs, cheese, parsley, salt, and pepper. Spread ¼ cup bread crumb mixture over each escarole quarter; moisten bread crumb mixture lightly with oil. Roll ham and escarole mixture together, jelly-roll fashion; tie with thread or secure with toothpicks. Set aside.

Heat 2 tablespoons oil in a skillet and sauté garlic for 2 minutes. Add roll-ups and brown lightly on all sides. Pour in reserved liquid; cover and simmer 8 to 10 minutes. Discard thread or toothpicks and serve hot.

SERVES: 4

VARIATION: Boil escarole and quarter as directed. Spread with cooked sausage meat (1 link or patty per quarter); roll and continue as directed above.

Crocchette di Cavoli
CABBAGE CROQUETTES

1 medium head cabbage   ⅓ cup grated Parmesan cheese
1½ quarts water   2 tablespoons flour
1 egg   ½ teaspoon salt
6 sprigs parsley, minced   ¼ teaspoon black pepper
1 small onion, minced   ¼ cup olive oil

Cut cabbage in quarters; remove core from each piece. Wash with cold water; place in a kettle and cover with water. Bring to a boil and boil gently, uncovered, until cabbage is tender—20 to 30 minutes. Drain; cool; chop.

Combine chopped cabbage with egg, parsley, onions, cheese, flour, salt, and pepper. Heat oil in a skillet and slip rounded tablespoons of cabbage mixture into hot oil. Flatten croquettes slightly with spatula; fry until golden—3 to 5 minutes on each side. Add more oil to skillet if necessary. Serve hot.

SERVES: 6

Cavolo in Padella
SAVORY SKILLET CABBAGE

Savory Skillet Cabbage has been in the annals of my family for over two centuries. It's simply delicious; even vegetable haters have succumbed to its natural charms.

¼ cup olive oil   ½ cup water
1 medium onion, chopped fine   Salt and black pepper
1 medium head cabbage,   ¼ pound Romano cheese, cut
    shredded   in slivers
2 carrots, sliced

In a large skillet or electric frying pan, heat oil and sauté onions for 3 minutes. Add shredded cabbage and carrots and sauté for 5 to 8 minutes, turning and stirring frequently. Pour in water and salt and pepper to taste. Sprinkle cabbage with cheese slivers; cover and simmer slowly, turning occasionally, until cabbage is tender—20 to 30 minutes.

SERVES: 6 to 8

Melanzane Farcite

SPICY EGGPLANT HALVES

3 medium eggplants
¼ cup olive oil
1 medium onion, chopped
1 large tomato, skinned, chopped
½ teaspoon salt
¼ teaspoon black pepper
6 anchovies, chopped (reserve oil)

6 black Italian or Greek olives, pitted, chopped
2 tablespoons capers
1 teaspoon orégano
⅓ cup grated caciocavallo cheese
⅓ cup bread crumbs

Remove and discard stems from eggplants. Cut them in half, lengthwise. Remove pulp with grapefruit knife and spoon, leaving shells ½ inch thick. Chop pulp and set aside with shells. Preheat oven to 400° F.

In a skillet, heat oil and sauté onion until soft. Add eggplant pulp and sauté until lightly browned—5 to 8 minutes. Stir in tomato, salt, pepper, anchovies, olives, capers, and orégano. Add more oil if necessary and simmer mixture for 10 minutes.

Stuff eggplant shells with mixture. Combine cheese and bread crumbs; sprinkle over stuffing. Sprinkle bread crumb mixture with reserved anchovy oil. Place shells in an oiled baking pan; bake until tender and browned—30 to 40 minutes. Serve hot or at room temperature.

SERVES: 6

Carciofini al Forno

SNAPPY ARTICHOKE HEARTS

3 tablespoons olive oil
2 10-ounce packages frozen artichoke hearts, thawed (or 2 No. 2 cans artichoke hearts, drained)

⅔ cup Italian-style bread crumbs
2 cloves garlic, minced
1 2-ounce can anchovies

Pour olive oil in a shallow casserole. Perheat oven to 400° F. Add artichoke hearts; turn to coat sides with oil. Sprinkle with bread crumbs, garlic, anchovies, and anchovy oil. Bake 20 to 25 minutes.

SERVES: 6 to 8

Frittura di Carciofini

CRISP-FRIED ARTICHOKE HEARTS

1½ cups bread crumbs
⅓ cup grated Parmesan cheese
2 tablespoons minced parsley
⅛ teaspoon onion salt
¼ teaspoon garlic salt
Freshly ground black pepper

2 10-ounce packages frozen artichoke hearts, thawed (or 2 No. 2 cans artichoke hearts, drained)
2 or 3 eggs, slightly beaten
1½ quarts vegetable oil for deep-frying

Combine bread crumbs, cheese, parsley, onion salt, garlic salt, and pepper to taste. Dip artichoke hearts first in eggs, then in bread crumb mixture, coating well on both sides.

Heat oil in a frying kettle to 370° F. (a small piece of bread browns evenly in 1 minute). Add artichoke hearts, a few at a time, and fry until golden—3 to 5 minutes on each side. Remove with slotted spoon and drain on absorbent paper. Serve hot.

SERVES: 6 to 8

TIP: Deep-fried foods should always be served hot; keep food warm in oven at 250° F. until all pieces are fried.

Cardune Fritte

FRIED CARDOONS

1 large bunch cardoons
1 lemon, cut in half
Flour

Olive oil
Salt and freshly ground black pepper

Remove and discard roots, leaves, and tough outer stalks, and scrape strings from cardoons. Wash well with cold running water; drain. Cut stalks into 4-inch pieces; rub cut ends with lemon to prevent discoloration.

Place stalks in a kettle; cover with lightly salted water and bring to a boil. Boil gently until cardoons are tender—35 to 45 minutes. Drain. Dredge stalks in flour and pan fry in ½ inch hot oil until golden on both sides. Drain on absorbent paper; salt and pepper to taste; serve hot.

SERVES: 4 to 6

NOTE: *Cardune* (Sicilian dialect) are called *cardi* in Italian, and in English they are also referred to as burdocks.

Insalata d'Arugula e Filetti di Pomodori
ARUGULA AND LITTLE BEEFIES SALAD

Italians and gourmets eat arugula "straight," as suggested in this recipe. The variation is recommended for first-time arugula skeptics.

2 bunches arugula	Juice of 1 lemon
4 plum tomatoes (little beefies), sliced	Salt and freshly ground black pepper
⅓ cup olive or salad oil	

Remove and discard root ends from arugula. Wash well with cold water; drain; dry with absorbent paper being careful not to crush or bruise leaves. Break into bite-size pieces and chill with tomatoes for at least 30 minutes. Just before serving, mix arugula and tomatoes with oil, lemon juice, and salt and pepper to taste.

SERVES: 4

VARIATION: Toss ½ bunch arugula (chopped), 1 head romaine lettuce, 1 cup artichoke hearts (in marinade), and 6 to 8 black olives with 1 teaspoon orégano, ⅓ to ½ cup olive oil, 2 to 3 tablespoons vinegar, and salt and pepper to taste.

NOTE: Arugula or rugula is a very tasty salad green with a most unusual flavor. Although Italian in origin, it is also called rocket, rocket cress, or garden rocket in various sections of the country.

Ricci di Melanzane al Forno

BAKED EGGPLANT URCHINS

1 medium onion, chopped	6 small oval eggplants
Olive oil	½ pound caciocavallo cheese,
1 No. 2 can tomato purée	cut in slivers
½ cup water	1 can anchovies, chopped
½ teaspoon salt	½ cup chopped celery leaves
⅛ teaspoon black pepper	2 cloves garlic, cut in half

In a saucepan, sauté onions in 2 tablespoons oil until they are soft. Pour in tomato purée, water, salt, and pepper. Simmer slowly for 10 to 15 minutes. Preheat oven to 400° F.

While sauce is simmering, remove stems from eggplants and pare skin, from top to bottom, every other half inch. With sharp knife, make slits in eggplants at random and fill with cheese slivers, anchovies, and celery leaves. Tie each eggplant with string to keep stuffing enclosed. In a skillet, heat 2 tablespoons olive oil and sauté garlic halves for 2 minutes. Add eggplants and brown lightly on all sides. Discard garlic.

Transfer eggplants to a casserole. Pour sauce over them and bake 30 to 40 minutes. Remove strings before serving.

SERVES: 6

Zucchine al Formaggio

CHEESED ZUCCHINI

2 tablespoons olive oil	Salt and freshly ground black
1 small onion, minced	pepper
1½ pounds zucchini, thinly	2 tablespoons water
sliced	
2 ounces Romano cheese, cut in	
slivers	

In a large skillet, heat oil and sauté onion until golden. Add zucchini and brown lightly on both sides. Sprinkle cheese slivers over slices; season with salt and pepper to taste. Add water; cover and simmer until zucchini is tender and translucent—about 10 minutes.

SERVES: 4

Bieda e Pomodori in Padella

SWISS CHARD AND TOMATO MEDLEY

1 large Swiss chard (about 1½   2 tablespoons olive oil
   pounds)   1 cup canned tomatoes, chopped
Salt   Freshly ground black pepper
1 small onion, chopped

Remove and discard core and bruised and tough outer leaves from Swiss chard. Wash with cold water and drain. With a sharp knife, separate stalks from leaves and cut stalks into 2-inch pieces. Place stalks in a small kettle; cover with salted water and boil gently until stalks are tender—about 10 minutes. Add leaves and cook 5 minutes longer. Drain.

In a saucepan, sauté onion in oil for 3 minutes. Pour in tomatoes and simmer for 5 minutes. Add Swiss chard and salt and pepper to taste, and simmer for 5 minutes longer.

Pomodori alla Piana degli Albanesi

GRECIAN TOMATOES

1 cup rice   3 tablespoons pine nuts
2 cups water'   (pignoli)
Salt   1 tablespoon minced basil
1 tablespoon butter   (fresh or dried)
6 large, ripe tomatoes   Olive oil

In a saucepan, combine rice, water, 1 teaspoon salt, and butter. Bring to a boil; stir well; cover; lower heat; simmer slowly until water has been absorbed—15 to 20 minutes. Preheat oven to 400° F.

Cut a ½-inch slice across stem end of each tomato and discard. Hollow centers with grapefruit knife and spoon, leaving ½-inch shells. Chop pulp and mix with cooked rice, pine nuts, basil, 2 tablespoons olive oil, and salt to taste. Brush shells with oil and place in an oiled casserole. Bake for 10 to 15 minutes. Baste once or twice with drippings during baking. Serve warm or at room temperature.

SERVES: 6

Pomodori Conditi
TOMATO RELISH

2 cups Italian parsley (flat leaf), chopped
3 medium ripe tomatoes, chopped
6 scallions, chopped

Juice of 2 lemons
2 to 4 tablespoons olive oil
Salt and freshly ground black pepper
4 anchovies, chopped (optional)

Toss parsley, tomatoes, and scallions together. Add lemon juice, oil, and salt and pepper to taste; mix well. Garnish with anchovies if desired.

SERVES: 4 to 6

Melanzane alla Parmigiana
EGGPLANT PARMESAN

This version of eggplant Parmesan is baked in a single layer, permitting its blending flavors to be distinguished.

2 eggplants (about 3 pounds)
Salt
Olive oil
1 onion, chopped
1 clove garlic, cut in half
1 8-ounce can tomato purée
½ cup water
3 fresh basil leaves (or 1 teaspoon dried)

Freshly ground black pepper
2 cloves garlic, minced
1 pound mozzarella cheese, cut in slices
½ cup grated Romano cheese
Fresh basil leaves

Remove stems from eggplants; cut into ½-inch slices and salt liberally. Drain for 1 hour on absorbent paper, weighted down with bread board.

Heat 2 tablespoons oil in a saucepan and sauté onion and garlic halves for 3 minutes. Add tomato purée, water, basil, ½ teaspoon salt, and ⅛ teaspoon pepper. Bring to a boil, cover, and simmer for 15 to 20 minutes. Preheat oven to 400° F.

Rinse salt off eggplant slices and dry with absorbent paper. In a large skillet, heat ¼ cup oil and sauté minced garlic for 2 minutes. Fry slices until golden—3 to 5 minutes on each side. Add more oil if necessary. Drain on absorbent paper.

Arrange fried eggplant slices on an oiled baking pan; spread with 1 tablespoon sauce, 1 slice mozzarella, and 1 teaspoon grated cheese per slice. Bake until cheese is melted and lightly browned and eggplant slices are cooked through—10 to 15 minutes. Arrange slices on a heated serving platter; season with freshly ground pepper to taste and garnish with fresh basil leaves.

SERVES: 6 to 8

Peperonata
SWEET PEPPER FRY

Olive oil
2 large green peppers, cut in 2-inch strips
2 large red peppers, cut in 2-inch strips
2 large onions, chopped
1 tablespoon wine vinegar

2 tablespoons water
2 large ripe tomatoes, skinned, chopped, seeded
½ cup green Sicilian olives, pitted, chopped
Salt

In a large skillet, heat ¼ cup olive oil; add green and red peppers and sauté for 5 minutes. Add onions and sauté 5 minutes longer. Mix vinegar with water and pour over pepper mixture. Stir in tomatoes, olives, and salt to taste. Cover and simmer slowly until peppers and onions are cooked—15 to 20 minutes.

SERVES: 4 to 6

Insalata di Ceci
CHICK-PEA SALAD

2 No. 2 cans chick-peas, drained
1 bunch scallions, chopped
¼ cup chopped parsley

Juice of 1 lemon
⅓ cup olive or salad oil
Salt and freshly ground pepper

Mix ingredients together. Let stand 30 minutes before serving (always serve at room temperature).

SERVES: 4 to 6

Tortino di Carciofini
DELICATE-SHARP ARTICHOKE PIE

CRUST:
2 cups sifted flour
Dash of salt
⅔ cup lard (or ¾ cup
   shortening)
⅓ cup ice water

FILLING:
2 cloves garlic, minced
2 tablespoons olive oil
2 10-ounce packages frozen
   artichoke hearts, thawed
4 eggs, slightly beaten
½ cup grated caciocavallo
   cheese
8 ounces mozzarella, chopped
Salt and freshly ground black
   pepper

Place flour and salt in mixing bowl; cut in lard with pastry blender or two knives until mixture resembles small peas. Sprinkle ice water, a tablespoon at a time, over mixture, adding to driest part each time. Mix gently with fork until all is moistened. Gather up with fingers, form into ball. Divide in half.

Roll one half between two pieces of waxed paper to ⅛-inch thickness and 1 inch larger than a 9-inch pie pan. Fold in half and fit loosely into pan, working gently and carefully. Set aside. For top crust, roll out other half as directed above and set aside.

Preheat oven to 450° F.

Sauté garlic in hot oil for 2 minutes. Add artichoke hearts and brown lightly on both sides. Transfer to mixing bowl and stir in eggs, caciocavallo, and mozzarella. Season with salt and pepper to taste. Pour mixture into pie pan. Cover with top crust; trim off all but ½ inch of excess dough. Turn under, sealing the two crusts together. Flute with index finger, pressing dough gently between thumb and index finger of other hand. With point of sharp knife, cut air holes in design of your choice on top crust. Bake at 450° F. for 15 minutes; reduce heat to 350° F. and bake until golden brown—about 30 minutes.

SERVES: 6 to 8

NOTE: Artichoke pie is perfect as a hot hors d'oeuvre, a first course, or a luncheon meal. It may be frozen and thawed out 1 hour in advance of serving. Then, heat in a preheated oven at 350° F. for 10 to 15 minutes.

Insalata di Lenticchie

PEBBLE (LENTIL) SALAD

1 pound lentils	1 cup chopped parsley
Water	1 cup olive or salad oil
1 tablespoon salt	Juice of 1 to 2 large lemons
1 medium onion, quartered	Salt
1 medium red onion, sliced, separated into rings	Freshly ground black pepper

Rinse lentils and remove bits of rock. Cover with water and soak for 30 minutes. (If processed lentils are used, soaking is not necessary.) Drain; cover with fresh water to 2 inches above lentils; add 1 tablespoon salt and onion quarters. Bring to a boil; cover and simmer until lentils are tender but not mushy—20 to 30 minutes. Drain; discard onions and chill.

Put chilled lentils in a large salad bowl; mix with onion rings, parsley, olive oil, lemon juice, and salt and pepper to taste.

SERVES: 6 to 8

Spinaci alla Muffoletto

SPINACH BOUQUET À LA MUFFOLETTO

2 pounds fresh spinach	⅓ cup Italian-style bread crumbs
¼ cup water	
2 to 4 tablespoons olive oil	2 tablespoons grated Parmesan cheese
Salt	
Freshly ground black pepper	Garlic salt

Remove tough stems, roots, and discolored leaves from spinach. Put leaves in colander and rinse several times with cool water until free of sand.

Pour water into a large kettle; add spinach; cover and bring to a boil. Lower heat and cook only 3 to 5 minutes. Turn heat off; stir in oil, salt and pepper to taste.

Combine bread crumbs with cheese and garlic salt and pepper to taste. Cover spinach with bread crumb mixture; moisten with a sprinkling of olive oil. Cover and let stand 10 minutes before serving.

SERVES: 4

Olive Condite

OLIVE RELISH

1 pound green Sicilian olives, pitted, crushed
2 stalks celery with leaves (inner stalks), chopped fine
1 medium onion, chopped
⅓ cup olive or salad oil
3 tablespoons wine vinegar
Salt and freshly ground black pepper
2 cloves garlic, crushed

Combine ingredients and toss, coating vegetables well with salad dressing. Let stand at room temperature for at least 2 hours before serving.

SERVES: 6

Melanzane ai Quattro Formaggi

EGGPLANT-CHEESE QUARTET

This savory casserole alternates eggplant slices, tomato sauce, and a quartet of cheeses into a rich, sharp and "meaty" combination.

4 medium eggplants
Salt
Olive oil
1 medium onion, chopped
1 clove garlic, minced
2 cups fresh or canned tomatoes skinned, chopped
4 sprigs fresh mint (or 1 tablespoon dried)
¼ teaspoon black pepper
¼ pound provolone cheese, sliced
¼ pound mozzarella cheese, diced
¼ pound natural Gruyère or Swiss cheese, chopped
¼ pound grated Parmesan cheese
¼ cup butter

Remove stems from eggplants and cut into ½-inch slices. Salt liberally on both sides and place on absorbent paper, weighted down with a heavy platter or board. Drain for 1 hour. Rinse salt off and dry slices with absorbent paper.

In a saucepan, heat 2 tablespoons olive oil and sauté onions and garlic for 3 minutes. Pour in tomatoes, mint, and pepper; simmer for 10 to 15 minutes. Preheat oven to 350° F.

In a large skillet, heat ¼ cup oil and brown eggplant slices on both sides. (Add more oil during browning, if necessary.) Drain on absorbent paper.

In a buttered casserole, spread one ladle of sauce and one layer eggplant slices; spoon sauce over them and cover with provolone slices. Add a second layer of eggplant slices, sauce, and mozzarella cubes. Cover with a third layer of eggplant slices, sauce, and Gruyère cheese. End with a fourth layer of eggplant slices, sauce, and grated Parmesan cheese; dot with butter. Bake for 30 to 40 minutes. Serve hot or at room temperature as an appetizer, entrée, or side vegetable.

SERVES: 6 to 8

Funghi Ripieni al Forno
STUFFED MUSHROOM CAPFULS

24 large mushrooms	¼ cup grated Romano cheese
Lemon juice	¼ cup minced parsley
¼ cup olive oil	¼ teaspoon salt
1 clove garlic, minced	⅛ teaspoon black pepper
1 small onion, minced	Olive oil
1 cup bread crumbs	

Preheat oven to 350° F.

Brush baking pan with oil. Wash mushrooms with cold water. Remove stems; chop finely and reserve. Put caps on baking pan, stem side up. Sprinkle with lemon juice; set aside.

Heat oil in a skillet; sauté mushroom stems, garlic, and onion for 5 minutes. Remove from heat and stir in bread crumbs, cheese, parsley, salt, and pepper. Fill caps with mixture and sprinkle with olive oil. Bake for 15 minutes.

SERVES: 6

Broccoli Fra Diavolo
DEVILED BROCCOLI

2 tablespoons olive oil	Flour
2 cloves garlic, minced	½ teaspoon crushed red pepper
2 10-ounce packages frozen broccoli, thawed	Salt

In a skillet, heat oil and sauté garlic for 2 minutes. Dredge broccoli in flour and fry in hot oil until lightly browned on all sides. Sprinkle with red pepper and salt to taste; cover and cook over low heat until broccoli is tender—8 to 10 minutes.

SERVES: 6 to 8

Carote al Marsala

CARAMELIZED CARROTS WITH MARSALA

¼ cup butter	¼ cup dry Marsala wine
2 No. 2 cans whole baby carrots, drained	1 teaspoon sugar
	Salt

In a saucepan, melt butter; add carrots and simmer for 3 minutes. Add Marsala wine, sugar, and salt to taste. Cook slowly, turning occasionally, over moderate heat until sauce is reduced by one half—5 to 8 minutes.

SERVES: 4 to 6

NOTE: Use fresh Car-ettes (2 bunches) instead of canned carrots. Scrape Car-ettes; cover with water and boil gently until tender— about 8 to 10 minutes. Continue as directed above.

Antipasto di Peperoni e Acciughe

ANTIPASTO ANCHOVY-PEPPERS

Here's a simple and popular antipasto that's colorful and zesty. It's also an excellent companion to beef and veal dishes.

4 large red or green peppers	1 can anchovies
2 tablespoons olive oil	Freshly ground black pepper

Preheat oven to 400° F.

Cut peppers in half; remove and discard stems, seeds, and sponges. Rinse with cold water and dry with absorbent paper. Place peppers, skin side up, under a hot broiler until skins are browned—3 to 5 minutes. Cool. Remove skins by peeling or rubbing them off; cut peppers in strips and arrange in a shallow baking dish with olive oil and oil from anchovies.

Bake for 10 minutes. Cool; arrange on individual serving plates topped with anchovies and freshly ground pepper to taste.

SERVES: 6 to 8

Ortaggi Freddi alla Giardiniera
PICKLED GARDEN VEGETABLES

1 small head cauliflower, cut in flowerets, sliced
2 carrots, cut into 2×½-inch strips
2 stalks celery, cut in 1-inch slices
1 large green pepper, cut in 2-inch strips
1 medium red pepper, chopped
1 clove garlic, crushed
½ teaspoon thyme
½ teaspoon celery salt
2 tablespoons capers
½ teaspoon ground savory
1 bay leaf
1 cup water
1 cup olive or salad oil
1 teaspoon salt
4 peppercorns, crushed
2 tablespoons sugar
1 cup cider vinegar
½ teaspoon powdered saffron
Freshly ground black pepper

In a large kettle, combine ingredients and stir. Bring to a boil, cover, and simmer for 5 to 8 minutes (vegetables should be firm). Cool; marinate in refrigerator for at least 4 hours or overnight. Drain well and sprinkle with freshly ground pepper before serving. Pickled garden vegetables are served as an antipasto, relish, or salad.

SERVES: 6 to 8

Spicchi d'Arancioe Cipolle in Insalata
ORANGE AND ONION SALAD

Blood oranges are cultivated in Sicily, and an occasional supply is found in American markets during the winter months. At any rate, this salad is just as refreshing when made with navel or eating oranges.

4 large navel oranges, chilled
1 medium red onion, sliced, separated into rings
¼ cup olive or salad oil
Salt and freshly ground black pepper

Peel oranges with sharp paring knife as you would peel an apple. Starting at either end, peel below skin, removing inner membrane as well as skin. Cut out orange sections and place in a bowl. Add onion rings, oil, salt, and pepper to taste. Toss well so as to coat oranges and onions with salad dressing evenly. Let salad stand at room temperature for 30 minutes before serving.

SERVES: 4 to 6

Capunatina

EGGPLANT SALAD

Capunatina, the internationally famous eggplant medley, combines the gems of the Sicilian vegetable kingdom into a rich sweet and sour salad, served either warm or cold.

2 large ripe eggplants (about 3 pounds)
Salt
Olive oil
2 large onions, chopped
4 stalks celery, chopped
1 No. 2½ can whole tomatoes
2 fresh basil leaves (or 1 teaspoon dried)

1 teaspoon salt
½ teaspoon black pepper
½ cup capers
1 cup Italian green olives, pitted, chopped
1 tablespoon sugar
1½ tablespoons vinegar

Remove stems from eggplants and discard. Chop unpeeled eggplant and salt liberally; drain in colander for 1 hour. (Excess water and bitter flavor will drain off.) Rinse off salt and dry with absorbent paper. Set aside.

Heat 3 tablespoons olive oil in a large skillet; add onions and celery and sauté for 5 minutes. Pour in tomatoes; add basil, salt, and pepper. Simmer for 10 minutes. Add capers and olives and cook for 10 minutes longer. Set aside.

In another large skillet, sauté eggplant in ⅓ cup hot olive oil. (Add more oil if necessary to prevent it from sticking; eggplant absorbs a lot of oil as it cooks.) Combine sautéed eggplant with sauce mixture in a large saucepan, stirring until both are evenly mixed. Sprinkle sugar and vinegar over mixture and stir. Cover and simmer slowly for 10 to 15 minutes. Serve warm or cold as an appetizer, salad, or accompanying vegetable.

SERVES: 6 to 8

VARIATION: Add 3 tablespoons pine nuts (pignoli) and 3 tablespoons seedless black raisins to the basic recipe.

SAUCES

Sicilian sauces are like Sicilian women—honest and uncomplicated, but also piquant, distinct, and mellow. They are not sophisticated by nature, but they are certainly genuine in flavor and give value to any dish they embrace.

Unlike French sauces, they are simple to prepare and very basic indeed. The repertoire of Sicilian sauces is small, but resplendent in freshness and savoriness. Cream sauces are nonexistent in Sicily, except for *salsa besciamella* (white sauce), which is used as a filling in rice croquettes and baked pasta casseroles.

The honorable tomato plays the leading role in a bevy of sauces that marry pasta dishes successfully. *Sugo,* a tomato sauce made with a meat base, is the most popular tomato sauce. *Marinara* sauce, a fresh tomato and herb combination, is another traditional favorite that braces fish, pasta, and rice dishes particularly well.

Agrodolce (sweet and sour) sauces have as prominent a place in Sicilian cooking as tomato sauces. Their composition includes combinations of raisins or currants, wine or vinegar, capers, pine nuts, olive oil, herbs, and seasonings which add zing to bland vegetables, fish, poultry, and game.

Salmoriglio, a blending of olive oil, lemon juice, salt, pepper, garlic, and herbs, is an excellent marinade or basting sauce for fish and white meat roasts. Or it may be poured over sizzling grilled fish just before serving.

One last but typical popular sauce, made basically with anchovies, tomatoes, and bread crumbs, is used to savor spaghetti. Variations of anchovy sauce are created to blend with fish and meat.

Salmoriglio

LEMON SAUCE

Sicilians regularly pour salmoriglio over grilled, roasted or fried fish. Parsley is changed to orégano, basil or rosemary at will. Salmoriglio is also a good basic marinade for both fish and poultry.

1 cup olive oil
½ cup fresh lemon juice
2 cloves garlic, minced
¼ cup chopped parsley

1 teaspoon salt
¼ teaspoon freshly ground
   black pepper

Combine all ingredients and blend well. Lemon sauce may be made in advance and stored in the refrigerator. It must be left at room temperature for 1 hour before using.

SERVES: 4 to 6 (makes about 2 cups)

Ragù alla Siciliana

SICILIAN MEAT SAUCE

¼ cup olive oil
1 medium onion, chopped fine
2 cloves garlic, cut in half
3 stalks celery, chopped fine
1 pound stewing veal
½ pound pork (shoulder)

1 No. 2½ can tomato purée
1 cup water
1 teaspoon salt
¼ teaspoon pepper
1 tablespoon dried mint or basil
½ cup peas

Heat oil in a large saucepan and sauté onions, garlic, and celery for 3 to 5 minutes. Add veal and pork and brown on all sides. Pour in tomato purée, water, salt, pepper, and mint. Bring to a boil, cover, and simmer slowly until meat is tender—about 1 hour. Remove meat; cool and shred. Return to sauce and stir in peas. Simmer for 5 minutes longer. Correct seasoning if necessary and discard garlic before serving.

SERVES: 6 to 8 (makes about 2 quarts)

NOTE: This sauce is also called *grassato*.

Salsa di Acciughe

ANCHOVY SAUCE

Finfish, shellfish, spaghetti, and linguine are all marriageable partners for anchovy sauce. Their delicate and somewhat bland flavors balance and support the piquancy of the sauce.

½ cup butter
¼ cup olive oil
6 cloves garlic, sliced paper-thin

1 2-ounce can anchovies
Freshly ground black pepper

Melt butter over moderate heat; do not brown. Add olive oil, garlic, anchovies in their oil, and pepper to taste. Blend and cook until anchovies are dissolved. Pour over cooked fish, spaghetti, or linguine and serve immediately.

SERVES: 4

Salsa di Sesamo
SESAME SAUCE

1 cup dry white wine	½ teaspoon crushed red pepper
½ cup olive oil	1 teaspoon salt
⅓ cup sesame seeds, toasted	2 cloves garlic, minced

Combine and blend ingredients well. Pour over cooked fish or meat roasts. If used to baste roasts, do not toast sesame seeds in advance.

SERVES: 4 to 6 (makes about 2 cups)

Salsa al Pomodoro
RUBY SAUCE

This jewel of a sauce is ruby-red in color, thick and pulpy in texture, and sweet in taste. It's excellent over fresh or commercially made pastas, fish dishes, and poultry.

2 tablespoons olive oil	3 sprigs fresh basil (or 1
1 medium onion, chopped	tablespoon dried)
2 cloves garlic, cut in half	5 sprigs parsley
1 No. 2½ can plum or whole	1 teaspoon salt
tomatoes	¼ teaspoon black pepper
1 6-ounce can tomato paste	

Heat oil in saucepan and sauté onion and garlic until golden— about 3 minutes. Add tomatoes, tomato paste, basil, parsley, salt, and pepper and bring to a boil. Cover and simmer slowly for 1 hour. Correct seasoning if necessary. Discard garlic and parsley before serving.

YIELD: About 1½ quarts

Salsa di Conserva di Pomodori

WINTER'S TOMATO SAUCE

Winter's Tomato Sauce is economical during the winter months, when fresh tomatoes are expensive, but actually it is an ideal sauce all year round. It's so simple to prepare, and basic enough to be served with meat or fish dishes and over pasta, rice, and pizza.

3 tablespoons olive oil
1 large onion, chopped fine
3 cloves garlic, cut in half
2 7-ounce cans tomato paste
3 cups water

3 sprigs fresh mint (or 1 tablespoon dried)
1 teaspoon salt
¼ teaspoon pepper

In a large saucepan, heat oil and sauté onions and garlic until onion is soft. Add tomato paste and sauté for 3 minutes. Pour in water; season with mint, salt, and pepper. Bring to a boil; cover and simmer slowly for 30 to 45 minutes. Discard garlic and correct seasoning if necessary.

YIELD: About 1½ quarts

Salsa di Funghi e Pomodori

MUSHROOM AND TOMATO SAUCE

Mushroom and tomato sauce may be teamed with fish, poultry, spaghetti, and rice dishes.

2 tablespoons olive oil
1 medium onion, chopped
2 cloves garlic, cut in half
1 No. 3 can (2 pounds 3 ounces) plum tomatoes in purée (or 2 pounds fresh plum tomatoes)

¼ cup chopped Italian parsley (flat leaf)
1 teaspoon salt
¼ teaspoon pepper
½ pound mushrooms, sliced lengthwise

In a large saucepan, heat oil and sauté onion and garlic until golden—about 3 minutes. Add tomatoes, parsley, salt, and pepper and bring to a boil. Cover; lower heat and simmer slowly for 30 minutes. Add mushrooms and simmer 10 minutes longer. Correct seasoning if necessary and discard garlic before serving.

SERVES: 6 to 8 (makes about 2 quarts)

Salsa Marinara

QUICK SAUCE SAILOR STYLE

Quick and easy superlatively describe Salsa Marinara. Its fresh flavor adds a touch of spring and summer to pasta, fish, and poultry dishes.

2 tablespoons olive oil
1 bunch scallions, chopped fine
1 No. 3 can (2 pounds 3 ounces) whole tomatoes (or 2 pounds fresh)

4 sprigs fresh basil (or 1 tablespoon dried basil)
1 teaspoon salt
¼ teaspoon freshly ground black pepper

In a large saucepan, heat oil and sauté scallions for 3 to 5 minutes. Stir in whole tomatoes, basil, salt, and pepper. Bring to a boil; cover and simmer slowly for 30 minutes. Correct seasoning if necessary.

SERVES: 6 to 8 (makes about 2 quarts)

TIP: If fresh tomatoes are used, plunge them into boiling water for 1 to 2 minutes to facilitate removal of skins and stems.

Sugo di Carne e Pomodori

MEAT AND TOMATO SAUCE

Time-saving recipes are essential to every busy homemaker, but the proof of the pudding is in the eating. Meat and Tomato Sauce satisfies both these principles; it saves time and produces an excellent thick sauce.

2 tablespoons olive oil
1 medium onion, chopped fine
2 cloves garlic, cut in half
1½ pounds ground beef
1 No. 2½ can tomato purée

1 cup water
1 tablespoon dried orégano or basil
1 teaspoon salt
¼ teaspoon black pepper

Heat oil in a large saucepan and sauté onion and garlic until golden. Add ground beef and brown for 5 minutes, stirring frequently with spatula to separate meat and to brown evenly.

Pour in tomato purée, water, orégano, salt, and pepper. Bring to a boil; cover and simmer slowly for 1 hour. Discard garlic before serving. This thick, meaty sauce is excellent over ravioli, pizza, spaghetti, and lasagne.

SERVES: 6 to 8 (makes about 2 quarts)

THE SPICE
AND HERB RACK

Sicilian food is flavored with a pinch of discrimination and a dash of adventure. Americans overspice and overherb Italian cooking, thinking that's how it should be. Actually, Sicilians have a rather light hand in seasoning. Using a modicum of reasonably well-known herbs and spices, they brighten up a dish, making it more desirable. In other words, the natural flavor of the food is enhanced, not camouflaged or changed. Usually one or two herbs and spices are used for accent, or to make a dish sparkle. When more are blended, their flavors intermix smoothly and evenly.

Fresh herbs, such as rosemary, basil, mint, parsley, and orégano, are inexpensively and readily available in Sicily. It's possible to buy them in open markets or at wine and oil stores in almost any city. In the United States, Italian grocers carry a small variety of fresh herbs along with a large selection of dried and freeze-dried herbs.

A Sicilian spice and herb rack contains:

ANISETTA (ah-nee-set'-tah)

ANISE: An aromatic herb with a pleasant warm taste. Used principally in the manufacture of liqueurs, anise oil and anise seed are both used to flavor pastries, cookies, cakes, and breads. Anise is popular throughout Eruope, Greece, and the Middle East.

AGLIO (ahl'-yoh)

GARLIC: For centuries, garlic has been considered a bulb with miracle healing powers. Sicilians still consider it part of nature's medicine chest to cure intestinal disorders, worms, skin diseases, and wounds, and even to drive away evil spirits. Garlic's sturdy cloves, with their strong odor and flavor, are today employed chiefly for culinary purposes. Garlic is used in many sauces, salad dressings, meats, fish, poultry, game, and vegetables, *but sparingly*. The purpose is not to smother the flavor, but to enhance it.

BASILICO (bah-zee'-lee-koh)

BASIL: Although native to India, basil has been widely cultivated in Europe and particularly in Italy. I don't know of an Italian garden or windowsill without it. In fact, Italians would bottle the essence if they could, and sell it as a perfume—their love for basil is that strong. Tomatoes, cooked or raw, and basil make a delicious duet. Pizza, fish, salads, and meat are also nicely complemented with this herb.

CANNELLA (kahn-nell'-lah)

CINNAMON: Cinnamon stick is used more often than ground cinnamon; its highly aromatic brown bark occasionally flavors meats and game and often spices cakes, puddings, and pastries.

CAPPERI (kah'-pay-ree)

CAPERS: Capers, the unopened flower buds of low prickly shrubs, are small and drab green in color. They are grown in abundance principally in countries bordering on the Mediterranean Sea. Sicilian capers are much larger and meatier than those from any other part of the Mediterranean. Pickled or salted, they are added to sauces, and are particularly good with fish and tomatoes. They also add a nice accent to salads and are especially good when combined with green olives, celery, and onions.

CHIODO DI GAROFANO (kee-oh'-doh dee gah-roh-fah'-noh)

CLOVE: This nail-shaped spice, introduced to Europe by the Arabs, is actually the unexpanded bud of an evergreen tree. Dark brown in color and strong in flavor and aroma, cloves wake up desserts and accent game nicely.

CIPOLLA (chee-poll'-lah)

ONION: It would seem that Sicilians chop onions in and over every dish. They use a heavy hand with onions, which perhaps accounts for their piquant and strong bite in some dishes. Onions are plentiful and inexpensive and are often baked whole with a sprinkling of salt and pepper or stuffed for variation.

FINOCCHIO (*fee-nock'-kee-oh*)

FENNEL: Fennel is a fragrant, umbelliferous, perennial plant symbolizing flattery and heroism. It is completely edible, from its tiny aromatic seeds to its lacy, fragrant leaves. Usually the bulb is quartered, iced, and eaten raw like celery. The seeds are culled from the wild variety and added to meats' and fresh hot or sweet sausages. Fennel is available from November through early spring in Italian-American markets.

MAGGIORANA (*mahdj-djoh-rah'-nah*)

MARJORAM or ORÉGANO: Marjoram is a perennial plant of the mint family and of several species. Two varieties are used as the characteristic flavoring in many dishes:

1) *Origano,* or wild marjoram, has a strong, distinct aroma and is used primarily on pizza, meats, and fish.

2) *Maggiorana,* or sweet marjoram, is fragrant and aromatic, but is not as powerful as *origano*. It is added to soups, stews, and fish dishes.

MENTA (*men-tah'*)

MINT: This delicate herb gives the most welcome accent to fresh fruit drinks, fresh tomatoes and tomato sauces, fish, pizza, and many vegetables. There is no comparison in flavor and fragrance between fresh and dried mint. Fresh mint is available only during the spring and summer, and for the most part only in Italian markets. Therefore, I suggest growing it; it's worth it. Purchase some from a nursery or ask any Italian lady over forty to give you a few leaves from her garden. Mint roots easily and grows rapidly and abundantly; you can dry or freeze the excess for use in the winter months.

NOCE MOSCATA (*noh'-chay moss-kah-tah'*)

NUTMEG: Added to sweet pastries, ricotta dishes, and some pasta dishes. If ground just before using, greater zest and freshness will result.

OLIVE (*oh-lee'-vay*)

OLIVES: Olives are almost a national symbol of Italy. The olive tree flourishes well on the arid terrain of Sicily, providing her with one of the basic ingredients of the cuisine and also a thriving industry. Olive oil is used exclusively in cooking. Butter is rarely used, since milk from cows is used for cheese. For this reason, butter for many years was unknown to the masses. The most popular olives in Sicily are small, oil-cured black olives that remind me of prunes, for they have the same wrinkled skins and rich, dry condensed texture. Green olives are grown primarily around the areas of Mt. Etna and Catania. They are medium in size, a little bitter in flavor, and are packed whole or cracked (with pits removed) in plain brine or brine with spices.

PEPE (*pay'-pay*)

PEPPER: Freshly ground black pepper seems to be used almost exclusively in seasoning although red pepper appears occasionally. Both are aromatic, extremely hot, and pungent in taste.

PIGNOLI (*pee-nyoh'-lee*)

PINE NUTS: Pine nuts grow in the cone of stone pine. They are narrow, small (about a third of an inch long), cream-colored, mild, and slightly oily in flavor. Sicilians use them so much in cooking they should be called Sicilian nuts. They perk-up sauces, meats, sweet and sour dishes, cookies and pastries.

ROSMARINO (*ross-mah-ree'-noh*)

ROSEMARY: Rosemary is a beautiful evergreen shrub with a pleasant odor and a bitterish flavor, which changes to a delicate taste after cooking. Excellent with poultry, fish, lamb, and pork.

SALE (*sah'-lay*)

SALT: Sea salt, or marine salt, from the salt lagoons of Sardinia provides all of Italy, including Sicily, with salt. According to my palate, food cooked with sea salt is much tastier. Nutritionists claim it to be healthier too!

SALVIA (*sahl'-vee-ah*)

SAGE: A garden plant, sage is used today solely for cookery, whereas formerly it was used for its medicinal qualities. (Its name in Italian means "to save.") Sage leaves are a dull gray-green in color, velvety in texture, and curl when dried. Often teamed with liver, sage is also added to stuffings, fowl, and fish dishes.

SEMI DI SESAMO (*say'-mee dee say'-sah-mo*)

SESAME SEEDS: Although native to India, sesame seeds were cultivated in Sicily by the Arabs. The golden seeds are eaten as food and also yield an emollient oil. Sicilians call them *giugiulaina* and use them in baking sprinkled generously over long loaves of bread, clustered on *foccace* (crusty rolls) and *biscotti* (cookies).

TIMO (*tee'-moh*)

THYME: Garden thyme is both mild and spicy with a distinct aromatic fragrance—a favorite in salad dressings, sauces, meat, and poultry.

VANIGLIA (*vah-e-nee'-lyah*)

VANILLA: Vanilla bean is more popular than vanilla essence. The bean is stuck into a jar of confectioners' sugar to be used later in pastries, desserts, and icings.

ZAFFERANO (*dsahf-fay-rah'-noh*)

SAFFRON: An expensive herb derived from the crocus plant. It takes seventy-five thousand crocuses, each providing three stigmas, to produce one pound of saffron. Its rich color and subtle flavor season and color soups, fish stews, and sauces.

FRUITS
OF THE EARTH

While driving from the hills of Palermo to the valleys of Agrigento, up north again to the steep slopes of Mt. Etna and continuing along the coast to Messina, one becomes intoxicated with fragrant air. Many beautiful fruit orchards and groves grace the countryside, producing a perfumelike aroma unequaled by any bottled essence.

Golden pears, jade-green grapes, ruby-red cherries, emerald-green figs, yellow and red melons, blood oranges, vibrant-yellow lemons, small and sweet nectarines, and cactus fruit are Sicily's prized harvest of fruits.

Cactus fruit, or *fichi d'India,* was brought to Sicily from the West Indies by the Spaniards and has become the national fruit and symbol of the island. There are several varieties, but the fruit from Catania and Messina is most highly prized for its sweetness and succulent pulp. Lavender, green, and yellow in color, this fruit has a subtle, delicate flavor; it is also called prickly pear for the little prickly needles on the skin. Exportation to the United States is frequent, even though California and Mexico grow this fruit in abundance.

Melone alla Gelatina di Frutta
BEAUTIFUL STUFFED MELON

1 package strawberry Jell-O	1 cantaloupe or honeydew
1 cup boiling water	melon
¾ cup cold water	1 fresh peach, peeled, diced
¼ cup strawberry Marsala	1 fresh pear, peeled, diced
wine	

In a bowl, dissolve Jell-O in the boiling water. When dissolved, add the cold water and wine. Refrigerate.

Cut 1-inch slice from one end of melon. (If melon does not stand upright, remove a thin slice from other end, being careful not to open end.) Remove and discard seeds and membrane. Pour in Jell-O and refrigerate.

When Jell-O begins to set, add peach and pear and intermix. Refrigerate until Jell-O is firm.

When ready to serve, cut melon horizontally into 1-inch slices. Remove and discard melon rind from each slice. Serve on individual fruit plates.

SERVES: 6 to 8

Granita di Melone Verde

HONEYDEW ICE

1 cup sugar	2 tablespoons lemon juice
1 cup water	2 tablespoons ginger Cointreau
2 cups chopped honeydew pulp	

Dissolve sugar in water and cool. Purée honeydew pulp with lemon juice and Cointreau. Add cooled syrup to honeydew purée and blend. Pour mixture into a freezer container and freeze until firm—about 4 hours—or overnight.

SERVES: 4 to 6

Pesche al Vino

PEACHES IN RED WINE

Sicilians and/or Italians have been flavoring fruit with wine (or vice versa) for as long as time remembered. The fruit-flavored wine is drunk during the meal and the fruit is eaten for dessert. Peaches are the most popular, since they take to wine so well. During the winter months, diced apples and orange slices are used.

Allow 1 peach per person (peeled and pitted). Cut in half or quarters or slice. Place in a tall pitcher; cover with dry red wine. Soak fruit for 30 minutes to 1 hour before serving. The longer the fruit soaks, the more flavored the wine and peaches become.

Granita di Prugna

PLUM ICE

1 No. 2½ can purple plums	1 cup water
1 cup sugar	1 egg white

Drain plums; reserve liquid. Pit and chop plums. Heat plum liquid with sugar and water. Bring to a boil and boil gently for 5 minutes. Cool. When cool, beat in egg white and add plums. Pour into freezer container and freeze.

When semifrozen, remove from freezer; transfer to bowl and beat for 1 minute. Pour back into container and freeze.

SERVES: 6

Melagrana Sorbetto

POMEGRANATE SHERBET

1 cup sugar	½ pint heavy cream, whipped
1 cup water	3 or 4 drops red food coloring
1 cup pomegranate syrup	3 pomegranates
(available in gourmet shops)	Mint leaves

Heat sugar and water together until sugar has dissolved. Pour in pomegranate syrup and stir. Chill. Fold in whipped cream. Blend in 3 or 4 drops of red food coloring for pomegranate hue. Pour into freezer container and freeze.

Cut pomegranates in half; scoop out seeds and reserve. Fill empty shells with pomegranate sherbet. Garnish with pomegranate seeds and mint leaves. Serve immediately.

SERVES: 4

Gelato di Fichi

FIG ICE CREAM

1 No. 2 can figs, drained, chopped	2 tablespoons Strega liqueur
½ pint heavy cream, whipped	½ cup hazelnut meats, roasted, chopped
¼ cup confectioners' sugar	
⅓ cup mixed candied fruit, minced	

Combine all ingredients in a large bowl. Pour into freezer container and freeze until firm (about 4 hours) or overnight.

SERVES: 4 to 6

VARIATION: Quarter 1 dozen fresh figs; cover with ½ cup Strega liqueur; chill. Portion into sherbet glasses; scoop fig ice cream over chilled figs. Dollop with whipped cream and sprinkle with toasted hazelnuts.

Granita di Limone
LEMON ICE

Juice of 12 lemons	Rind of 2 lemons, grated
5 cups water	1 egg white
2 cups sugar	

Squeeze lemons and discard seeds and skins. Combine water and sugar in a saucepan. Bring to a boil and boil gently for 5 minutes. Cool. Stir in lemon juice and rind. Using whisk, beat in egg white. Pour mixture into ice cube trays or freezer container.

When lemon ice is semifrozen (2 to 3 hours), remove from freezer; transfer to bowl and beat for 1 minute. Pour back into container and freeze.

SERVES: 8 to 10

Coccodè
FROZEN FRIED EGGS

When a hen lays an egg in Sicily, she croaks, "*Coccodè.*" Sicilian humor glimmers throughout this recipe in concept, content, and presentation. Frozen *zabaione* (egg-wine custard) is shaped to simulate fried eggs. (Three "egg yolks" are arranged in a *cocotte* [egg] pan, and whipped cream is piped around them to simulate egg whites.) Everyone does a double take when this dessert is served; at first glance, one really believes they're fried eggs. It's so funny to watch people's reactions; they begin tasting with trepidation and are happily surprised to find these are the best "frozen fried eggs" they ever tasted.

6 egg yolks
6 tablespoons sugar
¾ cup Marsala wine
½ pint heavy cream, whipped

½ pint heavy cream, whipped
(for decoration)
Confectioners' sugar

In top section of double boiler and away from heat, combine egg yolks with sugar. Beat with a whisk until thick and smooth. Place over hot water (in lower section) and beat in wine until mixture is very thick and hot (the consistency of soft custard). Be sure not to boil mixture; keep heat moderate. Remove from heat and cool.

Pour custard gradually over whipped cream and fold in. Pour into freezer container and freeze (3 to 4 hours or overnight)'. When firm, shape with a spoon to simulate egg yolks. Fill pastry bag with whipped cream sweetened with confectioners' sugar to taste. Pipe cream around yolks to simulate egg whites.

SERVES: 6 to 8

NOTE: *Zabaione, or Marsala custard*—allow 2 egg yolks, 2 tablespoons sugar and 2 tablespoons wine per person. Cook as directed above; pour into sherbet glasses and serve warm and foamy. Doctors consider it a restorative food as well as being a delicious and easy dessert.

Fragole alla Crema
E-Z STRAWBERRY CREAM

½ pint heavy cream
¼ cup confectioners' sugar
1 package frozen sliced strawberries, thawed

Whip cream and sweeten with confectioners' sugar. Fold in strawberries and their liquid. Pour into sherbet glasses and chill for at least 2 hours.

SERVES: 4 to 6

VARIATION: Strawberry cream may be frozen and served sliced with fresh strawberries.

Gelselmo

CHOCOLATE-CHIP WATERMELON MOLD

This adorable-looking delicious dessert appeals to children of all ages. It is shaped to look like a small watermelon, with chocolate chips representing the seeds and pistachio nuts the rind.

1 envelope gelatin (1 tablespoon)
¼ cup cold water
1 cup boiling water
¼ cup sugar
¼ cup chocolate chips, cut in half

1½ cups seeded, chopped watermelon
¼ cup pistachio nuts, grated

Soften gelatin in cold water. Stir in boiling water and sugar until sugar is dissolved. Pour into 1-quart oval mold or round bowl. Refrigerate. When gelatin is beginning to set, intermix chocolate chips and watermelon; return to refrigerator until firm.

When ready to serve, invert onto serving plate. Hold a hot damp cloth over mold, and shake mold to release. Sprinkle with pistachio nuts.

SERVES: 4 to 6

Aranci Caramellati

CARAMEL ORANGES

6 large firm navel oranges
2 cups water
2 cups sugar

½ cup Grand Marnier or brandy
2 pieces cinnamon stick

With sharp small knife, start peeling oranges at stem end, cutting below white membrane in sawing motions, and removing skins in a spiral. Make sure no white membrane is left on oranges. Do not discard orange peels; set them aside for making candied orange peel.

Combine sugar, water, Grand Marnier, and cinnamon stick in a large skillet and heat until sugar is dissolved. Then, bring mixture to a rolling boil and boil gently until syrup feels thickish—15 to 20 minutes. Dip oranges in syrup, turning them to coat all sides.

Arrange oranges in crystal bowl and spoon syrup over them. Wave spoonfuls of spun sugar every which way, forming thin, long threads. Serve oranges warm or cold.

Spun Sugar: Combine 1 cup sugar, ¼ cup water, and ½ tablespoon glucose† or ¼ cup corn syrup in a heavy saucepan. Heat until sugar dissolves; cook to hard-crack stage (285° F.—when 1 scant teaspoon of syrup is dropped in 1 cup cold water, it separates into hard brittle threads).

SERVES: 6

† Glucose is available in drugstores and gourmet shops.

Bucce d'Arancia Candite
CANDIED ORANGE PEEL

Plunge orange peels in boiling water and boil until peel is soft—about 10 minutes. Drain and cool. Press out excess water and remove white membrane with spoon. With kitchen shears, cut orange peels into 3×¼-inch strips. Place in ready-made syrup from Caramel Oranges* or make syrup as directed in recipe for Caramel Oranges. Cook strips in syrup until they take on a transparent look and most of the syrup has boiled away—10 to 15 minutes. Drain in colander and cool. When cool enough to handle, separate and place on a greased baking sheet. Allow to stand until strips feel fairly dry. Sprinkle with enough sugar to give a crystallized look. Use as needed and store in an airtight jar in refrigerator.

VARIATION: Prepare candied orange peel as directed but do not place on baking sheet to dry. Dip in sweet or semisweet melted chocolate; separate and place on greased baking sheet or waxed paper to set chocolate.

TIP: Grapefruit rind is also delicious candied. Prepare as directed above.

Pesche al Limone
LEMON-PEACHES

> 8 large ripe peaches
> Juice of 2 lemons
> Granulated sugar

Plunge peaches in boiling water for 1 to 2 minutes. Cool and peel off skins. Cut them in half; remove and discard pits. Slice peaches into a bowl; squeeze lemons directly over slices, turning them to coat all sides. Sprinkle with sugar to taste. Chill. Let stand at room temperature for 10 minutes before serving.

SERVES: 4 to 6

Macedonia di Frutta
FRESH FRUIT SALAD

Macedonia di frutta is a multimixture of the very freshest and ripest fruit of the season, cut in varied bite-size shapes and flavored with sweet wine or liqueur.

Make ten selections from the suggested list below and shape as directed. Sprinkle fruit liberally with Marsala wine or kirsch or Maraschino liqueur and sugar to taste. Intermix and marinate fruit in refrigerator for at least 2 hours.

cantaloupe balls	pomegranate seeds
watermelon balls	apricot halves
honeydew balls	pineapple cubes
peach slices	pitted cherries
pear cubes	strawberries, blueberries,
diced apples	raspberries
orange sections	seedless grapes
grapefruit sections	banana slices
nectarine slices	papaya cubes
fig quarters	mango cubes
plum halves or quarters	persimmon slices

Brush apples, pears, and bananas with lemon juice to prevent discoloring. Serve fruit salad in a large crystal bowl, a watermelon shell, or individual fruit shells (melon, pineapple, orange, or grape-fruit).

Fresh fruit salad is always refreshing as an appetizer or dessert. Whipped cream, flavored with vanilla sugar, may be dolloped over each serving with a sprinkling of toasted nuts (pistachio, almonds, or walnuts).

Frutta Candita
FRUIT CONFECTIONS

3 tangerines, peeled, sectioned
½ pound grapes (with stems)
½ pound fresh cherries (with stems)
1 pint fresh strawberries (with stems)
2 cups sugar

2 cups water
2 tablespoons Grand Marnier or brandy
Bonbon wrappers†
Green leaves (crystallized sugar) †

Remove seeds from tangerine sections by cutting slits in skins; discard seeds. Pluck grapes from bunch, but leave stems on. Wash fruit with cold water and drain.

Combine sugar, water and Grand Marnier in a saucepan and heat. After sugar dissolves, cook to the hard-crack stage (285° to 300° F.) Use candy thermometer or test by dropping a little syrup from a teaspoon into a cup of cold water. Syrup should separate in hard brittle threads. Watch carefully; do not let syrup go above 300° F.

Dip fruit with stem or fork into hot syrup, turning to coat all sides. Place on a greased baking sheet and let stand until syrup is set. Arrange in individual bonbon wrappers or place on a doilied serving plate. Decorate with leaves.

SERVES: 6 to 8

NOTE: While dipping fruit, keep heat on low to prevent sugar from setting.

† Available in gourmet or spice shops.

Fragole al Marsala

STRAWBERRIES WITH MARSALA

> 1 pint fresh strawberries
> Granulated sugar
> ⅓ cup Marsala wine

Place strawberries in colander and rinse with cold water. Drain and remove hulls. Slice and sugar to taste. Let stand 30 minutes at room temperature to draw out natural juices. Pour Marsala wine over strawberries and chill.

SERVES: 4

NOTE: Wild strawberries are tiny in size and have a delicious, delicate flavor. In Sicily, they are as readily available as the cultivated variety. In the United States, they are sometimes sold in country markets or fancy produce stores. However, both cultivated and wild strawberries can be used for this recipe.

Frullata di Frutta

ICED FRUIT SHAKE

Frullata di frutta is a refreshing and nourishing drink at any time of the day. Add an egg and leave out the ice for breakfast in a glass. Any combination of fresh, frozen, or canned fruit to your liking may be used.

½ McIntosh apple, cored (leave skin on)
½ cup cantaloupe pulp
½ peach, peeled
½ banana
6 or 7 strawberries
2 lemon slices

1 orange quarter, chopped (leave skin on)
1 cup milk
4 to 6 ice cubes or 1 cup sherbet
2 to 4 tablespoons sugar

Add fruit to blender gradually with milk until fruit is blended. Turn blender on low speed, stopping and starting, with additions every few seconds. Drop in ice cubes or sherbet; add sugar and blend until mixture is smooth. Serve immediately.

SERVES: 2

Melone all'Oro Siciliano

MELON WITH SICILIAN GOLD LIQUEUR

1 Cranshaw or Persian melon   ½ cup Sicilian Gold liqueur
2 fresh papayas, sliced (or 1   Fresh mint leaves (for
   No. 2 can, drained, cubed)   garnishing)

Scoop flesh from melon with melon-ball cutter. Arrange melon balls and papaya slices in dessert dishes. Sprinkle with Sicilian Gold and chill. Before serving, garnish with fresh mint leaves.

SERVES: 4 to 6

NOTE: Serve melon balls flavored with a liqueur of your choice with toothpicks for hors d'oeuvre.

Fichi d'India

INDIA FIGS

India figs, or prickly pears, appear in American markets during the winter and early spring months. The fuzzy prickly spots can be avoided by holding the pear by its ends with one hand and peeling the skin off lengthwise with a sharp paring knife in the other. De-fuzzed pears are also available and may be handled fearlessly.

4 India figs, peeled
¼ cup kirsch liqueur

Slice or cube fruit. Sprinkle with kirsch and chill. Serve with toothpicks for hors d'oeuvre or with forks for dessert.

SERVES: 4

VARIATION: Make fruit kebabs using cubes of prickly pears, pineapple, and bananas alternately with Maraschino cherries.

Fichi Freschi Gelati

ICED FRESH FIGS

Fresh figs are the "plums" of nature's bounty. Their soft, plump bodies exude a delicate sweetness that is capable of sending any mortal soul into ecstasy. Unfortunately, except in California and

Florida, fresh figs are available only during the summer months and during the Christmas holidays. The canned and dried variety, available all year round, are useful in baking and dessert cookery but cannot compare to the delicacy of fresh figs.

The best way to serve them is *au naturel*. Peel them carefully; arrange them on a doilied serving dish garnished with fresh mint sprigs; chill until they are icy cold. They are an excellent dessert after any meal. They may also be served for a first course. Wrap them in thin slices of Italian ham (prosciutto) and serve chilled. *Delicioso* and low in calories too!

Caldarroste

ROASTED CHESTNUTS

> 2 pounds chestnuts
> 2 to 4 tablespoons water

Preheat oven to 425° F. Cut 2 slits, criss-cross fashion, on flat sides of chestnuts. Place them in a shallow baking pan with water. Roast for 25 to 30 minutes. Serve warm with dry or sweet wine. Chestnuts are also delicious roasted over a charcoal fire.

Pere al Forno con Panna

BAKED PEARS AND GINGERED CREAM

> 8 firm pears
> 1⅛ cups sugar
> ½ teaspoon lemon rind
> 4 cups dry red wine

Peel pears with vegetable peeler; leave stems on. Preheat oven to 350° F. Mix sugar, lemon rind, and wine in shallow baking dish. Place pears in baking dish; turn them to color them evenly. Bake until pears are tender—about 50 minutes. Baste and turn pears frequently. Serve warm or chilled with Gingered Cream.

GINGERED CREAM: *Combine and blend:*

½ pint heavy cream, whipped
¼ cup confectioners' sugar
1 tablespoon grated fresh ginger
  (or 1 teaspoon dried)

Castagne Candite
CANDIED CHESTNUTS

2 pounds chestnuts
Water
2 pounds sugar
½ cup corn syrup

1 vanilla bean, chopped
2 pints vanilla ice cream (or 1
  pint heavy cream, whipped)

Cut slits, criss-cross fashion, in flat sides of chestnuts with point of sharp knife. Cover with water and boil for 15 minutes. Cool long enough to handle and peel off shells and inner skins. Drain. Cover with water and boil until barely tender—about 25 minutes. Drain.

Bring sugar, corn syrup, and vanilla bean to a rolling boil. Boil until mixture begins to brown. Add chestnuts and let stand 5 minutes. Transfer to a wire rack and drain for 2 hours. Reheat syrup; return chestnuts to syrup and let stand 5 minutes. Return to rack and drain overnight.

Next day, repeat process twice. When ready to serve, line dessert dishes with 4 to 6 candied chestnuts each. Cover with 1 scoop ice cream or whipped cream and dot with 2 or 3 more candied chestnuts.

SERVES: 8

DESSERTS, DESSERTS

"In Coqna Pficitur Anima"
"In the Kitchen, the Soul Reaches Perfection"

The mark of many great cuisines is to end a delectable meal with brilliance, dignity, and confection. I take my *toque blanche* (chef's hat) off to Sicily for its delectable *dolci*. It was the Arabs who first taught the Sicilians how to make desserts, but it was the Sicilians who gave a new style to dessert making.

Procopio Cotelli, a Palermitano, opened the famous Café Procope in Paris, and it was he who first introduced *gelato* (ice cream) to the European Continent.

In addition to *gelato,* Sicilians make ices that elevate the spirit to a higher plane. Lemon, plum, strawberry, raspberry, and coffee flavors are especially noteworthy. Sicilians like to eat their fresh-fruit ices sandwiched in brioche rolls—different, simple, filling, and so good.

Cassata, a multilayered sponge cake filled with alternating layers of sweetened ricotta cheese mixed with candied fruit and chocolate and covered with sweetened whipped cream, and *cannoli,* flaky pastry shells filled with sweetened ricotta, mixed citron, grated chocolate, and pistachio nuts, are two Sicilian specialties that have become international favorites. Sicilians make an assortment of *biscotti* (cookies), but are credited as the originators of *angellini,* golden cookies shaped like fingers and rolled in sesame seeds, *pignoli,* round clusters of hardened meringue studded with pine nuts, and *pasta reale,* a version of marzipan made with ground pistachio nuts instead of almonds.

Has your sweet tooth begun to ache by now? If so, dash into the kitchen and perfect your soul!

Biscotti alla Mamellata di Mandorle

ALMOND MARMALADE TARTS

Signora Zitto of Cefalù, Sicily, gave me this recipe—it's her favorite. After I made these luscious tarts, they became my favorite too.

FILLING:
1 pound ground almonds
2 cups sugar
1 cup water
4 ounces semisweet chocolate, grated

DOUGH:
1 cup shortening
1 cup sugar
1 egg yolk
4 cups sifted flour
1 teaspoon cream of tartar
1 teaspoon baking soda
½ cup milk
3 tablespoons grated lemon rind
Confectioners' sugar

Place almonds, sugar, and water in a medium saucepan. Bring to a boil; boil gently until mixture resembles a thick paste—15 to 20 minutes. Mix in chocolate and set aside.

Cream shortening with sugar; stir in egg yolk. Sift flour, cream of tartar, and baking soda together. Add gradually to shortening mixture with milk and lemon rind. Mix well, forming a smooth dough. Gather up with fingers and form into a ball. Cover with a cloth and refrigerate for 30 minutes. Preheat oven to 400° F. Grease 2 baking sheets.

Roll dough out, between two pieces of waxed paper, into thin sheets, ⅛ inch thick. Cut into small shapes or rounds (1 inch in diameter). Spoon filling onto dough shapes; cover with same shape and press edges together with fork. Place on greased baking sheets and bake until tarts are lightly browned—about 10 minutes. Sprinkle with confectioners' sugar before serving.

YIELD: Approximately 4 dozen

Biscotti con Pignoli

PINE NUT COOKIES

1 pound almond paste
2 cups sugar
4 egg whites, slightly beaten

2 to 3 ounces pine nuts (pignoli)

Preheat oven to 350° F. Lightly grease baking sheets.

Cream almond paste, sugar, and egg whites together until mixture is smooth—about 3 minutes with electric mixer. Drop by rounded teaspoons onto baking sheets, 1 inch apart. Sprinkle with 6 to 8 pine nuts and bake until lightly browned—15 to 20 minutes.

YIELD: Approximately 6 dozen

Bianco Mangiare
MELTING MOMENTS PUDDING

2 cups milk	1 tablespoon grated lemon rind
½ cup sugar	⅓ small almond chocolate bar,
2½ tablespoons cornstarch	grated (2 to 3 tablespoons)

Pour milk, sugar, cornstarch, and lemon rind in top section of double boiler. Place over gently boiling water (lower section), stirring constantly, until pudding thickens—about 10 to 12 minutes. Pour into dessert or custard cups and cool. Sprinkle with grated chocolate and refrigerate until ready to serve.

SERVES: 4

Pan di Spagna al'Anice
ANISE SPONGE CAKE

5 egg whites	1 teaspoon pure anise extract
Pinch of salt	1 cup sifted flour
1 cup sugar	1 teaspoon baking powder
5 egg yolks, slightly beaten	Confectioners' sugar

Preheat oven to 375° F. Grease a standard loaf pan.

In a large bowl, beat egg whites until soft peaks form. Sprinkle salt and sugar gradually over whites; continue beating until mixture is stiff. Fold in egg yolks and anise extract, blending well.

Sprinkle flour and baking powder gradually over egg mixture, folding in well after each addition. Pour batter into greased loaf pan. Bake for approximately 30 minutes. Remove from oven and wait 5 minutes before turning onto cooling rack. When cool, dust top with confectioners' sugar.

SERVES: 8 to 10

Budino di Castagne e Cioccolato con Panna
CHOCOLATE CHESTNUT LOAF

2 pounds chestnuts (or 2 large cans whole chestnuts, drained)
1 quart milk
½ cup butter, melted
6 ounces chocolate syrup
¼ cup Strega liqueur
½ pint heavy cream, whipped
2 tablespoons confectioners' sugar
10 glazed cherries
⅓ cup pistachio nuts, toasted

If using fresh chestnuts, cut slits, criss-cross fashion, in flat sides of chestnuts with point of sharp knife. Cover with water and boil for 15 minutes. Drain. Cool enough to handle and remove shells and inner skins. (Canned chestnuts need no special preparation.) Pour milk in saucepan; add fresh or canned chestnuts and simmer slowly until chestnuts are tender (add more milk if necessary)—30 to 40 minutes.

Put chestnuts through ricer or blender and combine with butter, chocolate syrup, and Strega. Pour mixture into buttered standard loaf pan. Refrigerate for at least 2 hours. Unmold onto doilied serving platter and frost with whipped cream sweetened with confectioners' sugar. Decorate with cherries and pistachio nuts. Cut in slices and serve.

SERVES: 10 to 12

Struffoli
HONEY BALLS

Struffoli, or honey balls, look uniquely festive and are prepared traditionally for Christmas and St. Joseph's Day. They are piled high in wreath rings, pyramid forms, and dome shapes for guests to pick at while sipping their after-dinner espresso.

2 cups water
1 cup margarine or shortening
¼ teaspoon salt
4 cups sifted flour
10 large eggs
16 ounces honey
½ cup pine nuts (pignoli), toasted
⅓ cup candied orange peel
½ cup (multicolored) cake-decorating sprinkles

Preheat oven to 350° F. Grease two baking sheets lightly. Have eggs at room temperature.

Place water, margarine, and salt in a saucepan and bring to a boil. Remove from range and cool for 3 minutes. Stir in flour and mix well. Return to heat and cook, stirring constantly, until mixture forms a ball and leaves sides of pan—about 1 minute. Remove from range and cool for 5 minutes.

Add eggs to mixture, one at a time, beating hard for approximately 1 minute after each addition. Fill pastry bag with batter and pipe small rounds (the size of marbles) 1 inch apart onto baking sheets. (Or drop by half teaspoons onto baking sheets.) Bake until lightly browned—about 25 minutes. Remove from oven and cool on wire racks.

In saucepan, heat honey until it comes to a rolling boil. Boil for 5 minutes, being careful not to let it boil over. Dip puffs, approximately 12 at a time, into honey and roll around to coat evenly. Remove with slotted spoon onto a plate. Continue until all puffs are dipped. Wet hands with cold water and stick puffs together forming wreath rings, pyramids, or dome shapes. Decorate with toasted pine nuts, candied orange peel, and multicolored cake-decorating sprinkles.

SERVES: 10 to 12

Pasta Reale

PINE NUT FUDGE

Pasta reale, marzipan's twin sister, is equally famous in eastern Sicily, particularly in the Messina province. Originally it was made with pistachio paste, but today it is made with pine nut paste, since the cost of pistachio nuts has become prohibitive.

FUDGE:
½ cup pine nuts, ground
2 cups confectioners' sugar
1 teaspoon lemon juice
1 egg white
½ cup (4 ounces) pine nuts

ICING:
½ cup confectioners' sugar
Grated rind of 1 lemon
1 tablespoon lemon juice

In a medium bowl, combine ground pine nuts, confectioners' sugar, lemon juice, and egg white; mix until paste is smooth. Add whole pine nuts and intermix. Turn onto sheet of aluminum foil; roll into a log, 1 inch thick, using foil for backing. Chill in refrigerator.

Blend icing ingredients together until smooth. Icing will be thin and liquidy. (Add 1 teaspoon water if icing is too thick.) Frost log with icing and return to refrigerator until icing is set. Store in refrigerator until ready to serve. Slice in thin patties before serving. YIELD: Approximately 2 dozen patties

Teste di Turchi

TURKS' HEADS

Sicilians mockingly named this dessert after the Turks who invaded them. Their resentment is evident in both the name and the nature of the dessert. Nonetheless, *Teste di Turchi* is a delicious blending of flaky pastry and soft custard cream.

CUSTARD:
2 cups milk
2 egg yolks
2 tablespoons cornstarch
½ cup sugar
1 teaspoon vanilla
1 tablespoon rum

DOUGH:
2 cups sifted flour
Pinch of salt
3 large eggs
1½ quarts frying oil

Multicolored and chocolate cake-decorating sprinkles

In the top section of a double boiler, mix milk, egg yolks, cornstarch, sugar, and vanilla together. Place over hot water (in bottom section); cook, stirring constantly, until custard thickens—10 to 15 minutes. Remove from heat and cool. Stir in rum and refrigerate.

Place flour and salt in a bowl; make a well in center and drop in eggs. Mix well; gather up dough with fingers and form into ball. Turn onto lightly floured board and knead until dough is smooth and satiny—5 to 8 minutes. Roll out into thin sheets (about ⅛ inch thick) and cut into 2-inch squares.

Pour oil into frying kettle. Heat to 370° F. (1-inch cube of bread browns evenly in 1 minute). Drop squares, a few at a time, into hot fat and lightly brown—approximately 30 seconds on each side. Squares expand and brown quickly; work fast and stay with it. Remove with slotted spoon and drain onto absorbent paper. Continue until all squares are cooked.

Spread custard over wafers and decorate with multicolored and chocolate sprinkles.

YIELD: Approximately 5 dozen

NOTE: Wafers keep for 1 week if stored plain. Spread with custard when ready to serve. After a heavy meal, wafers provide a light dessert if served with a dusting of confectioners' sugar instead of custard cream.

Biscotti all'Anice
ANISE TOAST

3 cups sifted flour	1 cup sugar
1 tablespoon baking powder	5 egg yolks
¼ teaspoon salt	1 tablespoon pure anise extract
5 egg whites	

Preheat oven to 375° F. Grease two baking sheets.

Sift flour, baking powder, and salt together. Set aside.

In a large bowl, beat egg whites until soft peaks form. Sprinkle sugar gradually over whites; continue beating until mixture is stiff. Fold in egg yolks and anise extract, blending well.

Sprinkle flour mixture gradually over egg mixture, folding in well after each addition. Pour batter, forming 3×14×¾-inch rectangle, onto each baking sheet. Bake at 375° F. until cake tester inserted in center comes out clean—about 30 minutes.

Remove from oven and cool for 15 to 20 minutes. Cut slices across rectangle, 1 inch thick. Place slices on their sides, on ungreased baking sheets and toast at 400° F. until lightly browned on sides—8 to 10 minutes.

YIELD: Approximately 2½ dozen

CASSATA (*Version I*)

Cassata comes in two versions: as a rich cheese-, fruit-, and cream-filled layer cake or as a triflavored ice cream cake—both are superb.

CAKE:

1 package orange supreme cake mix
1 package vanilla pudding mix
½ cup vegetable oil

4 eggs
½ cup orange juice
½ cup milk
1 teaspoon grated orange rind

CHEESE FILLING:

2 pounds ricotta cheese
2 tablespoons confectioners' sugar
⅔ cup mixed candied fruit (orange rind, citron, pineapple, cherries), chopped fine

4 ounces sweet chocolate, coarsely grated
⅔ cup brandy, Maraschino liqueur, or rum
1 pint heavy cream, whipped

Preheat oven to 350° F. Grease 10-inch tube pan.

In a large mixing bowl, combine cake ingredients and mix until batter is smooth—about 5 minutes. Pour into greased tube pan and bake until done—45 to 50 minutes. (Cake should be firm yet springy to the touch. Insert toothpick in center; if clean when removed, cake is done.) Remove from oven and wait 5 minutes before inverting to cool.

In a large bowl, combine ricotta, confectioners' sugar, candied fruit, chocolate, and brandy. Fold in whipped cream and refrigerate.

Cut cake into ½-inch slices. Grease a 3½- to 4-quart china or ceramic bowl. Line bottom of bowl (*and sides of bowl*) with cake slices. Cover with some of the cheese mixture. Continue layering cake slices and cheese mixture alternately until bowl is filled, ending with cake slices on top. Refrigerate for 6 hours or overnight. When ready to serve, loosen sides with spatula; invert bowl onto serving plate and frost.

FROSTING:

½ pint heavy cream, whipped
3 tablespoons confectioners' sugar

1 ounce semisweet chocolate
½ cup Maraschino cherries
⅓ cup pistachio nuts

Sweeten whipped cream with confectioners' sugar and use to frost entire cake. Using a vegetable peeler, shave chocolate over top and sides of cake. Decorate with cherries and pistachio nuts.

SERVES: 10 to 12

NOTE: Pound or sponge cake may be used in place of orange supreme cake. Cassata may be frozen (without frosting). Thaw for 1 hour; frost and serve.

CASSATA (Version II)

1 pint French vanilla ice cream,
  slightly softened
2 tablespoons Strega liqueur
2 pints cherry vanilla ice cream,
  slightly softened
2 tablespoons Maraschino liqueur
½ cup mixed candied fruits
1 pint pistachio ice cream,
  slightly softened

⅓ cup pistachio nuts
1½ pints heavy cream, whipped
6 tablespoons confectioners'
  sugar
Green and violet flowers
  (crystallized sugar)

Place a 2½-quart bombe mold in freezer. Mix softened vanilla ice cream with Strega liqueur. With spoon, press evenly inside the chilled mold, making a ½-inch layer. Freeze until firm.

Mix softened cherry vanilla ice cream with Maraschino liqueur and candied fruits and press evenly over the vanilla layer, making a 1-inch layer. Freeze until firm.

Mix softened pistachio ice cream with pistachio nuts and press into center of mold. Freeze until firm.

When ready to unmold, let cassata stand at room temperature for 5 minutes. Invert onto serving plate. Hold a hot damp dishcloth over mold, and shake mold to release. Sweeten whipped cream with confectioners' sugar and place in pastry bag with flowered decorating tip. Pipe whipped cream in rows to cover entire mold. Decorate with green and violet flowers (crystallized sugar). Return to freezer until dessert time. Slice in wedges and serve on doilied dessert plates.

SERVES: 14 to 16

Ravioli Dolci alla Elizabetta

ELIZABETTA'S SWEET RAVIOLI

FILLING:

½ ring (½ pound) dried figs, chopped
Grated rind of 1 large orange
Grated rind of 1 large lemon
1 cup seedless raisins
½ cup hazelnuts, chopped

½ cup almonds, chopped
½ cup walnuts, chopped
1 teaspoon nutmeg
¼ cup sugar
⅔ cup chocolate syrup
2 cups sweet Marsala wine

Grind or blend figs, orange and lemon rind, raisins, hazelnuts, almonds, and walnuts together. Use medium blade of grinder or blend to coarse consistency. (Add 2 tablespoons water if mixture is too thick for grinding or blending.) Transfer to a large saucepan and stir in nutmeg, sugar, chocolate syrup, and Marsala wine. Cook over moderate heat, stirring constantly, for 15 to 20 minutes. Cool and set aside.

DOUGH:

4 cups sifted flour
1 cup sugar
½ teaspoon salt

6 large eggs
2 eggs, slightly beaten
1½ quarts frying oil

In a large bowl, sift flour, sugar, and salt together. Make a well in center and add 6 eggs. Mix well. Gather up with fingers to form ball. Turn onto lightly floured board and knead until dough is smooth and satiny—10 to 15 minutes. Cut dough into four sections; roll out each section into a thin sheet, ⅛ inch thick. Cut 2-inch rounds with ravioli or biscuit cutter. Place 1 rounded tablespoon of filling in center of each round. Brush edges with 2 eggs, slightly beaten, and cover with another round, sealing edges with fingers or fork.

In frying kettle, heat oil to 370° F. (1-inch cube of bread browns in 1 minute). Carefully drop a few ravioli at a time in hot oil. Fry until golden brown on one side—about 3 minutes; turn; fry until golden brown on other side. Remove with slotted spoon and drain on absorbent paper. When ready to serve, sprinkle liberally with vanilla sugar.†

YIELD: Approximately 4 dozen

† *Vanilla sugar*—Chop 2 vanilla beans and mix in 1 box of confectioners' sugar. Store in cupboard for use in pastry cookery.

Spumetti

CHOCOLATE-HAZELNUT MERINGUES

1 pound hazelnut meats or
  cashew nuts, coarsely
  chopped
1 pound confectioners' sugar
  (1 box)

1 ounce cocoa (or 2
  tablespoons)
2 teaspoons cinnamon
About 5 to 6 egg whites

Preheat oven to 325° F. Cut baking pan liner paper or brown paper to fit 2 baking sheets and grease lightly.

Put hazelnuts, confectioners' sugar, cocoa, and cinnamon in a large bowl; add egg whites and mix well until mixture is well blended—about 5 minutes. Wet hands with water and break off small pieces of mixture (about 1 tablespoon) and shape into round balls. Place on baking sheets, 1 inch apart, and bake for approximately 30 minutes.

YIELD: Approximately 3½ dozen

NOTE: Use glass measuring cup for measuring egg whites.

Fiorelli

WAFER ROSETTES

FROSTING:
1 pound ricotta cheese, drained
½ cup confectioners' sugar
1 teaspoon vanilla
1 teaspoon cinnamon
½ cup hazelnuts, toasted,
  chopped
½ cup glazed cherries, chopped

WAFERS:
1 egg
1 cup milk
½ teaspoon salt
1 cup sifted flour
2 tablespoons sugar
1½ quarts frying oil

Combine ricotta with confectioners' sugar, vanilla, and cinnamon. Refrigerate.

In a medium bowl, beat egg with milk and salt until blended. Gradually stir in flour and sugar and beat until batter is smooth.

In frying kettle, pour oil and heat to 370° F. (1-inch bread cube browns evenly in 1 minute). Heat rosette iron in hot oil for 1 minute. Shake off excess oil.

Dip hot iron in batter to top of iron (do not allow batter to go over top of iron or wafers will stick to iron). Immediately immerse in hot oil. As soon as rosette begins to brown, lift iron, and let rosette drop into hot oil. Turn and brown lightly on other side. (Work quickly since wafers brown in seconds.) Drop rosettes, a few at a time, in hot oil until batter is finished. Remove with slotted spoon onto absorbent paper. When cool and ready to serve, frost with ricotta cheese mixture, toasted nuts, and cherries.

YIELD: Approximately 30 wafers

VARIATIONS: Frost rosettes with custard cream and dollop with whipped cream and nuts.

For weight-conscious dessert lovers—serve light and lovely rosettes with only confectioners' sugar dusted over them.

Cassatine

MINI CHEESE-FILLED TARTS

PASTRY:
1 cup shortening
¼ cup hot water
¼ cup dry red wine
¼ cup honey
1 teaspoon vanilla extract
2 teaspoons orange juice
3 tablespoons orange rind
4 egg yolks
4 cups sifted flour
¾ cup sugar
1 teaspoon baking powder
1 teaspoon salt

CHEESE FILLING:
1 pound ricotta cheese, drained
½ cup confectioners' sugar
2 ounces semisweet chocolate, coarsely grated
2 tablespoons grated orange rind
1 tablespoon orange-blossom water
¼ cup candied citron, minced
½ cup slivered almonds, toasted

Place shortening in a large bowl, and pour hot water, wine, honey, vanilla, orange juice, and orange rind over it. Cream ingredients together; beat in egg yolks. In another bowl, sift flour, sugar, baking powder, and salt together. Combine with shortening mixture; mix until dough is smooth and soft. Gather up with fingers and form a ball. Cover dough with cloth and refrigerate until firm. Preheat oven to 400° F. Grease *small* muffin cups.

Combine ricotta cheese, confectioners' sugar, grated chocolate, orange rind, orange-blossom water, and citron. Refrigerate.

On a lightly floured board, roll dough into sheets ¼ inch thick. Cut in rounds to fit muffin cups. Place in greased muffin cups, pressing gently with fingers to fit cups. Bake until tarts are browned—about 10 minutes. Cool tarts before removing from pans.

Fill tarts with cheese filling and sprinkle with toasted slivered almonds. Serve immediately or refrigerate until ready to serve.

YIELD: Approximately 4 dozen

Biscotti di Giugiulena
SESAME COOKIES

½ cup sesame seeds	¼ teaspoon salt
¼ cup water	½ cup shortening
2½ cups sifted flour	2 eggs, slightly beaten
½ cup sugar	¼ cup milk
2½ teaspoons baking powder	1 teaspoon vanilla extract

Preheat oven to 400° F. Grease two baking sheets. Moisten sesame seeds with ¼ cup water. Set aside.

Sift flour, sugar, baking powder, and salt together. Cut in shortening with pastry blender or two knives until mixture resembles coarse cornmeal. Stir in eggs, milk, and vanilla; mix until dough is smooth. Gather up with fingers and form into a ball. Cut ball into 4 pieces.

On a lightly floured board, roll pieces with palms of hands, forming long ropes ½ inch thick. Cup ropes into 2-inch lengths. Spread moistened seasame seeds on a flat surface; roll cookies over them, coating well. Place cookies, 1 inch apart, on greased baking sheets. Bake until cookies are browned—10 to 12 minutes.

YIELD: Approximately 3 dozen

NOTE: Sesame cookies are also called *biscotti di regine* or *angellini* in other parts of Sicily and Italy.

Biscotti di Cioccolata
CHOCOLATE SPICE COOKIES (*Version I*)

1 cup shortening
1 cup brown sugar, well
  packed
3 cups sifted flour
1 teaspoon baking soda
½ teaspoon salt
1 teaspoon cinnamon
½ teaspoon nutmeg
½ teaspoon ginger

½ teaspoon ground cloves
½ teaspoon ground allspice
½ cup milk
1 teaspoon vanilla extract
½ cup cocoa
1 cup dark raisins, softened
  in warm water
1 cup walnuts, chopped
Grated rind of 1 orange

Preheat oven to 400° F.; grease two baking sheets. Cream shortening with brown sugar in a large mixing bowl. In another bowl, sift together flour, baking soda, salt, cinnamon, nutmeg, ginger, cloves, and allspice. Add sifted ingredients slowly to creamed shortening mixture. Add milk and mix thoroughly. Add vanilla, cocoa, drained raisins, chopped walnuts, and orange rind, and stir until all ingredients are well blended.

Shape 1 heaping teaspoon cookie mixture into small balls and place on baking sheets, 1 inch apart. Bake for 8 to 10 minutes. After cookies have cooled, frost with Lemon Icing* (below).

YIELD: 5½ to 6 dozen

Glassatura di Limone
LEMON ICING

2 cups confectioners' sugar
3 tablespoons lemon juice
2 teaspoons milk

1 cup Maraschino cherries,
  cut in halves

Blend confectioners' sugar, lemon juice, and milk together until smooth. Icing should be thin and liquidy. When cookies have cooled, spread icing over tops. While icing is still soft, place a cherry half on each cookie.

Biscotti di Cioccolata alla Sorella Marù

SISTER MARY LOU'S
CHOCOLATE SPICE COOKIES (*Version II*)

1¼ cups shortening
2 cups sugar
4 eggs
5 cups sifted flour
1 teaspoon baking soda
4 teaspoons baking powder
½ teaspoon salt
1 teaspoon cinnamon
½ teaspoon ground cloves
½ teaspoon ground allspice
½ teaspoon nutmeg

½ teaspoon black pepper
1¾ cups cocoa
¾ cup buttermilk or sour milk
1 tablespoon orange rind
¼ cup orange juice
2 or 3 drops red food coloring
½ cup seedless raisins, softened with ¼ cup water
1 cup nuts, chopped fine

Preheat oven to 400° F. Grease four baking sheets.

Cream shortening with sugar; add eggs and beat well. Sift flour, baking soda, baking powder, salt, cinnamon, cloves, allspice, nutmeg, black pepper, and cocoa together. Add dry ingredients alternately with buttermilk to shortening mixture, mixing well after each addition. Blend in orange rind, orange juice, and red food coloring. Fold in raisins and nuts.

Drop by rounded teaspoons onto greased baking sheets, 1 inch apart. Bake for 8 minutes (do not overbake). Cool cookies on wire racks and frost.

YIELD: 12 dozen

FROSTING:
4 egg whites
1 teaspoon cream of tartar
1 pound confectioners' sugar
1 teaspoon vanilla

Beat egg whites with cream of tartar until whites are foamy. Gradually add confectioners' sugar and continue to beat until all the sugar is added and mixture is smooth. Blend in vanilla. Spread or brush on cooled cookies.

Cremolata di Caffè
COFFEE CUSTARD

2 cups light cream
½ cup espresso coffee, extra strong
5 egg yolks
2 tablespoons cornstarch
½ cup sugar
Pinch of salt
2 tablespoons coffee cordial
½ pint heavy cream, whipped

Scald light cream; make espresso coffee; set both aside.

Combine egg yolks, cornstarch, sugar and salt in top half of double boiler. Place over hot water in bottom boiler and gradually pour in scalded cream, stirring constantly. Cook until custard thickens—about 5 minutes. Remove from heat and cool.

Stir in coffee cordial and espresso; blend. Fold in whipped cream. Pour mixture into sherbet glasses and chill for at least 2 hours. SERVES: 6 to 8

Buccelato
FIG-PRESERVE PASTRY WREATH

Buccelato is a time-consuming pastry, but certainly worth every minute of it. Its flaky pastry and fig-preserve filling is a happy combination of flavors and textures. It looks and smells impressive, too!

FIG-PRESERVE FILLING:
1 pound dried figs, chopped
2 tablespoons water
8 ounces apricot preserve
½ cup pine nuts (pignoli)
½ cup slivered almonds
1 teaspoon pure anise extract

Pasta Sfogliata (PUFF PASTE):
1 cup (2 sticks) sweet butter, softened
2 cups flour, chilled
½ teaspoon salt
½ cup ice water
1 egg yolk, slightly beaten

Grind or blend figs with 2 tablespoons water into a smooth paste (use medium blade of grinder). Transfer to a saucepan and mix with apricot preserve, pine nuts, almonds, and anise extract. Cook over moderate heat, stirring often, for 10 minutes. Remove from heat and set aside.

Place butter in a bowl; sprinkle with ¼ cup of the flour and knead thoroughly. Form mixture into brick shape; wrap in waxed paper and chill in coldest part of refrigerator for 15 minutes.

Place remaining chilled flour and salt in a bowl and mix with ice water. Mix until mixture holds together; gather up with fingers and turn onto a lightly floured board. With fingertips, gently knead until dough is pliable and smooth—8 to 10 minutes. Wrap loosely in waxed paper and refrigerate for 10 minutes.

Place dough on a lightly floured board and roll into an $8 \times 9 \times \frac{1}{2}$-inch rectangle. Place the butter brick in center of rectangle and fold one third of the dough over the butter, and then fold the remaining portion of the dough over this. Press open edges of top and bottom together. Turn rectangle upside down so it presents a smooth surface to you, and roll it to the size it was originally. (Always roll away from you; never return the rolling pin toward you.)

Now fold again as before; one third to the center and the other third over the folded part. Press bottom and top edges together. Wrap loosely in waxed paper and refrigerate 15 to 30 minutes. Repeat rolling, folding and chilling, four more times, always facing the open ends (those not folded over) toward you. (Mark dough with fingertip impression to keep track of turns.) Preheat oven to 400° F.

Finally, roll dough into a $20 \times 8 \times \frac{1}{2}$-inch rectangle. Spread with fig-preserve filling, ¼ inch thick, over half of dough (along length). Lift other half to cover filling; seal open edges with egg yolk and press firmly with fingers. Lift onto ungreased baking sheet and twist into a wreath (ring).

Cut leaves and flowers from leftover dough; brush one side with egg yolk and paste them on wreath. Bake about 40 minutes. Cool before glazing.

Apricot Glaze: Heat ½ cup apricot preserve with 2 tablespoons water for 8 to 10 minutes. Brush over tops and sides of pastry; wait 5 minutes and repeat.

SERVES: 8 to 10

NOTE: Leftover fig-preserve filling should be poured into an airtight jar and stored in refrigerator. Leave at room temperature for 15 minutes before using. It's an excellent preserve.

CANNOLI

Sicilians are the creators of *cannoli* (fried pastry horns filled with a delicious mixture of sweetened ricotta cheese, chocolate, candied fruit, and nuts). In my opinion, they are the most delectable of pastries. I bow in thanks to Sicily for this marvelous creation.

SHELLS:
- 2 cups sifted flour
- 2 tablespoons shortening or lard
- 1 teaspoon honey
- ¼ teaspoon salt
- ¾ cup Marsala wine

- 1 egg, slightly beaten
- 1½ quarts vegetable oil
- Metal tubes (6×¾ inches—available in gourmet shops)

FILLING:
- 1 pound ricotta cheese, drained
- ½ cup confectioners' sugar
- 2 ounces semisweet chocolate, coarsely grated
- 3 tablespoons chopped citron
- ½ teaspoon cinnamon
- 2 tablespoons crème de cacao
- 12 strips candied orange
- 12 glazed cherries
- ½ cup pistachio nuts, toasted, chopped

Combine flour, shortening, honey, and salt, wetting mixture gradually with Marsala wine. Knead with fingers until dough is firm. Shape into ball; cover with cloth and let stand for 1 hour.

Combine ricotta cheese with confectioners' sugar, grated chocolate, citron, cinnamon, and crème de cacao. Refrigerate until ready to use.

After 1 hour, cut dough in half and roll into thin sheets ¼-inch thick. Using a sharp knife, cut dough into 4-inch squares. Place metal tubes diagonally across squares. Wrap dough around each tube by overlapping the two opposite points. Seal points with beaten egg, pressing together with fingers.

In frying kettle, heat vegetable oil to 370° F. (1-inch bread cube browns evenly in 1 minute). Drop tubes carefully, a few at a time, into hot oil. Fry on all sides until shells acquire a deep golden brown color. Remove with slotted spoon and drain on absorbent paper. When cool enough to handle, gently remove tubes from shells. Set shells aside to cool on absorbent paper. Continue until all shells are fried.

Fill pastry bag with cheese filling and pipe filling into ends of shells (or spoon filling into shell ends). Place 1 strip candied orange on one end of shells, a glazed cherry on the other end. Sprinkle both ends with pistachio nuts.

YIELD: 1 dozen

NOTE: Shells store well in airtight containers. Filled shells may be frozen.

VARIATION:

HAZELNUT-BUTTERCREAM FILLING:
½ cup butter
1 box confectioners' sugar
2 tablespoons crème de cacao

1 cup hazelnuts, chopped fine
2 to 3 tablespoons cocoa
2 to 4 tablespoons milk

Combine all ingredients and mix until mixture is smooth, thick, and creamy. Fill as directed above.

Cucidati
FIG COOKIES

FILLING:
1 ring (1 pound) dried figs, chopped
1 cup seedless raisins
Rind of 1 large orange
½ pound walnut or hazelnut meats, roasted and chopped
1 cup honey
½ cup bourbon whiskey
1 teaspoon cinnamon

PASTRY:
2½ cups sifted flour
½ cup sugar
2½ teaspoons baking powder
¼ teaspoon salt
½ cup butter or margarine
2 eggs
½ teaspoon vanilla
¼ cup milk

ICING:
½ box confectioners' sugar (1½ cups)
Juice of 2 lemons
Multicolored cake-decorating sprinkles

Preheat oven to 400° F. Grease two baking sheets.

Grind or blend figs, raisins, orange rind, and walnuts together. (Add 2 tablespoons water if mixture is too thick for grinding.) Use medium blade and grind to a coarse consistency. Stir in honey, whiskey, and cinnamon; mix well. Set aside.

Sift flour, sugar, baking powder, and salt together. Cut in butter with pastry blender or two knives until mixture resembles coarse cornmeal. Stir in eggs, vanilla, and milk and mix until dough is smooth. Gather up with fingers and form into a ball.

Turn onto a lightly floured board and roll out ¼ inch thick. Cut dough into 4-inch strips. On one half of strip, spread a row of filling 1 inch thick. Fold over dough half to cover filling. With fingers or fork, press edges together to seal filling in. Slicing on a slant, cut filled strip into 1-inch slices. Repeat process until dough and filling are finished.

Place slices on greased baking sheets 1 inch apart and bake until slices are lightly browned—15 to 20 minutes. Remove from oven and cool on wire racks.

Combine confectioners' sugar and lemon juice; mix into smooth glaze. Glaze cookies with icing and decorate with multicolored sprinkles.

YIELD: Approximately 5 dozen

VARIATION: Cut dough into star, round, or crescent shapes with cookie cutter. Place 1 rounded tablespoon of filling in center of dough; cover with same dough shape and press edges together with fork. Cut small slits, criss-cross fashion, on top of each cookie. Bake and ice as directed above.

NOTE: *Cucidati* store well for weeks in an airtight container. Filling and dough may be made in advance and stored in refrigerator for 1 week.

THE WINES
OF SICILY

Wines produced in Sicily are strong and rich in flavor, sparkle like fire, and are sweet and aromatic with deep, changing reflections.

The merits of Sicilian wines are many, but Marsala wine is world-renowned for its quality and flavor. Strange as it may seem, an Englishman named John Woodhouse invented Marsala wine. He knew how heartily and readily Madeira wine was consumed in England; therefore, being ingenious and enterprising, he discovered that Marsala and Madeira were at about the same latitude. At the end of the seventeenth century, he opened a wine factory in the little Sicilian city of Marsala. He produced a wine as good as Madeira, which soon became the favorite of the wealthy in England. In fact, Woodhouse's success inspired so many Englishmen to settle in Marsala that the English government established a consulate there.

Marsala wine is dry and sweet, warm and generous, with a characteristic aroma. The dry variety is used in cooking or for an aperitif, and sweet Marsala is used in desserts.

Muscatel is another favorite wine made in many regions of Sicily, but Muscatel from Syracuse and Pantelleria (a small island southwest of Sicily) is the finest. It was first produced in the seventh century by King Pollius, who brought the vines to Syracuse from Biblina, in Thrace, where they originated. Muscatel is a sweet dessert wine that is also served between meals. It is full-bodied and velvety, and its aroma is penetrating.

Other notable Sicilian wines and liqueurs are charted by province, distinguishing characteristics, and availability in the United States. Unfortunately, the selection of Sicilian wines exported to America is narrow, because of poor promotion and distribution.

PROVINCE	NAME	TYPE	COLOR	WHEN TO SERVE	AVAILABLE IN U.S.
Palermo	Partinico Bianco	Dry	Pale straw	Aperitif	No
	Marsala Fine	Moderately sweet (17% alcohol)	Golden yellow	Dessert wine	Yes
	Marsala Superior	Moderately sweet (18% alcohol)	Golden yellow	Dessert wine	Yes
	Marsala al Caffè	Sweet, coffee flavor	Amber	Aperitif and dessert wine	Yes
	Marsala alla Fragola	Sweet, straw-berry flavor	Amber	Aperitif and dessert wine	Yes
	Marsala alla Mandorla	Sweet, almond flavor	Amber	Aperitif and dessert wine	Yes
	Crema Marsala	Sweet; similar to sherry in flavor	Amber	Aperitif and dessert wine	Yes
	Marsala all'Uovo	Sweet, eggy flavor	Amber	Aperitif and dessert wine	Yes
Trapani	Segesta	Moderately dry	Pale straw and garnet red	With fish and poultry With red meats, roasts	Yes

PROVINCE	NAME	TYPE	COLOR	WHEN TO SERVE	AVAILABLE IN U.S.
Ragusa	Cerasuolo di Vittoria	Dry and slightly bitter	Cherry	When young, good table wine; when aged, aperitif	No
Syracuse	Albanello di Siracusa	Dry and slightly bitter	Golden yellow	Aperitif	No
	Eloro Bianco	Dry	Deep straw	With fish	No
	Muscatel di Noto	Moderately sweet	Bright amber yellow	Aperitif	Yes
	Muscatel di Siracusa	Fairly sweet	Bright amber yellow	Aperitif	Yes
	Eloro Rosso	Dry	Garnet red	Table wine; with roasts	No
Catania	Etna Bianco	Dry and delicate	White	With fish, fowl	No
	Etna Rosato	Dry and fragrant	Pink	With meat, fish, poultry	No
	Etna Rosso	Dry	Vivid ruby red	Table wine; when aged, with red and white meat, roasts, and game	No

PROVINCE	NAME	TYPE	COLOR	WHEN TO SERVE	AVAILABLE IN U.S.
Taormina	Taormina wine	Dry	Pale straw	With fish	No
	Cappo Rosso	Dry	Pink	Good table wine	No
	Faro	Dry	Vivid ruby red	Excellent with red and white meat, roasts, fowl, and game	No
Messina	Capo Bianco	Dry and delicate	Pale straw	With fish	No
	Malvasia di Lipari	Sweet and delicate	Golden yellow	Dessert wine	No
	Mamertino Dry	Dry and sweetish	Golden yellow	With fish	No
	Mamertino Sweet	Sweet and velvety	Golden yellow	Dessert wine	No
Liqueurs (throughout Sicily)	Sicilian Gold	Sweet	Pale straw	After dinner	Yes
	Mandor Crema	Sweet	Amber	After dinner	Yes
	Anisette	Sweet	White	After dinner	Yes

INDEX

Aglio, 167
Agnello alla Cacciatora, 103–4
Albanello di Siracusa Wine, 210
All Souls' Day, 22
Almond Blossom Festival, 9
Almond Marmalade Tarts, 188
Almond Paste, Marzipan of, 15–16
Anchovies,
  Antipasto with Peppers and, 156–57
  Fried Spaghetti with, 39
  Fritters, Dad's Special, 119
  Pizza Toppings with, 117, 118, 121
  Sauce, 162–63
  for Squid, 70
Angel's Hair with Bread Crumbs, 44
Anise, 189
  Sponge Cake, 189
  Toast, 193
Anisetta. *See* Anise
Anisette Liqueur, 211
Antipasto, Anchovy-Pepper (*di Peperoni e Acciughe*), 156–57
Apple Fritters, Holiday, 116
Apricot Glaze, 203
Aranci Caramellati, 178–79
Arancini, 52–53
Arrosti: (Roast Meats). *See* Beef, Lamb, Veal
Artichoke Hearts,
  Crisp-Fried, 146
  Pie, 152

Rice with Olives and, 55
  Snappy, 145–46
Artichokes, Stuffed, 133
Arugula Salad, 147
  Tomato and, 147
Asparagus Omelet, 60–61

Baccalà con Olive in Umido, 73
Basil (*Basilico*), 168
Bass, Fish Stew with, 76
Beans,
  and Escarole, Stewed Cannellini, 133–34
  Royal Fava, 134
  Salad with String, 140–41
  and Tomatoes, String, 142–43
Beef,
  Birds in Wine Sauce, 86–87
  Boiled Dinner, 91–92
  Cannelloni from the Valley of the Temples, 35–36
  and Eggplant Casserole, 49–50
  Eggplants Stuffed with, 132
  Hamburgers, Nutty Broiled, 104–5
  Liver, Saged, 90
  Macaroni Casserole, Eggplant and, 49–50
  Macaroni Casserole, Eggy, 32–33
  Meatball Soup, 27
  Meatballs, Spicy Fried, 104
  Meatloaf, Three-Meat, 85
  Onions Stuffed with, 132

Peppers Stuffed with, 140
Ravioli, Spinach and, 44–45
Rice Croquettes with, 53
Roast, Red Wine Sirloin, 97
Rolled, in Tomato Sauce, 88–89
Roll-Ups, 98
    Variation, 97
Sauce, Tomato and, 165
Sausage Tiranno with, 101–2
Spinach Loaf, Stuffed, 95–95
and Spinach Ravioli, 44–45
Steak, Breaded and Broiled, 87
Steak, Piquant Shell, 92–93
Steak Palermo Style, Sirloin, 88
Steak in Spicy Tomato Sauce,
    90
Bianco Mangiare, 189
Bieda e Pomodori in Padella,
    149
Biscotti. See Cookies
Bistecca. See Beef
Bollito de Manzo, 91–92
Bonata, 94–95
Braciole di Pesce Spada, 75
Bread, 114–26
    Cheese, Pepper-Speckled, 177
    Fritters, Anchovy, 119
    Fritters, Holiday, 116
    Golden Braid, 125–26
    of Monreale, Artichoke-Shaped,
        123–24
    Pizza. *See* Pizza
    Sandwich Surprise, Baked, 122
    Sassy Carnival Rolls, 122–23
    Sesame-Seed Rolls, 124–25
Broccoli, Deviled, 155–56
Broccoli Affogati, 138
Broccoli Fra Diavolo, 155–56
Buba cu l'Uova, 13
Bucce d'Arancia Candite, 179
Buccelato, 202–3
Budino di Castagne e Cioccolato,
    190

Bulgur, Cùscusu with, 17–19
Burdocks (Cardoons), Fried,
    146–47
Buttercream Filling, Hazelnut, 205

Cabbage, Croquettes, 144
    Savory Skillet, 144
Caciocavallo Cheese, 65
Cake, Anise Sponge, 189
    Cassata, 194–95
Calamari. *See* Squid
Caldarroste, 184
Calf's Liver. *See* Veal
Calzoni, 122
Cannella, 168
Cannellini Beans and Escarole,
    133–34
Cannelloni from the Valley of the
    Temples, 35–36
Cannoli, 204–5
Capelli d'Angelo with Bread
    Crumbs, 44
Capers, 168
    Sauce for Chicken, 112
Capo d'Anno, 7–8
Capo Bianco Wine, 211
Capon with Sausage Stuffing, 109
Capperi. See Capers
Cappone Ripieno con Salsiccia,
    109
Cappo Rosso Wine, 210
Capunatina, 158–59
Caramel Oranges, 178–79
Carciofi alla Nanna Greco, 133
Carciofini al Forno, 145–46
Cardoons (Cardune) Fried, 146–
    47
Carrots (*Carote*) with Marsala,
    Caramelized, 156
Cashew Nut-Chocolate Meringues,
    197
Cassata, 194–95
Cassatine, 198–99

Castagne Candite, 185
Cauliflower,
　Fritters, Holiday, 116
　and Pasta Shells, 43
　Rosettes, Black and White, 129
　Salad, 135
　Smothered, 138
Cavolfiore Fritto con Olive, 129
Cavolo in Padella, 144
Cerasuolo di Vittoria Wine, 210
Cheese, 64–66
　Bread, Pepper-Speckled, 117
　Calzoni, 122
　Cannoli Filling, 204–5
　Cassata Filling, 194
　Cruller Filling, 11
　Eggplant Quartet, 154–55
　Eggplant Sandwiches with, 131
　Frosting for Wafer Rosettes, 201
　Omelets. *See Eggs*
　Pasta Dishes. *See* Pasta
　Pizza. *See* Pizza
　Ravioli Filling, 46
　Salad, Salami and, 136
　and Spleen Sandwiches, 105
　Sassy Carnival Rolls with, 122–23
　Squid with Ricotta Stuffing, 79
　Tart Filling, 198–99
　Torte, Rice, Meat and, 56
　and Ziti Casserole, Baked, 33
Cherries, Candied Confection with, 181
Chestnuts,
　Candied, 185
　Chocolate Loaf, 190
　Roasted, 184
Chicken
　Breasts, Elegant Stuffed, 113
　Cacciatore, 110–11
　in Caper Sauce, 111

　Deviled, 108
　with Eggplant, 111–12
　Lemon-Broiled, 108
　in the Pot, 111
　Rice, Cheese, and Meat Torte, 56–57
　Roll-Ups (Variation), 97
　with Sausage Stuffing, Capon, 109
　with Tuna Sauce, Messina Style, 107
Chick-Peas,
　Croquettes, 139–40
　Salad, 151
　Soup, 3, 27
　and Wheat Kernels, 3
Chiodo di Garofano, 168
Chocolate, Chestnut Loaf, 190
　-Chip Watermelon Mold, 178
　Hazelnut Meringues, 197
　Spice Cookies, 200–1
Christmas, 4–6
Cinnamon, 168
Cipolle. See Onions
Clams, Pizza Topping with, 120
　Rice Fisherman Style with, 55–56
Clove, 168
Coccodè, 176–77
Codfish, Fish Stew with, 76
　Messina Style, 71
　Stew, 73
Coffee Custard, 202
Companatto o Soffritto di Frattaglie, 105–6
Conchiglie con Cavolfiore, 43
Coniglio in Agrodolce, 109–10
Cookies,
　Anise Toast, 193
　Chocolate-Hazelnut Meringues, 197
　Chocolate Spice, 200–1

Fig, 205–6
Pine Nut, 188–89
Pistachio, 22
Sesame, 199
Wafer Rosettes, 197–98
Costolette (cutlets). *See* Veal; etc.
Cozze alla Marinara, 69
Cracked Wheat, Cùscusu with, 17–19
Cream, Frosting for Cassata, 194–95
    Gingered, 184
    Strawberry, 177
Cremolata di Caffè, 202
Crocchette. See Croquettes
Croquettes,
    Cabbage, 144
    Chick-Pea, 139–40
    Egg, 35, 63
    Rice, 52–53
    Sardine, 69–70
Crosetti, 47
Crullers, 11–12
Cuccia, 2
Cucidati, 205–6
Cucumber Salad, 135
Cùscusu, 17–19
Custard,
    Coffee, 202
    Marsala, 177
    "Frozen Fried Eggs," 176–77
    Turks' Heads with, 192–93
Cuttlefish, Fish Stew with, 76
    Macaroni with, 42

Desserts, 186–206. *See also* Fruit
    Almond Marmalade Tarts, 188
    Anise Sponge Cake, 189
    Anise Toast, 193
    Cannoli, 204–5
    Cassata, 194–95
    Cheese-Filled Tarts, 198–99
    Chocolate-Chestnut Loaf, 190
    Chocolate-Hazelnut Meringues, 197
    Chocolate Spice Cookies, 200–1
    Coffee Custard, 202
    Fig Cookies, 205–6
    Fig Preserve Pastry Wreath, 202–3
    Frozen Fried Eggs, 176–77
    Honey Balls, 190–91
    Marsala Custard, 177
    Marzipan, 15–16
    Melting Moments, 189
    Pine Nut Cookies, 188–89
    Pine Nut Fudge, 191–92
    Sesame Cookies, 199
    Sweet Ravioli, 196
    Turks' Heads, 192–93

Easter, 12–13
Eggplant,
    Cheese Quartet, 154–55
    Chicken with, 111–12
    Meat and Macaroni Casserole, 49–50
    Meat-Stuffed, Individual, 132
    Parmesan, 150–51
    and Pepper Medley, 129–30
    Peppers Stuffed with, 140
    Quails, 136–37
    and Rice, Palermo Style, 54–55
    Salad, 158–59
    Sandwiches, Breaded, 131
    Soup, 28–29
    Spicy Halves, 145
    Springtime, 130–31
    Urchins, 148
Eggs, 59–63
    Asparagus Omelet, 60–61
    Croquettes, 35, 63
    Easter Baskets, 13
    Ham Omelet Cake, 59–60

Lasagne with, 34
Meat and Macaroni Casserole with, 32–33
Mozzarella Omelet, 62
Peppers, Potatoes, and, 63
Poached, in Tomato Sauce, 62–63
Ricotta Omelet in Tomato Sauce, 60
Salad, Tomato and, 137
Scrambled, with Tomatoes, 62
Soup, Egg-Drop, with Mushrooms and Tomatoes, 26
Soup, Potato, 26
Spaghetti, Fried, with, 39
Spaghetti, Lenten, with, 34–35
Spinach-Cheese Omelet, 61
Eloro Wines, 210
Escarole and Cannellini Beans, Stewed, 133–34
and Ham Roll-Ups, 143
Etna Wines, 210

Fagiolini Casalinghi al Pomodoro, 142–43
Fanfarichi, 119
Farsumagru in Salsa di Pomodoro, 88–89
Fava Beans, Royal, 134
Fave dei Morti, 22
Fave del Re, 134
Fegato. *See* Liver
Fennel, 169
Fried Sardines, 76
and Lettuce Salad, 134
Ferragosto, 20–21
Festivals, 1–22
All Souls' Day, 22
Almond Blossom Festival, 9
Christmas, 4–6
Easter, 12–13
Grape-Gathering, 21

of the Madonna, Feast, 20–21
New Year's, 6–8
St. Agatha's, 8–9
St. John the Baptist's, 19–20
St. Joseph's, 10–12
St. Lucy's, 2–3
Sicilian Cart, 14–16
Tuna Kill, 16–19
Fette di Melanzane Ripieni, 131
Fettine di Vitello al Forno, 93–94
Fettine di Vitello alla Garibaldi, 93
Fettuccine, Spinach, with Tomato Sauce, 43–44
Fichi Freschi Gelati, 183–84
Fichi d'India, 183
Figs,
Cookies, 205–6
Fritters, Holiday, 116
Ice Cream, 175–76
Iced Fresh, 183–84
Pastry Wreath with Preserve Filling, 202–3
Finocchio. See Fennel
Fiorelli, 197
Fish and Seafood, 67–80. *See also* specific kinds
Cùscusu, 17–19
Fry, Combination, 77–78
Rice Fisherman Style, 55–56
Salad, Cold, 72
Stew Syracuse Style, 76
Focacce, 124–25
Fragole. See Strawberries
Frittatone alla Campagnola, 59–60
Fritteda, 25
Frittelline della Festa, 116
Fritters, Anchovy or Shrimp, Dad's Special, 119
Holiday, 116
Fritto Misto di Pesce, 77–78
Frittura di Carciofini, 146

Froscie (Omelets). *See* Eggs
Frostings. *See also* Icings
  for Cassata, Cream, 194–95
  for Chocolate Spice Cookies, 201
  for Wafer Rosettes, Cheese, 197–98
Fruit, 172–85. *See also* specific kinds
  Cassata with, 194–95
  Confections, 181
  Ravioli, 196
  Salad, Fresh, 180–81
  Shake, Iced, 182
Frullata di Frutta, 182
Frutta Candita, 181
Fudge, Pine Nut, 191–92
Funghi. See Mushrooms
Fusilli al Forno, 32–33

Garlic, 167
Gelato di Fichi, 175–76
Gelselmo, 178
Gingered Cream, 185
Giorno dei Morti, Il, 22
Glassatura di Limone, 200
Glaze, Apricot, 203
Gnocchi with Meat Sauce, 38
Gnocculli, 38
Granite. See Ices
Grapefruit Peel, Candied, 179
Grapes, Candied Confection with, 181
Grassato, 162

Haddock, Cùscusu with, 18–19
Halibut, Fish Fry with, 77–78
Ham,
  Eggplant Sandwiches with, 131
  and Escarole Roll-Ups, 143
  Omelet Cake, 59–60
  Pizza Topping with, 120

Sassy Carnival Rolls with, 122–23
Haslet Stew, 105–6
Hazelnut-Buttercream Filling, 205
Hazelnut-Chocolate Meringues, 197
Herbs and Spices, 167–71
Honey Balls, 190–91
Honeydew. *See* Melon

Ice Cream, Cake (Cassata), 195
  Fig, 175–76
Ices,
  Honeydew, 174
  Lemon, 176
  Plum, 175
Icings. *See also* Frostings
  for Fig Cookies, 205–6
  Lemon, 200
  for Pine Nut Fudge, 91–92
Incanestrato Cheese, 65
Insalate. See Salads
Involtini (Roll-Ups). *See* specific meats

Lamb,
  Haslet Stew, 105–6
  Rice, Potatoes, and, Hunter's Style, 103–4
  Roast, Mama Lucia's, 95–96
  Spleen and Cheese Sandwiches, 105
  Stew, Spring, 101
Lasagne, New Year's and Carnival, 34
Lasagne, Zucchini and Meat Pie with, 47
Leaves of Paste alla Pirandello, 37–38
Lemon-Broiled Chicken, 108
Lemon Ice, 176
Lemon Icing, 200
Lemon Peaches, 180

Lemon Sauce, 161–62
Lenticchie con Salsicce al Formo, 94
Lentils,
  Baked Sausages over, 94
  Salad, 153
  Soup, 24–25
Lettuce and Fennel Salad, 134
Linguine with Squid Sauce (*in Salsa di Calamari*), 41–42
Liqueurs, 211
Liver,
  Broiled Pork, 89
  Haslet Stew with, 105–6
  Saged, 90
  Tangy Calf's, 100
Lumache in Umido, 79
Lungs, Haslet Stew with, 105–6

Macaroni. *See also* Pasta
  Casserole, Eggplant, Meat, and, 49–50
  Casserole, Eggy Meat and, 32–33
  with Cuttlefish, 42
Maccheroni con le Seppie, 42
Macedonia di Frutta, 180–81
Mafalda, Zucchini and Meat Pie with, 47
Maggiroana, 169
Malvasia di Lipari Wine, 211
Mamertino Wines, 211
Mandor Crema Liqueur, 211
Manteca Cheese, 65
Marjoram, 169
Marsala Custard, 177
  "Frozen Fried Eggs" with, 176–77
Marsala Wines, 208, 209
Marzipan, 15–16
Mattanza, La, 16–19
Meat, 81–106. *See also* specific kinds

Haslet stew, 105–6
  Sauce, 165
    Sicilian, 162
Meatballs,
  Pizza Topping with, 120
  Soup, 27
  Spicy Fried, 104
Meatloaf, Three-Meats, 85
Melagrana Sorbetto, 175
Melanzane. *See* Eggplant
Melon,
  Beautiful Stuffed, 173–74
  Ice, Honeydew, 174
  with Sicilian Gold Liqueur, 183
  Watermelon Mold, Chocolate-Chip, 178
Melone. See Melon
Menta, 169
Meringues, Chocolate-Hazelnut, 197
Mille Foglie alla Pirandello, 37–38
Milza Ripiena, 103
Minestra di Ceci, 27
Minestra di Melanzane, 28–29
Minestrone, 134
  Sweet and Sour, 25
Minestrone di Lenticche, 24–25
Minestrone di Trippa, 29
Mint, 169
Mozzarella Cheese. *See* Cheese
Mozzarella Fritta con Uova, 62
Mullet in Orange Sauce, Baked Rolled Fillet, 74
Muscatel Wines, 208, 210
Mushrooms, with Pine Nuts, Baked, 138
  Sauce of Tomato and, 164
  Stuffed Capfuls, 155
Mussels, Fish Stew with, 76
  Pizza Topping with, 120
  Sailor Style, Steamed, 69

Nasello. *See* Whiting
Natale, 5–6
New Year's, 6–8
Noccioline di Manzo in Brodo, 27
Noce Moscata, 169
Noodles. *See* Pasta
Nutmeg, 169

Octopus, Seafood Salad with, 72
Olive Condite, 154
Olives, 170
  Relish of, 154
Onions, 168
  Herbed Pearls, 142
  Salad, Orange and, 157–58
  Stuffed, Palermo Style, 132
Orange Peel, Candied, 179
Oranges,
  Caramel, 178–79
  Salad, Onion, 157–58
  Sauce, for Mullet, 74
Orégano (*Origano*), 169
Oréganoed Pork Chops, 99
Ortaggi Freddi alla Giardiniera,
  157

Pan di Spagna al'Anice, 189
*Pane con Formaggio e Pepe al
  Forno,* 117
Pane di Monreale, 123–24
Panelle Croccre, 139–40
Panini Rustici, 122–23
Papayas and Melon with Sicilian
  Gold Liqueur, 183
Partinico Blanco wine, 209
Pasqua, 12–13
Pasta, 30–50
  Angel's Hair with Bread Crumbs,
  44
  Cannelloni from the Valley of
  the Temples, 35–36

Fettuccine, Spinach, with Tomato
  Sauce, 43–44
Gnocchi with Meat Sauce, 38
  Home-Made, 40–41
Lasagne, New Year's and Carni-
  val, 34
Lasagne, Zucchini and Meat Pie
  with, 47
Leaves of Paste alla Pirandello,
  37–38
Linguine with Squid Sauce, 41–
  42
Macaroni Casserole, Eggplant,
  Meat, and, 49–50
Macaroni with Cuttlefish, 42
Pasta con le Sarde, 45–46
Mafalda, Zucchini and Meat Pie
  with, 47
Perciatelli, Green and Silver, 45–
  46
Ravioli, Mama's, 46
Ravioli, Meat and Spinach,
  44–45
Ravioli, Sweet, 196
Rigatoni Donnafugata, 47–48
Shells and Cauliflower, 43
Spaghetti,
  Coachmen's, 40
  Fried, 39
  Green and Silver, 45–46
  Lenten, 34–35
  alla Norma, 48–49
Vermicelli with Bread Crumbs,
  44
Vermicelli, Fried, 39
Vermicelli Syracuse Style, 36–37
Wagon Wheels, Baked, 39–40
Ziti and Cheese Casserole, 33
Zucchini and Meat Pie, 47
Pasticcio di Riso, 56–57
Peaches, Lemon, 180
  in Red Wine, 174

Pears and Gingered Cream, Baked, 184–85
Pecorino Siciliano Cheese, 66
Pepato Cheese, 66
Pepe, 170
Peperonata, 151
Peperoni. See Peppers
Pepper, 170
Pepperoni, Pizza Topping with, 117
Peppers,
    Antipasto of Anchovies and, 156–57
    and Eggplant Medley, 129–30
    Fried Sweet, 151
    Potatoes, Eggs, and, 63
    Sausage-Stuffed, 141
    Stuffed Sunset, 140
Perciatelli, Green and Silver, 45–46
Pere al Forno con Panna, 184–85
Pesce Spada. See Swordfish
Pesche. See Peaches
Pie, Artichoke, 152
    Zucchini and Meat, 47
Pignoli. *See* Pine Nuts
Pine Nuts, 170
    Cookies, 188–89
    Fudge, 191–92
Piscistoccu a Missinisa, 71
Pistachio Cookies, 22
Pizza,
    Catania Style, 121
    with Four Toppings (*ai Quatro Gusti*), 120
    Instant, (*Espresso*), 116–17
    Muffoletto, 118
Plum Ice, 175
Polenta, Baked, 90
Pollo. *See* Chicken
Polpette de Carne Fritte, 104

Polpette di Carne alla Griglia, 104–5
Polpettone di Manzo, Maiale, e Vitello, 85
Pomegranate Sherbet, 175
Pomodori. See Tomatoes
Pork. *See also* Sausage
    Cannelloni from the Valley of the Temples with, 35–36
    Chops, Oréganoed, 99
    Chops, Tipsy, 86
    Cutlets in Marsala, 92
    Livers, Broiled, 89
    Meatloaf with, 85
    Meat Sauce with, 162
    Rice Croquettes with, 53
    Roll-Ups, 96–97
Potatoes, Egg Soup with, 26
    Eggs, Peppers, and, 63
    Lamb, Rice, and, 103–4
Poultry, 106–13. *See also* Chicken
Prickly Pears, 183
Prosciutto. *See* Ham
Pudding, Melting Moments, 189
Puff Paste, 202

Quaglie de Melanzane, 136–37

Rabbit, Sweet and Sour, 109–10
Ragù alla Siciliana, 162
Ragusana Cheese, 66
Ravioli, Mama's, 46
    Meat and Spinach, 44–45
    Sweet, 196
Relish, Olive, 154
    Tomato, 150
Ricci di Melanzane al Forno, 148
Rice, 51–57
    with Artichokes and Olives, 55
    Cheese and Meat Torte, 56–57
    Croquettes, 52–53

and Eggplant, Palermo Style, 54–55
Fisherman Style, 55–56
Lamb, Potatoes, and Hunter's Style, 103–4
Ring, Cold, 53–54
Tomatoes Stuffed with, 149
Ricotta. *See also* Cheese
Salata, 66
Rigatoni Donnafugata, 47–48
Riso; Risotto. See Rice
Rocket (Arugula; Rocket Cress) Salad, 147
Rosemaried Veal Roast, 85
Rosemaried Broiled Swordfish, 77
Rosemary (*Rosmarino*), 170
Rotellini al Forno, 39–40
Rugula (Arugula) Salad, 147

Saffron, 171
Sage, 171
Saged Calf's Liver, 90
Sagra dei Mandorli in Fiore, 9
Sagra della Vendemmia, 21
Salads,
Bean, String, 140–41
Beef Dinner, Boiled, 91–92
Cauliflower, 135
Cheese and Salami, 136
Chick-Pea, 151
Cucumber, 135
Egg and Tomato, 137
Eggplant, 148–49
Fennel and Lettuce, 134
Fruit, Fresh, 180–81
Lentil, 153
Lettuce and Fennel, 134
Orange and Onion, 157–58
Rice Ring, Cold, 53–54
Salami and Cheese, 136
Seafood, Cold, 72
Tomato and Arugula, 147
Tomato and Egg, 137
Tomato, Snow-Topped, 137
Tuna, 80
Salami, and Cheese Salad, 136
Sassy Carnival Rolls with, 122–23
Sale, 170
Salmoriglio, 161–62
Salse. See Sauces
Salsicce. See Sausage
Salt, 170
Salvia, 171
Sandwiches, Baked Eggplant, 131
Sandwich Surprise, Baked, 122
Sarde. See Sardines
Sarde a Beccaficu, 70
Sardines,
Butterflies, 70–71
Croquettes, 69–70
Fennel-Fried, 76
Green and Silver Spaghetti with, 45–46
Pizza Topping with, 118
Marinated Raw-Cooked, 75
Sauces, 160–65
Anchovy, 162–63
for Squid, 70
Caper, for Chicken, 112
Lemon, 161–62
Marinara, 165
Meat, 165
Sicilian, 162
Mushroom and Tomato, 164
Orange, for Mullet, 74
Pizzaiola, 90
Ruby, 163
Sailor Style, 165
Sesame, 163
for Whiting, 72
Squid, 41–42
Tomato. *See* Tomato Sauce
Tuna, Chicken with, 107
Sausage, 101–3
Baked, 102–3

Broiled, 102
Capon Stuffed with, 109
and Escarole Roll-Ups, 143
Fried, 102
Grilled, 102, 103
Hors d'Oeuvres, 103
Lasagne with, 34
over Lentils (Pebbles), Baked, 94
Peppers Stuffed with, 141
Pizza Toppings with Pepperoni, 117, 120
Tiranno, 101–2
Scacciata, 121
Scaloppine. See specific meats
Scallops, Cùscusu with, 18–19
Scarola e Cannellini in Umido, 133–34
Segesta Wine, 209
Semi di Sesamo. See Sesame Seeds
Sesame Seeds, 171
Cookies, 199
Rolls, 124–25
Sauce, 163
for Whiting, 72
Sfinge, 11–12
Shells and Cauliflower, 43
Sherbet, Pomegranate, 175
Shrimp,
Fish Fry with, 77–78
Fritters, Dad's Special, 119
Rice Fisherman Style with, 55–56
Seafood Salad with, 72
Sicilian Gold Liqueur, 211
Sicilian Cart Festival, 14–16
Sicilian Crullers, 11–12
Smelt. *See* Sardines
Snail Stew, 79
Sole Rolls in Tomato Sauce, 75
Soup, 24–29
Beef Dinner, Boiled, 91–92
Chick-Pea, 27

and Wheat Kernels, 3
Egg-Drop, with Mushrooms and Tomatoes, 26
Eggplant, 28–29
Egg and Potato, 26
Fish Stew Syracuse Style, 76
Lentil, 24–25
Meatball, 27
Minestrone, 134
Sweet and Sour, 25
Potato and Egg, 26
Tripe Chowder, 29
Vegetable, Fresh, 28
Vegetable, Sweet and Sour Minestrone, 25
Spaghetti,
Coachman's (*alla Carretiera*), 40
Fried, 39
Green and Silver, 45–46
Lenten (*di Quaresima*), 34–35
alla Norma, 48–49
Spicchi d'Arancioe Cipolle in Insalata, 157–58
Spices and Herbs, 167–71
Spiedini alla Siciliana, 98
Spinach,
and Beef Loaf, Stuffed, 94–95
and Beef Ravioli, 44–45
Bouquet à la Muffoletto, 153
Cheese Omelet, 61
Spinach Fettuccine with Tomato Sauce, 43–44
Spleen, Baked Stuffed Veal, 103
and Cheese Sandwiches, 105
Sponge Cake, Anise, 189
Spumetti, 197
Squid,
in Anchovy Sauce, Stuffed, 70
Casserole, Ricotta-Stuffed, 79
Fish Fry with, 77–78
Rice Fisherman Style with, 55–56
Sauce, 41–42

Seafood Salad with, 72
in Tomato Sauce, Stuffed, 68–69
*Stracciatella con Funghi e Pomo-
dori,* 26
Strawberries, Candied Confection
with, 181
Cream with, E-Z, 177
with Marsala, 182
Struffoli, 190–91
Stufato di Agnello Primavera, 101
Sugar, Spun, 179
Vanilla, 196
Sugo di Carne e Pomodori, 165
Swiss Chard and Tomato Medley,
149
Swordfish, Cùscusu with, 18–19
Rolls in Tomato Sauce, 75
Rosemaried Broiled, 77
Sailor Style, 74

Tangerines, Candied Confection
with, 181
Taormina Wine, 210
Tarts, Almond Marmalade, 188
Cheese-Filled, 198–99
Teste di Turchi, 192–93
Thyme, (*Time*), 171
Tomato Sauce. *See also* Pasta
Beef, Rolled, in, 88–89
Beefsteak in Spicy, 90
for Codfish, 73
for Eggs, Poached, 62–63
Meat and, 165
Sicilian, 162
Mushroom and, 164
Pizza, 117, 118
Ruby, 163
Sailor Style, 165
for Spinach Fettuccine, 43–44
for Squid Casserole, 79
Winter's, 164
Tomatoes. *See also* Tomato Sauce

Grecian Stuffed, 149
Relish, 150
Salad, Arugula and, 147
Salad, Egg and, 137
Salad, Egg and, 137
Salad, Snow-Tipped, 137
and String Beans, 142–43
and Swiss Chard Medley, 149
Tonno in Salsa Agrodolce, 78
Torte, Rice, Cheese, and Meat,
56–57
Tortino di Carciofini, 152
Treccia Dorata, 125–26
Triglia al Forno, 74
Tripe Chowder, 29
Tuna,
Cùscusu with, 17–19
Fried Spaghetti with, 39
Salad, 80
Sauce, Chicken with, 107
Sweet and Sour, 78
Tuna Kill, The, 16–19
Turbot, Cùscusu with, 18–19
Turks' Heads, 192–93
Turnovers, Calzoni, 122

Uove. *See* Eggs

Vanilla (*Vaniglia*), 171
Sugar, 196
Vastieddi, 105
Veal,
Chop Casserole, 100
Chops, Herbed, 98–99
Cutlets with Marsala, 99
Cutlets Messina Style, 83
Cutlets Pizza, 93–94
Cutlets Sicilian Style, 83–84
Liver, Saged, 90
Liver, Tangy, 100
Meatloaf with, 85
Meat Sauce with, 162

Rice Croquettes with, 53
Roast alla Motta, 84
Roast, Rosemaried, 85
Rolls in Tomato Sauce, 91
Roll-Ups (Variation), 97
Scallops alla Garibaldi, 93
Spleen, Baked Stuffed, 103
Spleen and Cheese Sandwiches,
    105
and Zucchini Pie, 47
Vegetables, 127–59. *See also* Sal-
    ads; specific vegetables
Pickled, 157
Sauce for Vermicelli Syracuse
    Style, 36–37
Soup, Seasonal Fresh, 28
Soup, Sweet and Sour Mine-
    strone, 25
Vermicelli, with Bread Crumbs, 44
Fried, 39
Syracuse Style, 36–37
Viglia di Natale, La, 4–5
Vitello. See Veal

Wafer Rosettes, 197–98

Wagon Wheels, Baked, 39–40
Watermelon Mold, Chocolate-
    Chip, 178
Wheat, Cùscusu with Cracked,
    17–19
Kernels and Chick-Peas, 3
Whiting, Baked, in Sesame Sauce,
    72–73
Fried, Golden, 78
Stewed, 80
Wines, 207–11

Zabaione, 177
"Frozen Fried Eggs" with,
    176–77
Zafferano, 171
Ziti and Cheese Casserole, Baked,
    33
Ziti al Forno, 33
Zucchini,
    Baked Cheese, 141–42
    and Meat Pie, 47
    Sautéed Cheesed, 148
    Sweet and Sour, 139
Zuppe. See Soups